'As historian David Walker and translator Li Yao exchange their life histories, a fresh perspective on Walker's longstanding interest in the Asia–Australia relationship emerges. Sometimes droll, often poignant, always engaging, *Happy Together* is a story of parallel lives, contrasting national histories and an enriching cross-cultural friendship.'

Graeme Davison, Emeritus Professor of History, Monash University

'This is that rare book which gives a completely new perspective on a well-trodden subject— in this case Australia and China, in a work of great ingenuity and fascination. Our literature on this subject is full of Australian actors and China experts, but with Chinese actors barely visible. By contrast this contribution introduces two companion actors, an Australian, David Walker, and a Chinese expert on Australia, Li Yao, who has become not only an expert but a leaven in China–Australia cultural relations. In writing that is at times elegiac and very moving, Li Yao's story evokes what it was actually like to be tossed in those violent political currents that tore China apart in the mid-twentieth century, to remain optimistic and emerge into a fulfilling and successful career. The ingenuity and impact of the book lies in the interweaving of Li Yao's story with the counterpoint story of his fellow author, eminent historian and elegant writer David Walker, each story a metaphor for the vastly different histories of China and Australia over these last seventy years. Their relationship has become a catalyst for a ramifying array of other connections between China and Australia in the fields of writing, translation, publishing and historical research, a compelling story of the human and creative and happy relations that continue beneath the unhappy rhetoric of hostility and enmity of Australian politicians.'

Stephen FitzGerald, Australia's first ambassador to PR China and author of *Comrade Ambassador*

'In *Happy Together* we find that two academics of vastly contrasting upbringings—the South Australian-born David Walker and Li Yao who grew up in the turmoil of China's Cultural Revolution—can still find much in common. In this lyrical and elegant telling of their life stories, written together with David's wife Karen Walker, the "two Roosters" (both men were born in 1945) become the vessels through which we discover an Australia waking up to its place in Asia and a China undergoing a radical transformation. At several points, the lives of the scholarly Walker and the literary Yao cross—sometimes physically, such as when the pair embark on a trip through northern China together—or otherwise through shared experiences: both grew up in the countryside, with teachers for parents, and were bookworms from an early age. Occasionally the insertion of wry commentary creates a nexus between the men such as when David's grandmother tells her daughter one child was enough, or as the authors call it "Glasson's own one-child policy". But it is also how their lives contrast that makes this book so compelling with the rarefied world of Australian academia serving as a dramatic foil to the political upheavals of 1960s China.

Monica Tan, journalist and author of *Stranger Country*

This richly detailed memoir takes us on a remarkable journey through a tumultuous period of Chinese history. It is also an unforgettable celebration of a friendship between renowned scholar and gifted translator Li Yao, and David Walker, a distinguished Australian historian which bridges cultures, history, and life experience. An inspiring and insightful story for our times, and all times.

Alexis Wright, award-winning author of *The Swan Book* and *Carpentaria*

HAPPY TOGETHER

DAVID WALKER AND LI YAO
with KAREN WALKER

MELBOURNE
UNIVERSITY
PRESS

To the memory of
Li Tiren and Li Yueheng

献给

李体仁 李月恒

MELBOURNE UNIVERSITY PRESS
An imprint of Melbourne University Publishing Limited
Level 1, 715 Swanston Street, Carlton, Victoria 3053, Australia
mup-contact@unimelb.edu.au
www.mup.com.au

First published 2022

Text design by Sonya Murphy
Cover design by Nada Backovic
Printed in Australia by McPherson's Printing Group

A catalogue record for this book is available from the National Library of Australia

9780522878547 (paperback)
9780522878554 (ebook)

FASIC
FOUNDATION FOR AUSTRALIAN STUDIES IN CHINA

Contents

Abbreviations

AAP	Australian Associated Press
ACC	Australia China Council
ABC	Australian Broadcasting Commission
ALP	Australian Labor Party
ANU	Australian National University
ANZAC	Australia and New Zealand Army Corp
ANZUS	Australia, New Zealand and the United States
ASAL	Association for the Study of Australian Literature
ASC	Australian Studies Centre
ASIO	Australian Secret Intelligence Organisation
BBC	British Broadcasting Corporation
BFSU	Beijing Foreign Studies University
BHP	Broken Hill Proprietary
CIA	Central Intelligence Agency
CCP	Chinese Communist Party
CCTV	Central China Television
FASIC	Foundation for Australian Studies in China
IDP	International Development Program
IMNU	Inner Mongolia Normal University
KGB	Russian Committee for State Security
NSW	New South Wales
PLA	People's Liberation Army
RAAF	Royal Australian Air Force
IMPRP	Inner Mongolia People's Revolutionary Party
UK	United Kingdom
UNSW	University of New South Wales
USSR	Union of Soviet Socialist Republics

List of Illustrations

Image credits: *Unless otherwise stated all images are taken from the collections of Li Yao or David and Karen Walker*

CHAPTER 1

Searching for the ancestral village

In 1968 a middle-aged man struggles along a rough mountain road connecting Inner Mongolia with neighbouring Shanxi province. He is a primary school teacher, but first he is a Rightist. *Rightist?* What on earth was that? That meant someone thought to be against the Revolution. After enduring years of criticism and finger-pointing, he'd had enough. Abandoning teaching, he took to the open road.

He is a tall, gaunt fellow dressed in faded blue rags, at first glance a simple beggar. Look again. Over one shoulder is his beloved Chinese fiddle, the *erhu*. He is a talented musician. This man has had some education. At each village along the road, he strikes up a tune, singing folk songs of love and loss. Mongolian grassland songs are sad and mournful, full of yearning. Everyone knows them. Old and young join in when he sings:

> Swan goose
> In the sky
> Flying away from us . . .

When little children gather to hear the stranger, he bends down low and tells fantastic stories of magic, brave princes and far-away lands. When he tells stories about fierce lions, tigers and yellow-eyed wolves he growls and he prowls. The children scatter.

There have always been travelling musicians and storytellers in towns and villages across China. They were as familiar as drought, poverty and pestilence. Although the villagers had little enough for themselves, they offered simple food and shelter to this kind of stranger. As a child, Li Yao, the younger of the two writers of this story, knew this ragged traveller. He was Li Zhang, Li Yao's cousin, his great-uncle's son. In the early 1950s, Li Yao would often see Li Zhang during the holidays. At that time, Li Zhang was studying to be a teacher in Li Yao's hometown of Jining in Inner Mongolia. Everyone knew Li Zhang. He was a born entertainer who could play nearly every instrument: *erhu*, flute, zither and trumpet. He was a talkative fellow, full of jokes. A trickster. Now you see me, now you don't. There is an old saying in China, 'misfortune finds its way in by the mouth'. Even as a child, Li Yao sensed that people like his cousin who told one joke too many or who laughed loudly at the wrong time got into trouble. When Li Zhang was classified as a Rightist in 1957, no-one in the family was too surprised. He was a black sheep alright with a very big mouth. But the family was very surprised when he became a travelling beggar. The Li family were by no means rich, but they were respectable people. They had never raised a beggar.

As he began his journey to Shanxi, Li Zhang encountered his old Auntie, an ordinary peasant woman. One day Auntie heard noises in the street outside her tiny house. Peeping through the window she saw a skinny-looking fellow singing while beseeching passers-by to drop a coin into his bowl. He looked familiar. It was that rascal Li Zhang. Auntie cried at the sight of him. Such a talented fellow, reduced to this. She hurried him inside, insisting he should stay with her family, but he had other ideas. He was a man on a mission. 'Where are you going?' Auntie asked. 'I'm looking for our old hometown in Shanxi!' he told her. Auntie could not believe it, a fool's mission. 'No-one knows where we are from! Only your grandfather who died more than thirty years ago.' Tears came to Li Zhang's eyes. He could not explain why he wanted to look for the old hometown, even to himself.

During the Cultural Revolution, Li Zhang had suffered a lot as a Rightist. Perhaps he was searching for protection and solace, a refuge of sorts for his troubled soul. What a joke that was. Li Yao is adamant that no-one could find protection even in the remotest grasslands of Inner Mongolia, let alone in advanced Shanxi province. But Li Zhang had made up his mind. Waving goodbye to Auntie, he went on his way, searching for the Li family's ancestral home. As he went, he played his melancholy *erhu*, the sound carrying over valleys and mountains. Li Zhang, primary school teacher, Rightist, musician, prankster and beggar, Li Yao's cousin. No-one in the family saw him again.

In 2016, forty-eight years later, Li Yao appeared on the mountain roads of Shanxi province. He is also a teacher and would have been called a Rightist had he been a teacher in 1957 because he is also a talkative, sometimes silly man with the wrong kind of family background. Wrong, in any event, for those times. He too is looking for his old hometown. The two cousins have that in common, but the similarities end there. Li Yao can't play the *erhu*, he is not dressed in rags and he does not look at all like a beggar. But he does like singing. He loosens up after a cheering glass or two of potent *baijiu*, rice wine, liquid fire. It is a great Chinese tradition. All the Tang poets loved their wine. Six hundred years before Chaucer, one of the best-loved of them all, Li Bai, wrote in praise, not just of drinking but of getting plastered:

> Life in the world is but a big dream;
> I will not spoil it by any labour or care.
> So saying, I was drunk all the day
> Lying helpless at the porch in front of my door.

When encouraged by his friends—clapping, urging him on—Li Yao gets to his feet, smooths down his mane of dark hair and sings. Out come the favourite Mongolian folk songs: 'Swan goose, in the sky'. As night draws on and the drinks flow, so too do the songs and stories. Tomorrow is a long way off. It can look after itself.

There is another difference. Li Yao is not alone. He is travelling with his Australian friends, David and Karen Walker. How had they got to know Li Yao? In 2013, Li Yao had begun translating David's book, *Not Dark Yet: A Personal History*. No-one has translated more Australian writing into Chinese than Li Yao. He's been at it since

1980 and has covered a lot of ground, from May Gibbs' children's classic, *Snugglepot and Cuddlepie,* to Alexis Wright's prize-winning novel, *Carpentaria*. David's book, *Not Dark Yet,* was Li Yao's twenty-sixth Australian translation.

From the 1880s and moving across the twentieth century, *Not Dark Yet* tells the story of David's South Australian family. They were ordinary folk, teachers and small businesspeople for the most part, caught in the web of history: migrating, raising families and making homes through good times and bad. Li Yao gets to know David and Karen on long train trips through China. On their travels, Li Yao is good at supplying snacks: peanuts, cherry tomatoes, boiled eggs, apples, sandwiches. He keeps drawing supplies from his bag like a magician. Fellow passengers study this little party with interest.

The three travellers are all of an age. Li Yao was born in January 1946 while David came into the world in November 1945. Two births close in time but worlds apart. According to the twelve animals of the Chinese zodiac, both men are Roosters. Li Yao calls David 'elder Rooster', a fine title. Since 2004 David has been legally blind; he is very good at looking, not so good at seeing. But like any rooster worth his salt, he can shake his feathers and crow very loudly. Li Yao is not bad at shaking a feather or two either. And Karen? According to the Chinese zodiac she is a Fire Pig, born in July 1947. The Roosters are scribblers, the Fire Pig is a scientist. They make a strange trio.

The Chinese zodiac is serious business, dating back to who knows when. And the Rooster? What sort of a sign is that? In 1988 Li Yao met the witty Australian poet Fay Zwicky when she visited China. She also wondered what it meant to be a Rooster:

> I am a Rooster.
> Honest, frank, obliging, difficult
> to live with.
> Spot on so far. What's this?
> Vain? Despotic? Prickly about criticism?
> Perhaps there's nothing in it
> after all . . .

After translating *Not Dark Yet*, Li Yao tells David that he wants to have his own family story told, beginning with the migration of the Li family from Shanxi province to Inner Mongolia sometime in the late nineteenth century. Li Yao sees collaboration as the way to go, insisting that some of David's Australian story should be placed alongside his own.

They knew that life had dealt their families very different cards. The Li family had settled in Inner Mongolia, where Mongolian tribes had lived on the grasslands tending their herds of horses for many centuries. The Walkers had settled in inland South Australia, on a very old continent, home to its horse-less Indigenous peoples for 60 000 years. Yet these distant territories had their similarities: big skies, grasslands and vast spaces. The two men know that their families were small fry. Neither had produced big potatoes who had made any kind of mark on the national stage. They were not people who left lots of records. While Li Yao's family had journeyed by foot from Shanxi to Inner Mongolia, the Walkers had sailed from northern England to South Australia. They too were respectable people, in Australia by choice. There were no beggars, thieves or transported convicts in the extended Walker family.

One day, Li Yao, looking like a true Chinese scholar, with his longish hair combed back, announces that while he knew his family had come from Shanxi, it will prove impossible to ever locate their ancestral village. Li Zhang is long dead, Auntie too. Anyone who might remember where the old village might be is long gone. He seems happy with this state of affairs. As an historian, David grows impatient. He feels Li Yao has just given up on finding the village. David insists there must be some archival records, local papers, or oral histories. Something. 'But this is China!' Li Yao replies, a trifle impatiently. The lives of small potatoes are not recorded in Chinese archives or newspapers. That might happen in Australia, but not here. 'That may be right,' David replies 'but you haven't even tried. You can't know until you have made inquiries, done some looking. Besides, it would be exciting to try. Another journey, new cities to visit. Go on, what could be wrong with that?' Li Yao can't resist a chance to travel.

So, off we go by train and bus from Beijing towards Taiyuan, the capital of Shanxi province. First stop, the small city of Yuanuan, where we join Teacher Liu Junhong and her family for a fine meal in their roomy apartment on the eleventh floor of a large building complex typical of modern China. The next day we will speak at Yangquan Engineering College. The Vice-President and senior staff welcome us in their formally arranged meeting room. Big chairs and formal seating, arranged according to the size of the potatoes in attendance. The host must face the door. Speeches are delivered as the visitors sip their jasmine tea, then several books are exchanged, presented with both hands and a slight bow. There are toasts, photographs, good-humoured banter, then yet more photographs. No alcohol is served, anti-corruption measures now proscribe it.

The College has advertised a lecture on the writing and translation of *Not Dark Yet.* A huge poster with photos of the two Roosters stands at the entrance to a vast lecture theatre. A bell rings and in they pour, about five hundred staff and students. There are many questions—about writing and translation, climate change, the Australia–China relationship, and the status of Aboriginal Australians. Then comes the inevitable question on *The Thorn Birds*, the best-known and most loved Australian novel in China. A young man asks the final question, 'What is your attitude to death?' 'I am against it,' David replies. As we leave, a young girl presents him with a little crane, the Chinese symbol of longevity, folded from note paper.

We are taken to Yin Yuan village, a 400-year-old collection of buildings built for the Zhang family. Grey brick houses with curved tile roofs run down a series of eleven terraces, one below the other, carved into the hillside. In the valley below, disciplined vegetables march in uniform rows—corn, tomatoes, beans, cucumbers and eggplant. Throughout the village, carved stone screens at the entrances block the passage of evil spirits. Five workers play cards in one small courtyard. They shoot a quick glance at the foreigners before resuming their game. Nearby, a furry brown dog interrogates a pot of red flowers.

The following day we visit Xiao He, the 300-year-old seat of the prosperous Shi family of bakers and food suppliers. No stone was laid here without close attention to *feng shui*. The buildings look east towards nearby mountains. An obliging river runs below, just where it should be. Passing through intricate courtyards, we meet no-one except the caretaker, a member of the fourteenth generation of the Shi family. Ushering the party into a little room, he serves up his family speciality, fried doughnuts. Xiao He became famous as the home of Shi Pingmei, a brilliant young woman poet and writer. She is now remembered for her thwarted relationship with Gao Junyu, a founding member of the Chinese Communist Party (CCP) who died suddenly in 1925. Shi Pingmei herself passed away just three years later, aged only twenty-six. Declaring that 'Revolution and love are not contradictory', Premier Zhou Enlai ensured that she remains buried in Beijing at Tao Ran pavilion park beside her lover. It has become a romantic place of pilgrimage for young Chinese.

Further afield lies Dazhai. Through the 1950s to the 1960s, Dazhai's dashing Party Secretary, always seen wearing a distinctive headscarf, made his village famous. Villagers transformed its rocky hillsides into intricately sculptured terraces. While the unworthy Rightist, Li Zhang, was playing the fool in Jining, Dazhai's peasants—men, women and children—hauled rocks day in and day out. The results were so spectacular that Chairman Mao called upon his people to work for the Revolution and 'Learn from Dazhai'. Dazhai is now a heritage site. The rooms in the spartan village guesthouse retain their original furniture: a narrow iron-frame bed, a small reading lamp and a radio. Prominent leaders, including Premier Zhou Enlai and Mao's wife, Jiang Qing, stayed here. Mao had put little Dazhai on the map.

The next stop is the Local Chronicles Office in Taiyuan, the provincial capital. The only information Li Yao can provide is that his ancestors may have come from somewhere around Guoyang. Li Yao had learned this after talking to his much older and very frail half-brother who had a memory of Li Zhang setting out long ago for a village that sounded like Guoyang. The Director of the Chronicles Office is confident that he can help. Much discussion follows. He telephones his colleague Zhang Bin at the Yuanping Local Chronicles Office. Yuanping is a city near Guoyang and Zhang Bin is well-known as a walking encyclopedia on the area and its history. Zhang

Bin suggests that Li Yao's ancestors are likely to have come from a village called Li Sanquan. Many people called Li still live there and Zhang knows that many others had left this village in the past to go to Inner Mongolia.

Chen Yonggui, the village head, greeting visitors in Dazhai

We set off by train for Yuanping just an hour away from Taiyuan. It is the Dragon Boat Festival and the train is packed. A large man occupies one of our seats. Seeing foreigners waving tickets, he slinks away. People crowd the aisles. Li Yao presents us with coloured cotton wristbands, worn during the festival to 'ward off evil spirits'. The train moves through wide valleys edged in the middle distance with high, terraced hills. They are covered with a scrubby bush, not unlike saltbush country in South Australia. The valleys below are green with new crops of corn and wheat. Lines of newly planted trees march down the side roads.

The train's sound system plays jaunty Shanxi folk songs. The girl sitting opposite prefers her own music, delivered through enormous, furry headphones; she is a city girl returning home for the holiday in her new jeans and crisp white jacket edged with green. She is soon replaced by a sociable man in a blue striped business shirt and neat grey trousers. He has been making dumplings for the last fifty years. He tells Li Yao that around here they can grow many different types of vegetables and the fruit is excellent: peaches, apples, plums, walnuts and juicy 'acrobats'. Something has been gained in translation. A discussion ensues. Not acrobats, *apricots*. The dumpling maker says that many people did leave from this area for Inner Mongolia. He does not know much about Li Sanquan, but he has heard the name.

In Yuanping, the party stays at a hotel with rooms far more sumptuous than those on display in the Dazhai guesthouse. Everything is up to date in Yuanping. Zhang arranges for a car to take his visitors to Li Sanquan. A wide straight road lined with trees leads out of town. More fields of corn. It is too cold to grow rice here. The old town of Guoyang is about 20 kilometres away from the new town of Yuanping which has replaced it. As China modernises, this old town/new town pattern is repeated across the country. Guoyang is really old, dating from 311 CE. Zhang says Li Sanquan should be somewhere nearby. The car bumps down a narrow dirt road to reach a crossroad. After much discussion, we press on straight ahead. Signs of a village appear: broken stone walls, little houses that look as if they had been there forever, certainly since the 1890s. Is this Li Sanquan? So it seems. Zhang finds the house of the village head, Li Mingcai. It is a hot day and Li is wearing a white singlet and slacks. He leans forward, offering cigarettes and cups of green tea. A little dog with one eye open studies the intruders from under the table while Li Mingcai urges his shy daughter to try out her English on the foreigners.

Li Mingcai wastes no time getting down to business. He says 95 per cent of the 726 people in the village are called Li and invites some of the older villagers to come in and meet us. Li Yao passes around some of his old family photos. Li Mingcai on his part brings out a copy of the official Li family tree. A very exciting development. Although Li Yao can't find the name of his great-grandfather, a paragraph in the preface states very clearly that at the end of the Qing dynasty, some Li people moved to the Eighth Sumu, Zhuozi County, Inner Mongolia. Li Yao exclaims, 'No problem! This is the little place where I was born in Inner Mongolia! My forebears must have come from Li Sanquan! Li Mingcai and these people are my relatives!' Warm embraces all round. 'I am really very lucky! Far luckier than my cousin, Li Zhang! I am the only one of my generation to see the village my ancestors left more than one hundred years ago!' He shakes hands with his Australian friends, looks them in the eye and thanks them: 'I salute you my dearest friends.'

Li Sanquan is everything a traditional Chinese village should be. Narrow dirt streets, high walls around weather-beaten courtyard houses, mysterious doorways, little vegetable patches, old trees. Lots of stone and mudbrick. There are chooks and children flying in all directions, rather like an Australian country town in years gone by. The chooks are handsome bronze birds with bright red wattles. They cluck cheerfully and peck at the ground. The visitors are invited into a shady courtyard where, sitting on low stools, they eat their way through a mountain of watermelon. This family tells Li Yao that many years earlier some of their relatives had gone to Inner Mongolia by donkey in search of land and a better life.

We are taken up to Li Sanquan's small Buddhist temple. In front stands an old tree, festooned with cloth garlands to bring good fortune. The large trunk looks very old, but then again almost everything in Li Sanquan does. This is about to change. A new village has just been built and the villagers will soon be relocated there. Drawing closer, the first of the temple buildings looks fairly new. Li Mingcai says that the original was burned down by the Japanese in the late 1930s and it has now been rebuilt. At the back is a second, much older building with lively paintings still surviving on the back wall.

The two Roosters and the Fire Pig
with the villagers of Li Sanquan

Standing in the temple grounds, Li Mingcai explains how Li Sanquan got its name. Two thousand years ago, at the time of the Han dynasty, a big general, seeking a secure mountain retreat, camped with his troops not far from where the temple now stood. It had been a terrible journey through an empty, drought-ravaged land. The general could find no water anywhere. His soldiers were collapsing with thirst, their lips cracked and bleeding, faces burned brick red. Riding up on his horse, the general struck the ground three times with his sword and in an instant three springs bubbled up from the ground. With his grateful troops restored by the spring water, the general went on to defeat his enemies. Moving on, he left some of his soldiers behind to guard the precious springs. These men were the first to make Li Sanquan their home and if the story is to be believed, were Li Yao's ancestors. That was the story of the little village called Li Sanquan, 'Three Springs'.

CHAPTER 2

The strong devour the weak

There are twenty generations of people named Li documented in the family tree in Li Sanquan. Li Yao believes that his family lived there for many generations. Direct evidence is lacking because his great-uncle burned their family tree in 1951. At a time of disorienting change and recrimination when Mao's Land Reform Movement ordering land to be reassigned to the peasants gained momentum, any compromising documents showing the family to be landlords had to be destroyed.

Shanxi lies separated on three sides by barren mountain ranges and on the fourth by the Yellow River. It was a strategically important province, standing between Beijing to the east and the Muslim region of Xinjiang further to the west. Looking north–south, it provided a barrier protecting settled farmers in the central provinces from invading tribes in the Mongolian grasslands. Over its long history, Shanxi province ran the gamut from prosperity to privation.

During the Qing dynasty (1644–1912 CE), as little as 20 per cent of the land in Shanxi could be farmed. In 1913, the enterprising Australian traveller, Mary Gaunt, busy collecting material for her second book on China, found that, 'wherever among these stony hills there was a patch of ground fit for cultivation, though it was as tiny as a pocket handkerchief, it was cultivated'. Shanxi is notoriously stony and its fine villages and intricately terraced hillsides are an enduring monument to centuries of toil. Shanxi had no choice but to excel in hauling and shaping stone. The confined central valleys filled by fertile *loess* soil, blown in from the Gobi desert, sustained its largest communities. In the greatest of these basins lies the ancient city of Taiyuan, the capital of Shanxi province. Li Yao and his Australian friends enter Taiyuan through a massive gate topped by an impressive watch tower in a restored section of an old wall which had once enclosed the entire city.

Mary Gaunt had found it a slow and exhausting business getting to Shanxi from Beijing along roads that wound through narrow mountain passes. She concluded that the recipe for constructing a road in northern China was to take a piece of land too poor to farm, 'upset a stone wall over it', take care that the good large stones never lie evenly 'and you have your road'. Where the road turned sandy, carts carved deep ruts into the soil. In the nineteenth century, Shanxi's roads could only be travelled by pack animals: mules, donkeys, camels and, as ever across China, by people on foot. Far luckier than most, Mary, who was no sylph, was carried in a litter by hired hands who also carried her bulky luggage. Landlocked Shanxi had no access to ports. It was not until the early twentieth century that outright opposition to that newfangled invention, the railway, finally subsided.

Mary soaked up the sights as she travelled towards Taiyuan. It was spring. The shoots of new wheat were just showing above the ground and the plains were bathed in 'the golden sunshine of North China'. The sunlit plains and the invigorating air brought back memories of her childhood in Victoria. But all too soon she encountered large clouds of dust raised by pigs being driven along the road just as sheep were back home. Pigs were herded for long distances to arrive at harvest time when Shanxi farmers served hearty meals to their family and day labourers. Mary often saw inns used solely by pigs and their drivers. The stench, she said, was quite something, 'just a little taller than the average smell'.

Since earliest times there have been settlements around Taiyuan, when the ancestors of the modern Chinese began to practice agriculture. Millet, a small-grained cereal, was the staple crop in a region too cold and too dry to grow rice. These early people lived in small, thatched houses half buried in the earth for warmth, their little permanent settlements growing slowly into small walled towns where writing, pottery and bronze technology were developed.

The story goes that some of Li Yao's Shanxi forebears supplemented their modest farming income by making pots. Pottery is still an important industry in Shanxi. We visit a factory making traditional clay cooking pots, baked in fiery kilns. The workers are keen to pose for photographs with the foreigners from distant Australia. But something is not quite right. It takes considerable gesticulation, tugging and rearranging before the group is finally lined up in the correct order. David notices that one of the workers has lost an eye, the result of an accident unloading the kiln. When he warns the man not to lose the other eye, the worker laughs in agreement while his mates cheer. Later, as acknowledged ceramic enthusiasts, the party are taken on a cloak-and-dagger expedition down winding alleys to meet a collector of Neolithic pots. He shows off around fifty pots lined up on rough wooden planks. Some are damaged, others are very stylish three-legged beauties with pert handles, collectors' items.

The Fen River supplies Taiyuan with water. But drought has always stalked Shanxi farmers who need the rain to fall at exactly the right times to ensure good harvests. They are forever looking to the skies. If rain comes too late, no wheat can be grown, only millet and sorghum. David remembers how, as a student at the University of Adelaide, he once attended a lecture by Professor Otto van der Sprenkel, a name not easily forgotten. Van der Sprenkel argued that water management was the key to understanding Chinese civilisation.

Ancient chronicles tell how Yu the Great, founder of the myth-laden Xia dynasty, placed the first flood controls on the Yellow River with the aid of a yellow dragon and a black turtle. In nineteenth century Shanxi, the allocation of water to each village was carefully managed by local officials: 'hatch-keepers' to oversee correct water rotation and 'channel heads' watching the system as a whole. 'River books' documented all water use and were often consulted to resolve disputes. Whenever the rains faltered and water became scarce, the powerful dragons living in clear pools high in the mountains were courted in elaborate ceremonies. One year when the rains failed the governor ordered tiger bones to be thrown into the spring at the Jinci temples near Taiyuan hoping that rain would come when the dragon in the spring fought the tiger. In another year of drought, a dragon was executed outside the south gate of Taiyuan and his head was thrown into the Jinci spring. Sceptics doubted this would work, saying the head was not real, it was only made of paper.

Agricultural communities in north China lived in a state of constant insecurity. The climate was harsh and unpredictable. So too were their bellicose northern neighbours, against whom the high stone walls had been built. Nomadic herders from the northern grasslands invaded at regular intervals. Sweeping south, their great weapons were arrows, horses and speed. Yet the northern grasslands not only held the threat of conquest, they also stirred the brightest hopes of Shanxi people. Their fabled spaces fuelled dreams of land just waiting to be farmed.

Chinese towns of any size now have museums, handsome public buildings with imposing foyers. Here the once terrifying invaders of long ago are on display in life-size dioramas behind thick glass. There they are, the menacing Rong and the ferocious-looking Di people, long-haired and draped in animal skins. When a disciplined Jin army finally drove the Di people out of Shanxi, an early feudal state emerged, led by Duke 'Double Ears' Wen. He founded Jinyang, precursor of modern Taiyuan.

The antique city of Jinyang was vulnerable, it was captured, besieged, flooded and burned several times over. Once it was the grand capital of a Western Zhao kingdom (1046–771 BCE) stretching north into what is now Inner Mongolia. But when the Han dynasty (202 BCE–220 CE) moved their capital south to Xuzhou, it dwindled to a small military garrison. One year, Li Yao accompanies his foreign friends to the old Han city of Xuzhou where they descend by steep tunnels to the original Han tombs. In the nearby museum they are shown armies of small terracotta warriors, less famous than their full-sized counterparts in Xian. The museum staff insist on taking photographs before presenting their visitors with rubbings from the heavy stone carvings that once decorated the tombs. They reveal vivid scenes of ordinary life and simple pleasures.

With the founding of the great Tang dynasty (618–907 CE), Jinyang's days were over and the city of Taiyuan was established. During the Tang era, this new city prospered, becoming famous for its elegant palaces, extensive foreign trade and flourishing art, music and literature. The practice of Buddhism spread, at times promoted and at other times discouraged by Tang rulers. Taiyuan's fine provincial museum, a strikingly modern building shaped like an inverted pyramid, contains beautifully displayed Tang Buddhist statues, their drapery falling in subtle Hellenistic folds. There are also many Tang ceramic figures: courtiers, camels and horses, splashed with white, green and gold glaze. A small girl aged about eight, evidently a graduate from the national 'Training Young Museum Guides' program, explains each exhibit to a group of middle-aged Chinese tourists. Aspiring young guides must attend museum classes every Saturday afternoon for a year. What an inspired idea. There is no forgetting that assured little guide in Taiyuan.

Under the Tang emperor Taizhong, armies were sent deep into Central Asia to secure vital trade routes. Silk was the main export, woven by women from thousands of farming families. Horses for the army were the most sought after import. A Tang poet was intrigued and perhaps envious of the colourful adventures of the merchants:

> Traversing the oceans in search of pearls,
> Gathering jade on Chu's Mount Heng,
> North to buy Tangut horses,
> West to capture parrots in Tibet.

This trade changed the Chinese diet. Peas, spinach and garlic came in from the west. Pistachios and sesame were brought back from Persia, sugar and black pepper came from India, almonds from Turkestan, coriander from the Mediterranean and grape wine from Tashkent.

Eventually, the Tang dynasty collapsed and Taiyuan fell into decline. To the north momentous changes were underway. By 1206 CE, the formidable Chinggus (Genghis) Khan had united the Mongolian tribes. Before long, his horsemen attacked China and swept across the grasslands towards Europe to become embedded in Western imagination as the primal barbarian horde destroying all before it. In the late nineteenth century, whenever Australian colonists imagined an Asian invasion of their continent, as they were prone to do, they often conflated Mongolian hordes with their victims further south, the Han Chinese. Both became interchangeable contributors to a generic 'yellow man' with one calculating eye on empty Australia and the other on 'white womanhood'.

In 1890, a short invasion story, 'The Decline and Fall of the Australian Empire. A Chapter of Future History' appeared in *Melbourne Punch.* In the story, after landing in Australia's far north, the unstoppable Chinese drive south, 'laying the country waste on their march'. The Australian colonists fight gallantly to save Melbourne but are quickly overrun. All too soon, the standard of Emperor Hang Chow floats above the Victorian Parliament Building. A post-invasion conference, chaired by England, divides the spoils of victory. China, by right of conquest, takes over Victoria and New South Wales (NSW), forming the new province of 'Mongolia'. While Australian settlers of the time often expressed their fears of China in stories such as this, they were not so keen to acknowledge that their own forebears had invaded the Australian continent, turning the Indigenous peoples into outcasts in their own land.

During the Ming dynasty (1368–1644 CE), Taiyuan was primarily a garrison city, focused yet again on stopping incursions from the north by nomadic tribes. The Ming dynasty too was to fall. As unlikely as it might seem, two Australian writers, Charmian Clift and George Johnston, wrote an historical novel, *The Big Chariot* (1953), about the chaos that then ensued. When the Qing dynasty founded by Manchus from the north-east eventually rose to power, Taiyuan once again resumed its role as a trading centre. Shanxi merchants travelled into Russia and Central Asia, exchanging tea for furs, amber and European goods. When the Reverend Alexander Williamson from Scotland travelled to Shanxi in the 1860s, he was struck by the general prosperity of its walled villages and the abundance of foreign goods for sale in Taiyuan's numerous markets, finding there 'Russian woollen goods, exotic jewellery, matches and needles'.

Shanxi's banking and trading networks became famous across China. Each month, as the time for clearing fixed debts came around, a ceaseless stream of merchants could be seen in the streets of Taiyuan, carrying silver bullion. Provincial governments began to remit their taxes to the central government in Beijing via Shanxi banks which soon had branches all over China staffed by Shanxi men. The bankers wore costly embroidered clothes, lived in huge mansions and rode about on fine horses or in ornate carriages. Shanxi merchants remained influential down to the Chinese Revolution of 1911 and the Russian Revolution of 1917, which closed the Mongolian frontier. Shanxi then dwindled from a major trading corridor to an isolated backwater. Speaking Mandarin with a Shanxi accent, as the Li family did, became a mark of provincial backwardness.

During the mid-nineteenth century, many traditional industries provided Shanxi people with employment away from the farm. When Mary Gaunt stayed at the English Baptist Mission in Taiyuan, she was impressed by the 'shrieking of the greased wheelbarrows', the sounds of bells and gongs, and the 'shouting of hucksters'; all the busy sounds of 'an ancient people at work'. It struck her that these sounds had been heard when her own ancestors were 'naked savages hunting the deer and the bear and the wolf in the swamps and marshes of Northern Europe'.

Shanxi's mountains may be barren and stony but they bear rich seams of coal. Mountain villagers supported themselves in summer by growing millet and in winter by digging pits to get at the coal. The miners' lamps and fires lit up the night. A popular rhyme claimed Shanxi mines were as bright and numerous as the stars in the sky. Every year, at the Lantern Festival, people built towers of coal, lighting these 'fire pagodas' in their doorways to bring prosperity. Coal mining remains an important industry.

As we disembark in Yangquan, the first stop in the search for Li Sanquan village, we hear the rumble of heavy coal trucks. Trucks have chopped up Yangquan's roads, turning the drive to the city into a pantomime of drunken lurches, the sense of adventure underscored by the complete absence of seat belts.

Li Yao's paternal great-grandfather, Li Dabao, owned and farmed land near Li Sanquan village. It is not known for certain if he ever mined coal or made pots. But some clues about his circumstances can be gleaned from the life of the diarist Liu Dapeng who lived around the same time in another small Shanxi village. Liu Dapeng enjoyed a happy childhood, dancing, singing and jumping or travelling with his father to fairs and performances at the Jinci temples. With a small gang of other boys, he kept crickets, went fishing and engaged in elaborate games where King Yan, the king of Hell, would sit in judgement.

A Chinese girl and boy photographed by Mary Gaunt

The girls of the village could not join in these games. Mary Gaunt recalled two little girls she had seen in Shanxi, aged about eight and wearing neat cotton trousers under smocks of bright blue cotton. Their feet, tightly bound in embroidered shoes, were the size of those of a child of three. The little girls' cheeks were painted red but their haunted look could not be disguised. They moved with extreme difficulty. Until the early twentieth century, Shanxi was well known as the home of the bound foot. Girls with feet more than four inches long were thought unlikely to make a good marriage. Mary Gaunt describes the procedure: 'The toes, all except the big toe, are pressed back until they touch the heel' and kept in place by long cloth bands. Mary heard the girls crying each morning and evening when the bandages were bound ever more tightly. The only way to relieve the pain was to press the calf tightly against the side of the bed to interrupt the flow of blood to the feet. At times, to make the foot even smaller, the bone of the instep was broken with the back of a meat cleaver.

From the early twentieth century, the Shanxi government tried to stop foot-binding. Anyone who bound a child's feet, made shoes for bound feet or acted as a match-maker for a girl with bound feet was severely fined. The diarist Liu Dapeng's second daughter, born in 1900, was the first woman in her family not to have bound feet. Until that time, the only women with natural feet in Shanxi were servants or Protestant converts.

Despite the new regulations, the practice of foot binding hung on into the 1920s. Li Yao's mother had the terrible misfortune of being among the last to suffer. Her father insisted that her feet should be bound. He liked women with little feet. Even though his daughter cried day and night he could not be swayed. When the little girl's grandfather, a gentle man and respected teacher living in another village heard about this, he became very angry. There were terrible rows. The grandfather supported the new regulations banning foot binding. He threatened to bring a charge against his son and demanded that the bandages be removed. But it was too late. His little grand-daughter's feet were deformed beyond recovery. For the rest of her long life Li Yao's mother suffered great pain in her feet and legs, something Li Yao could neither forget nor forgive.

As a woman who remembered running barefoot in the Australian bush, Mary Gaunt was troubled by the lives of women with bound feet. They might be richly dressed in embroidered silks and satins, and with oiled, elaborately dressed hair but she thought of them as pets or dolls with painted faces. They walked as if their legs were made of wood, holding out their arms for balance. They had to spend their time indoors or confined to the internal courtyards of the houses. On her way to Taiyuan, Mary often noticed timid village women peeping at her from doorways, but only very rarely saw them outdoors or working in the fields.

At the age of eight, the diarist Liu Dapeng had begun studying at the local village school in conditions likely to have been much the same for Li Yao's great-grandfather, Li Dabao, if he had been lucky enough to receive some education. Schoolboys brought their own benches and tables to sit on, placing them outside under the eaves in summer and inside during winter. They were taught to sit upright with their feet together and to bow slowly and respectfully from the waist. They were to honour their schoolbooks, classic texts like *Elementary Learning* and *The Classic of Filial Piety*. They were to wash their hands before class and to read without touching the book itself. Paper with writing on it should always be treated with respect. As an old man clinging to Confucian precepts, Liu Dapeng could be seen thoughtfully picking up discarded cigarette papers near Jinci temple, because they had writing on them.

Traditional teaching inculcated important values. In a society where laws were often poorly enforced, filial piety, family relations, personal reputation and trust were vital. Throughout his life, Liu Dapeng interpreted every type of misfortune as punishment meted out by Heaven for his lapses in filial piety. When illness struck, Liu Dapeng would always blame himself for straying from the path of righteousness. The Li family may not have been as strictly traditional as the diarist. There is no way of knowing. But Li Yao is certain that Confucian values governed their behaviour.

Liu Dapeng was certainly much more educated than Li Yao's great-grandfather, Li Dabao. But in later life, when his prospects declined, the diarist came home to farm his own small piece of land where he followed the strict regimen of the agricultural year in a manner that Li Yao's great-grandfather would have known well.

When the ice thawed, the ground was fertilised with night-soil ahead of planting, a smelly but necessary beginning. Ploughing began in early spring. If the land was irrigated the main crop was wheat, followed by millet in the same year. On hillside fields further from water, only millet and sorghum would be grown. Another routine task in springtime was to repair the drainage channels ensuring that the winter wheat got adequate water. Liu Dapeng grew soybeans, yams, maize, cucumbers, green beans, peppers, turnips, leeks and radishes and three different types of cabbage.

With the onset of summer, hoeing, weeding and thinning of seedlings began. This back-breaking, but virtuous work provided a rich harvest of proverbs and lessons for life, 'if a man works hard the land will not be lazy and both large and small vats will be full'. In the full heat of summer it was said that 'you will eat as much as you sweat'. Weeding was a useful metaphor for right thinking. You do not have to be Chinese to encounter such exhortations. David's father, Gil, rarely lost an opportunity to point out how children who failed to do their homework would soon be 'weeded out'. Sweat was as much a sign of virtuous labour in outback South Australia as it was in Shanxi province. Biblical proverbs were well known in settler Australia. Everyone knew that seed falling on stony soil withered and died while the iron law of consequences was summed up in the biblical phrase, 'reap as ye shall sow'.

In Shanxi, when the winter wheat was ready to harvest, the busiest season of the year began. The diarist describes how he would hire several day labourers who worked as a group, pulling the plants up by the roots, singing as they went. Bundled into sheaves, corn was brought to the threshing floor. The different crops came in one after another: first winter wheat, then spring wheat, then millet. The women would cut the heads from the millet stalks, scattering them on the threshing floor where a donkey circled, pulling a stone roller. Grain was separated from chaff and spread to dry in the sun. There were also dates to harvest and cabbages to pickle and store for winter.

Even in bountiful years, there was often not enough grain in Shanxi to feed the people. Grain had always been imported, much of it from the Wei Valley of Shaanxi province over to the west, or from newly cultivated land in the Mongolian grasslands. At the height of its power in the eighteenth century, and well into the nineteenth, Qing officials took impressive measures to prevent famine in Shanxi during years of low rainfall. They maintained an extensive network of well-stocked state community granaries from which they released grain, keeping cereal prices down and providing emergency relief for the hungry. But between 1850 and 1878 the granary system fell apart as the state struggled to suppress major rebellions, particularly the massive Taiping Rebellion to the south. Taxes once used to maintain grain stores were diverted to military ends. Adding to the internal mayhem, the Qing state faced intensifying external threats from

Britain, Russia and Japan. Attempts to improve China's feeble naval defences and to secure the borders drained even more funds. Local elites lacked the power to transfer grain into the province. Defects also emerged in the transportation of grain by barge. Large stretches of the Grand Canal had silted up.

In the eighteenth century, the Portuguese and then the British solved their growing trade imbalance and made considerable profit by importing opium from India and selling it to China. As the opium habit spread, Shanxi farmers began to plant poppies instead of grain. Qing officials at first banned opium cultivation because it depleted the soil and deprived the state of taxes. When this prohibition was lifted in 1874, grain production in Shanxi declined sharply.

This combination of factors meant that Shanxi had little resilience when in 1876 a severe drought hit northern China. The province soon collapsed into horrific famine. Millions of people suffered acute privation as powerful global, regional and climatic forces coalesced. Conditions were well beyond the control of the decaying Qing dynasty or of small potatoes like the Li family who at the best of times just managed to keep their heads above water. Over one-third of Shanxi's population of 15 to 17 million either starved to death, died from famine-related disease or fled. It would take almost a century for the province to recover its pre-famine population. In a few short years, one of China's richest provinces had become one of the poorest.

There had been a global failure of monsoon rain. Through the years from 1876 to 1879 this caused an unusually severe drought, not only in the five provinces of northern China but over much of Asia. The resulting famine was one of the worst ever recorded. Scientists link such events to the warm extreme (*El Niño*) of the Southern Oscillation, a powerful movement of solar energy pushed by surface winds and ocean currents across the vast Pacific basin. During big *El Niño* events, normal patterns of aridity and rainfall are reversed, the extremely dry deserts of Peru experience thunderstorms while the humid jungles of Indonesia lack rain. The monsoons fail in western India, southern Africa, northern China and Brazil. As the pattern changes yet again, parts of Australia turn into a vast dust bowl, so dark during the day that the fowls stop flying and start to roost.

In China, no province was harder hit than Shanxi. An educated man called Liu Xing left an account of these famine years. In 1876 a severe summer drought began. By autumn the fields were so dry that it was difficult for farmers to sow their winter wheat. Grain prices rose sharply. The next year the spring rains failed and the land became so dry that even resilient crops died. When the autumn crops also failed, the streets filled with women begging for food. Grain prices were now far above what ordinary people could afford. With the famine came frightening social disintegration. Gangs armed with guns and rope whips roamed villages at night. Those with noodle soup to eat consumed it fearfully, their doors tightly closed. Starving people wandering the markets were beaten for grabbing dry beans and eating them raw.

The Imperial court made considerable if belated efforts to bring relief but were thwarted by the deterioration of the granary system. Cash was given rather than grain, but what could this purchase in a province with no food? Little grain came in from the Wei valley as it too was experiencing drought. Richard Forest, the British consul, travelling to Shanxi through the narrow Guguan pass saw how the mountain road was strewn with carcasses of men and beasts. Oxen, camels, mules and donkeys needed for transport were killed by people desperate for food. In ruined houses along the way he saw the living, the dying and the dead huddled together.

Even as the drought eased, misfortunes continued. Plagues of rats and locusts descended, wolves came down from the mountains, no-one slept at night. Infectious disease was rampant. The Governor of Shanxi wrote: 'In the earlier period of distress the living fed upon the bodies of the dead; next the strong devoured the weak; and now the general destitution has arrived at such a climax that men devour those of their own flesh and blood.'

First-hand accounts of this 'incredible famine' invariably portrayed it as a divine punishment. Heaven was surely displeased. One Shanxi poet attributed the catastrophe to the inauspicious movements of the planets, particularly Mars, Jupiter and Saturn. Others blamed a lack of filial piety. Sons 'secretly took opium'. Daughters-in-law were not well-behaved, gossiping about 'hair-pins and earrings'. The teachers 'were not strict', and the rich 'were not benevolent'. Years of prosperity had led to self-indulgence and excessive materialism. Frugality had to be emphasised. Grains should never be carelessly spilt or discarded, wastefulness was a great sin.

International audiences learned of the famine from shocked European consuls, traders and missionaries. The Reverend Timothy Richards, a Welsh Baptist missionary, led the way in calling for famine relief. Writing from Taiyuan, he sent searing reports of the disaster throughout the British Empire. None of this would have come as a surprise to the great scholar and economist Thomas Malthus who wrote in 1798 of famine as 'the last, the most dreadful resource of nature'. Richards as a missionary, would have known of its horrors from the *Book of Revelations*, where Famine is the Third Horseman of the Apocalypse, riding a black horse and carrying a set of scales.

In May 1878, the Adelaide *Advertiser* supported the Reverend Richards' appeal for funds to combat the famine, reprinting his reports of starving people eating rotten straw and roots while the 'hill-sides were swept clean for grass-seeds'. South Australians were asked not to turn their backs on their 'fellow creatures': 'A kind Providence has blessed us with abundance, and it will ill-become us, because of the indifference of race, to withhold . . . that help . . . which it is in our power to give.' The South Australian *Register* found deeper causes for the devastation in the deforestation that had occurred as Chinese people migrated north, made worse as starving peasants stripped surviving trees of their bark and leaves. While sympathetic to the plight of the starving, the *Register* continued to oppose Chinese migration.

In response to the famine, relief committees were soon established across Australia. In Burra, a little town in the mid-north of South Australia, the local paper, described how fund-raising activities were being organised by local churches. They divided Burra into nine fund-raising zones. In each, the local clergyman appealed for donations. One of the flock was David's great-grandfather, Thomas Walker, who had moved to Burra as a young man in 1873. At the age of four, Thomas had both ankles crushed in a terrible domestic accident. The bones were reset badly and for the remainder of his life he was forced to use crutches. As a prominent member of his local Methodist church, and as a man who knew something about hardship, Thomas Walker is sure to have contributed to the relief effort.

We have no records of the experience of Li Dabao. He lived through the famine but left no account of these years. To survive, his family must have had some land and sufficient resources to escape complete devastation, although family members may well have died. It strains credulity to imagine that funds donated by Thomas Walker could have reached the village of Li Sanquan. But multiple geopolitical, climatic and humanitarian forces were at work, drawing China and Australia into a more interconnected world.

CHAPTER 3

Breaking new ground

One late afternoon as we sit together eating watermelon in the courtyard of a house in Li Sanquan village, an old grandmother tells us how, long ago, some of her own family had decided to go north. They owned a donkey which had made the difficult journey somewhat easier. In the late 1890s, when hunger still stalked northern China, Li Yao's great-grandfather, Li Dabao, also thought it was time to leave. On the road there were always people ahead, around the next bend, over the next hill and more, always more following. Perhaps there was some comfort in numbers. Across his shoulders, Li Dabao carried a sturdy pole, a basket hanging at each end. One basket held the littlest children, the other, their big iron cooking pot. For colonial Australians, such images of a man carrying a heavy load with a pole across his shoulders became the accepted stereotype of the dogged 'Chinaman'.

Walking north from Shanxi was tough. When Mary Gaunt travelled this way in 1913, she complained that the road got 'worse and worse', sinking between high banks, hanging on to narrow ledges, or following a river bed through 'stony and forbidding' hills. After many days of walking, the Li family passed into Inner Mongolia through an old section of the Great Wall. A little further on, they stopped in the ancient river town of Xinghe. Xinghe already housed many migrants, some known to Li Dabao. Like most border towns it had its rogues and crafty opportunists, smuggling whatever they could lay their hands on through the barrier at the Great Wall. In

Xinghe, the men of the Li family found work as farm labourers, supplementing their income by making clay pots. It was hard going. As he recounts this, Li Yao ruffles his feathers and breaks into song. He is rather less impressed by the base coin of history than by the emotional appeal of folk songs. His song, *Going to Xikou,* tells how young married men from Shanxi moved north to find work. It describes the pain of parting rather than the day-to-day hardships of a poor family on the move:

> My love, you are leaving home to make money,
> I've no way of keeping you here any longer.
> Holding your hand, I say farewell at the gate.
> . . . Clinging to your sleeve,
> My heart is weeping, I long to go with you,
> But all I can do is wait for your return.
>
> My love, you are leaving home to make money,
> It hurts me so much it breaks my heart.
> How long will you be away from home?
> Will I have to wait for you until my hair turns grey?

We visit Xinghe County to meet Ms Guo, Chairman of the Wulanchabu Literary Federation. As the car passes through a wide valley between bare hills, David is taken back to the eroded landscapes of outback South Australia. Another memory. One day when he was a little boy, the afternoon sky suddenly turned dark as a tremendous dust storm rolled in from central Australia. His father had to reassure him, the sun had not gone away, it would be back again tomorrow.

Further on, the travellers are surprised to see healthy young pine and fir trees, compelling evidence of a sustained program of reforestation. Throughout north China, extensive tree planting is now common. On the outskirts of many small villages there are plots of tiny, well-schooled trees, a good little earner for a small farmer. There were very few trees in Xinghe when Li Dabao lived there. Even as late as the year 2000, the Chinese media warned that desertification and severe erosion in Xinghe County were causing sandstorms in

Beijing. Ms Guo is rightly proud of the transformation of bare hills into forest.

After the Li family had lived for a few years in Xinghe, though for exactly how long is quite unclear, Li Dabao's elder daughter married a merchant from Datong, a city just south of the Great Wall. This was a stroke of great good fortune. Her new husband, Merchant Niu, like many Shanxi traders at the time, had made a tidy sum out of the lucrative fur trade with Russia, selling pelts of fox, otter, squirrel, ermine and sable. Looking for investment opportunities he had bought land in Zhuozi County, near Wulanchabu on the grasslands of Inner Mongolia.

When Merchant Niu purchased his land, the Qing government was selling grassland in the Inner Mongolian provinces of Chahar and Suiyuan to Han people at a very affordable price. Zhuozi County at this time was still not actively farmed but was occupied by Mongol herdsmen. Merchant Niu hired Li Yao's grandfather, Li Hai (Li Dabao's eldest son) to farm his new land for him. So some time in the early 1900s, Li Hai, his three brothers and their wives and children travelled from Xinghe to settle in Zhuozi County.

Li Yao has no records for any of this, just broken fragments of stories and conversations overheard in childhood. Although his mother was a good storyteller, this was not her family history but his father's. Li Yao thinks that his father, Li Tiren, who was the fifth son and the seventh of Li Hai's ten children, was the last of the family to be born in Xinghe. Arriving in Zhuozi County, the Li family found nothing but a vast expanse of grassland stretching before them. While it seemed empty, appearances can be deceiving. Across that sweeping landscape, history had woven an intricate pattern of human occupation, appropriation and deadly conflict.

For three thousand years, the Mongolian plateau had been occupied by skilled horsemen, herding their flocks over great distances to exploit seasonal pastures. These were people of diverse ethnicities and languages. Shamans had taught them to worship the Supreme Spirit of the Sky. They grew a little millet and barley but farming always came a distant second to herding for these grasslands people.

Early on, one group of herders, the Xiongnu, drew the scattered grassland communities into a single large empire. This empire, like those that were to follow, soon fell into see-sawing patterns of engagement and hostility with the settled Chinese farmers to the south. Keeping peace on the borders required vigilance and ingenuity. The Chinese at first tried building walls, mighty walls, to keep the herders out. When this failed they turned to 'marriage for peace' or *heqin*, sending Chinese princesses north to marry the leaders of herder tribes.

David hears the story of Zhaojun, a great beauty from Hubei province, sent as a bride to the Xiongnu. One bright autumn morning, she left her home on horseback, wearing a red cloak and carrying her *pipa* or four-stringed lute. As she travelled, she grew melancholy thinking of the life she was leaving behind. Taking up her *pipa*, she began to sing softly to herself. A flock of snow geese flying south heard her song. Looking down, they were so overcome by her entrancing beauty that they forgot to flap their wings and fell from the sky. Zhaojun is now celebrated as one of the four famous beauties of China. She made a success of her marriage to a Mongol prince and when he died, agreed to become the wife of his successor. Although a risky move, contrary to Chinese practice, she made it work, bringing sixty years of peace to the border regions. Her grave now lies near the Inner Mongolian capital of Hohhot. The Tang poet Li Bai wrote:

> The moth eye-browed one, broken-hearted lies buried in the desert sand . . .
> Dying she leaves a green mound which moves the world to pity.

Her spirit lives on in the peony, the beautiful and greatly prized national flower of China, and her story reaches across the centuries in plays and poems, opera, film and television. It reached Australia in 1949 when Charmian Clift produced a script called 'Lady Bright' based on the life of Zhaojun, for ABC Radio.

The Chinese were to find that even the massive Great Wall of the Qin could not keep out the cavalry of Genghis Khan. As the great Mongol empire expanded, an increasing number of vassal rulers sought peace by presenting their daughters to Ghengis Khan as brides. In 1265 CE, Princess Maria Paleologina, daughter of a Byzantine emperor, started out from the city that is now Istanbul to marry the son of Genghis Khan. Finding that this son had died by the time she reached the grasslands, she married Ghengis' grandson instead. When he also died, thirteen years later, Maria at last was able to make the long journey home. She is still remembered in Istanbul at Kanile Kalise, the Church of St Mary of the Mongols, the only ancient Christian church in Istanbul not to have been converted into a mosque.

By 1206 CE, Genghis Khan had become the 'Great Khan' ruling a Mongol Empire stretching across Asia. He gave his nephew Kublai control of the Mongol-held territories in northern China. Consolidating his power, after Genghis died, Kublai Khan, proclaimed that a new Yuan dynasty led by Mongols would now rule China. But this dynasty proved short-lived, defeated by armies of Ming Chinese in 1368 CE. The last Yuan emperor was forced to retreat to the grasslands where his Mongol descendants continued to rule as Khans in Chahar province. Here they remained largely undisturbed until the first stirrings of yet another empire arose to their east at the beginning of the seventeenth century. The Manchurian war leader Nurcaci led his forces across the Great Wall to invade China. When Nurcaci died, his son Hong Taiji continued his father's campaign, first turning north to wrest control of Chahar from the Mongol Khan, then returning to the Chinese city of Shenyang. Here, he proclaimed himself the emperor of a new Qing dynasty, leader of a people he now called the Manchus.

Visiting Shenyang together, we explore Mukden Palace, with its beautiful yellow roof tiles, the residence of the first three Qing emperors. The Qing government valued Chinese settlers and encouraged them to migrate to Chahar province. Mongol resistance was swiftly put down. To ensure the Mongols stayed quiet, Chahar was kept under tight Manchu control. Chinese migration accelerated. While some Mongol princes grew wealthy by renting land to Chinese farmers, many poor Mongol herders were displaced from their traditional pastures and slid into poverty. Roman Catholic missionaries from

Belgium added to the mix of Mongol, Manchu and Han Chinese. By 1865 their Xiwanzi Mission in Chahar had around 5000 followers.

When Li Hai reached the site of his new farm, Li Yao says he found 'only a vast expanse of prairie'. The men quickly built a very simple hut in which to shelter, made from tree trunks, stacked straw and mud. Their life was very hard as they prepared the virgin land for planting. They worked from morning until night. Even the women with their little feet worked as men, helping to build the houses, and as Li Yao describes it, 'opening up the wasteland'.

Li Yao's grandfather, Li Hai

During this time, more and more Chinese arrived, taking advantage of cheap land and the chance of a new beginning. For the Li family the prospect of starting out again in such a desolate place, far removed from their ancestral home, must have been daunting. They felt on their own out there with bandits and ruffians roaming the grasslands. There were good markets for their grain down south in Shanxi, but it would be some time before they had grain to sell. When the Australian, George

'Chinese' Morrison, the London *Times* correspondent in Peking, came to inspect the new Trans-Manchurian Railway in 1897, a decade or so before the arrival of the Li family, he was unimpressed. Inner Mongolia was as 'treeless as the plains of Australia'. Nothing but 'windswept hills'. The only dwellings were the occasional Mongol yurts (*gers*) 'made of stretched sheepskin' and the rare station house 'half sunk into the ground' where you could pay for your meal 'with a slice sawn off a slab of brick tea'. He found it a 'poverty-stricken' place.

Did the Li family notice the environmental impact of their presence? Given their peasant background, they would have seen farming as an advance on herding, a better and more productive use of land. Did they notice that tigers, bears and deer and even the wolves so important to Mongolian culture were disappearing from the plains? Trees too were coming down. Trees had their uses, but what use were tigers and wolves to farmers who measured progress in terms of rich harvests? Besides, the sound of the marauding wolves who had come down from the mountains at the time of the great famine was not something Shanxi villagers would ever forget.

In 1891 the Australian James Campbell journeyed through Siberia into Mongolia, taking many notes. His reflections on his trip were widely circulated in Australian newspapers. Campbell, who grew up in the gold town of Ballarat, had an appetite for exotic travel. Not just a wealthy man, he was widely read and well connected. Shortly before his trip, he had become a member of the Legislative Council of Victoria. Travelling into Mongolia, Campbell was struck by its great empty spaces. He saw how the Qing government promoted Chinese settlement and found parallels with the process of indigenous displacement occurring in Australia and North America. But there was one crucial difference: where the Mongolians were being 'jostled' out, the 'native' populations of Australia and North America had been brutally pushed out by new settlers. He warned that the Han Chinese, and European Americans and Australians might themselves become 'the aboriginals of the future' when they in their turn encountered a 'superior race'.

Across the grasslands, Chinese numbers and influence continued to increase. Clashes broke out when the Mongols tried to collect rent.

As the Li family rented their land from Merchant Niu, Li Yao has no stories to tell about problems with the Mongols near Li village, the small settlement that gradually developed around the Li family farm. But as we race across the landscape on the fast train from Beijing to Suzhou, he recalls how Mongols did at times approach the Li family, asking for grain and food. Lapsing into silence, he looks out the train window.

Li Yao's parents always described his grandfather Li Hai as an intelligent and resourceful man. Although he had only studied for 'two winters and two springs' in a little private school, he could read and write. There appeared to be nothing he could not make or fix around the farm. David and Li Yao laugh ruefully at this discovery. Both had grandfathers who were practical men, good with their hands, but they themselves are quite unable to make, let alone fix, anything. Li Hai was not only a good farmer and businessman, he was also a skilful carpenter, stonecutter, potter and blacksmith. He and his wife Wang had seven sons, six of whom survived infancy. Li Yao's father, Li Tiren, was the fifth son, born on the fifth day of the twelfth lunar month of 1905. With six surviving sons and three daughters, Li Hai was a blessed man earning enough from the land to have some money over after paying his rent to Merchant Niu.

One year, after observing the sky and carefully studying the weather, Li Hai predicted that the coming year would be a particularly good one for buckwheat. He turned most of his land over to this grain and was rewarded with a bumper harvest, enabling him to buy a small piece of land for himself. From that time on, at each opportunity he added to his holdings. Old habits die hard. The Lis were Shanxi people and they are well known for their frugality. Li Yao thinks stinginess might be a better word. While Li Hai grew wheat and buckwheat, his family always ate cheaper food—corn, oats or potatoes. During the great mid-Autumn Festival celebrated with moon cakes, Li Hai allowed only half a moon cake per person. At Spring Festival, it was dumplings only. Li Hai was always saving to buy more land. By the time of his death in 1946, he had accumulated at least 90 hectares.

About thirty years before the Li family decided to move out of Shanxi, David's great-great-grandfather, William Walker, and his wife, Isabella, left Lincolnshire to face the long sea voyage to South Australia, a world away. South Australia, unlike NSW and Tasmania, was not a convict colony. Free settlers, particularly those adhering to the new non-conformist strands of Christianity, were to be the building blocks of South Australian colonisation. The colony became a 'paradise of dissent'.

There were three main paths out of the squalid inequality of early British industrial life. One path was by strict religious adherence, avoiding temptations like alcohol and gambling. Another was through political action as radical thinkers called for wholesale social change. A third path was to escape factory life altogether and try somewhere else. The immigrant with his trunkful of possessions waving goodbye to family and friends, perhaps never to return, became one of the stock figures of the nineteenth century. William and Isabella took the first and last of these three paths. They were Methodists, a fast-growing church community in a society where poverty and disease destroyed the lives of many working people. Methodists denounced the brutalising factory system and particularly abhorred one of its most pernicious symptoms: drunkenness.

There was no place for Aboriginal peoples in British plans for South Australian settlement. Seen at the time as 'Stone Age' people, unable to improve the land by agriculture, their role was to die out. The British believed that sturdy 'yeoman farmers' were what was needed. To them, farming land should be systematically distributed at an affordable price. South Australia's benefits were extolled throughout the United Kingdom. It was promoted as a salubrious land with gentle summers 'free from excessive heat' and praised for its extensive waterways, sheltered gulfs and fertile soils.

On arrival, William Walker laboured at removing tree stumps from Rundle Street, now the main shopping street in Adelaide, the state capital. When he heard of gold discoveries in Victoria, he took off for Mt Alexander near the town of Castlemaine, finding enough gold to buy a farm in the Adelaide Hills. Both the Li and Walker families started with life on the land.

William Walker's eldest son, John Thomas Walker (David's great-grandfather), did not remain a farmer. He moved to Burra in 1873 to open an 'emporium'. Burra is located on the traditional lands of the Ngadjuri, or 'peppermint gum tree people'. On the surrounding plains, in a time well before there was any light pollution, it was extraordinary to look up on a cold clear night at the overarching sky. Aboriginal Australians are the world's oldest astronomers, who used the slow passage of stars and planets to follow the passing of time, to navigate the flat lands around them, and to predict the weather. In winter, the southern sky is dominated by the kite-like constellation of the Southern Cross, known to the Ngadjuri, as the footprint of the great wedge-tailed eagle, Wildu. The Milky Way is Wali'bari, a river running across the sky, while the moon is called Bera. The sun is Jandu and about the sun a story survives, passed down through generations as recounted by Fred Warrior, Fran Knight, Sue Anderson and Adele Pring.

An old cannibalistic woman was travelling south towards the Eyre Peninsula with her two native dogs, one red, the other black. Anyone they met on their way, they killed and ate. Two Kudnu, or bearded lizard men, their throats covered in spiny dark-grey scales, were sent out to deal with the problem. They killed the dreadful old woman and her two dogs. But after this, the sun, Jandu, which until that time had always stayed in the sky, disappeared down into the underworld of the west and did not return. In desperation the Kudnu men hurled their boomerangs, west, then north, then south, but the sun did not come back. Finally they threw their boomerangs hard to the east and slowly, the sun returned.

The flat expanse and gently undulating hills around Burra resemble the grasslands near Li village, but the process of settlement was rather different. There was no sense in which European colonists were invited onto Ngadjuri lands. While the number of Ngadjuri people at the point of European contact is quite uncertain, by 1850 there were no more than seventy individuals left. They had been dispossessed, dispersed, killed in conflict or died from infectious diseases against which they had no immunity. They suffered an abrupt land grab by European pastoralists wanting good grazing for their sheep. In addition, from 1845, copper had been discovered which brought a rapid influx of miners to the area. Over the next thirty years, Burra became one of the world's leading suppliers of copper, attracting many adventurers including some Chinese. Handsome fortunes were made. John Thomas Walker saw a business opportunity, miners and pastoralists needed sturdy boots.

The first requirement of the European settlers when they came to Burra was for shelter. Their earliest efforts were crude wattle and daub structures later replaced by more permanent stone houses. They then put in wooden posts and yards and yards of smooth iron wire to fence their land. There are high walls around the houses but no fences around the fields in Li village.

While Li village to this day still supports a farming community, Burra's life as a mining town did not last long. When the copper ran out, people turned to wheat farming, against the stern advice of the South Australian Surveyor General, George Goyder. One new town was given the hopeful name 'Farina', the Latin word for flour. Farina soon had over 600 residents and up went a school, church, post office, saddlery, blacksmith's shop, two breweries, two hotels and a bakery.

To Goyder's surprise, the wheat harvest of 1870–71 was a great success while the crops of 1872–73 were superb. Railways were extended to bring the wheat to the nearest port. During the 1870s, as northern China sank deeper into drought, the Southern Oscillation brought heavy rains to South Australia. The widely held view that 'rain followed the plough' appeared to have been vindicated and nay-sayers like Goyder were derided. Nevertheless, as more and more hopeful wheat farmers moved onto the saltbush plains, Goyder continued to issue dire warnings that this region was suitable only for pasture.

The season of 1880 opened with good rains but then became very dry. It remained dry through winter. Red rust infected the wheat and swarms of locusts moved in. The settlers knew their Bible and thought of the words in Exodus:

> . . . the LORD, the God of the Hebrews, says: . . . I will bring locusts into your country tomorrow. They will cover the face of the ground so that it cannot be seen.

In 1880, crops failed. The season of 1881 proved just as bad. Farmers walked off their land, leaving behind their handsome stone farmhouses, built with so much optimism just a few years before. Some still stand there today.

Li Yao visited Burra in 2014, staying in a small room in the Paxton Square cottages, a complex of single-storey terrace housing built by the mining company for their Cornish workers in 1849. In the middle of the night he sensed a presence. Near the bed stood a lady in a beautiful long dress, holding the hand of a little girl. Li Yao reached out and touched her dress. It was very cold. He knew this was a ghost and he was afraid. But the woman told him not to be afraid, she was just there to get some biscuits for her daughter. Her little girl liked biscuits. Li Yao called out to his friend, Nick Jose, sleeping in the next room and then abruptly woke up. No-one was there. In the morning, when he told his story everyone agreed that he had seen a ghost, a not uncommon occurrence in Paxton Square cottages.

David doesn't see ghosts, but he could almost feel them, standing among rocks, earth and stunted saltbush 40 kilometres outside Burra where there had once been a town called Florieton. His family believes that some members of the Walker clan once lived here. Florieton is now very hard to find, swallowed by a landscape of biblical immensity. It takes the skills of Les Warnes, a Burra farmer, to locate it. Aged eighty-eight and unsteady on his pins, Les is an observant fellow. Seated in his old four-wheel drive, both hands on the steering wheel, he eases his vehicle smoothly down the Goyder Highway at a sedate 30 kilometres an hour. 'See that hill there,' he says, pointing, 'that's where the Woodcutters' Arms used to be.' There is not a tree in sight. Had it always been like this? Les is not so sure. He has seen an early photograph showing a long line of axe-men. The furnaces for the Burra coppermines had got through 100 tons of wood a day. In the forty years from 1845, that added up to a lot of trees.

David consults *The Cyclopedia of South Australia*. He finds that around the time when copper was discovered, the hills of Burra had been covered with gum trees and she-oak. 'There were extensive patches of scrub, the gullies were filled with shrubbery, wildflowers were very abundant' and the creek was lined with large gum trees. Within a dozen years, as goats roamed everywhere, the grasses, bushes and shrubs were eaten down to their roots and the trees had been carted off for fuel for the mines and homes. An era of 'bareness' had begun.

After half an hour of steady driving, Les pulls sharply off the road. Low blueish hills can be seen far away on the horizon. In the middle distance a thin line of trees marks the course of the Burra creek, dry more often than not. Easing his way through knee-high saltbush, Les points out a square stone well, still delivering water. Florieton had briefly been a stop along the main stock route from the Darling Downs in northern NSW leading all the way to Kapunda in South Australia where the great cattle baron, Sir Sydney Kidman, had his auction yards.

A closer look reveals some low stony walls, all that remained from the old buildings, each only a couple of rooms and a solid fireplace. Around the ruins assorted debris lay glinting: bits of weathered green and brown glass, some twisted wire, horseshoes and the metal nozzle of an oil lamp. On fragments of crockery, delicate floral patterns remained, suggesting a European elegance out of keeping with the desolation of their final resting place. German settlers had been drawn to Florieton. They can be seen lined up for a photograph taken outside the town's post office in 1914, not a good year to be German in Australia.

CHAPTER 4

Engaging the enemy

David finds a photograph. Arrayed before him are his grandmother, her sisters and other young women of Burra, dressed in kimonos, holding dainty fans and umbrellas. Evidently, in the first decade of the twentieth century, *Japonisme*, that Western enthusiasm for things Japanese, had made the unlikely journey to Burra. In 1914, Japan was Britain's gallant ally in the East. The Walker family's local Methodist church had decided the time was ripe to raise funds with a Japanese Fair. Walker and Sons buzzed with excitement at this lucrative encounter with rising Japan.

By the 1930s, the Walkers' attitude would certainly have changed. In Tokyo the militarists now had the upper hand. Japanese troops were strengthening their hold on Chinese territory, while the Chinese Nationalists led by Chiang Kai-shek struggled to govern their turbulent country. In northern China, warlords fought amongst themselves, while in the hinterland Communists built up the Red Army. The Walkers, while not following what was going on, would have felt that the Asian world to their north was becoming dangerously unstable.

Around this time, David's mother, Glasson, began training as a primary school teacher. She was an outgoing, intelligent but rather highly strung young woman, keen on the new balletic art of eurythmics. Gilbert was a steadying influence and smartly dressed too, a gentleman whose Burra-made shoes were always beautifully polished. They married in 1936 and began teaching together in Adelaide primary schools.

Li Yao's maternal grandparents, Yao Xianyun (right) and Li Hongzao

Li Yao's mother, Li Yueheng, also trained as a primary school teacher. Born in 1917, she was six years younger than Glasson. Her parents, Li Hongzao and Yao Xianyun, were peasants farming a little plot of land near the city of Fengzhen in Inner Mongolia. Close by, sections of the earthen Great Wall, surviving from the Ming dynasty, stretched across the countryside. Li Hongzao was an unreliable fellow, but his wife, a fine housekeeper, was much loved by her family. She encouraged her precious only child, Li Yueheng, to study. Girls at that time rarely attended school, especially when neither parent could read or write. But this little girl, her feet belatedly freed from bandages, came top of her class. Teacher Qiao soon learned of her abilities and helped persuade her parents to let her continue her schooling.

At the age of fifteen, Li Yueheng sought a place at teacher training college in Jining but the only vacancy went to a male student whose father was a powerful local man. Undeterred, in 1932, she travelled alone by train through turbulent northern China to take an examination in Hohhot. Only a year earlier, Japanese troops had created a small explosion on the railway line near Shenyang as a pretext for occupying the city. Soon after, they marched north to invade Manchuria where they set up the puppet state of Manchukuo. Shanxi and Inner Mongolia were evidently next in line.

Visiting Shenyang in 2013, David is very surprised to find himself standing on the railway line where the notorious 'Mukden Incident' had taken place. In northern China, it is the subject of many songs. Li Yao breaks into 'Along the Songhua River', telling how people fled from their homes after the awful events of 18 September 1931 (in Chinese, the month appears before the day): '9.18; 9.18'—*Jiu yi-ba, Jiu yi-ba*, the repeated line drives home the date. Shenyang now has an enormous 9.18 Historical Museum to ensure no-one forgets the beginning of the anti-Japanese war.

In the 1920s, the city of Mukden/Shenyang was controlled by the notorious warlord Zhang Xueliang. In 1923, William 'Farmer' Whyte, the smartly dressed editor of the Sydney *Daily Telegraph*, passed through Mukden's high city walls to get a look at the old city. He was intrigued by its 'strange, polyglot population—Chinese, Manchus, Japanese, Russians', including some of the most 'evil-looking faces' he had ever seen. Several months later, another Australian writer, G.C. Dixon, visited Mukden, again finding little to like. Its streets were unpaved, there was no sewerage system and he was disturbed to find rival Chinese and Japanese telephone exchanges. On meeting the warlord Zhang Xueliang, Dixon described him as a burly, somewhat dissolute but voluble fellow. If Zhang was not at his best then, worse was to come. By 1928 he was a morphine addict, a physical wreck who desperately needed taking in hand. That task fell to another Australian, a friend of 'Farmer' Whyte, the journalist W.H. Donald. As a Methodist, Donald knew all about the straight and narrow.

Born in Lithgow, NSW, in 1901 Donald had become a journalist in Hong Kong and China. Blunt to the point of rudeness, he did not speak Chinese and refused to eat Chinese food. Even so, he became very well known as a trusted advisor to Chiang Kai-shek and other Chinese leaders. After visiting Mukden, Donald took up the challenge of restoring Zhang Xueliang to full health. Gambling, loose women and the needle were banned, replaced by long walks, golf and clean living, and in 1933, a recuperative trip to Europe. Zhang returned to Mukden bursting with energy and new-found patriotism, even if somewhat too impressed with Nazi Germany. His health restored, Zhang was to live on to the age of 100.

In Shenyang, Li Yao arranged for his Australian guests to stay in the Liaoning Hotel. Opened in 1927 by the Japanese, it retains its Japanese proportions, cedar door frames and elegant rooms. It is easy to imagine the atmosphere of the 1930s when Zhang Xueliang mixed with Mukden sophisticates, spruce army officers and beautiful Chinese starlets. The visitors are taken to see Zhang's carefully restored residential compound, where Western clocks and chandeliers vie with ornate carvings, shuttered windows and curtained alcoves. Everything suggests that the warlord was a man of culture until the visitors reach the little Western-style 'tiger room'. Here, in January 1929 after inviting them to dine, Zhang had pulled out his pistol in front of his dinner guests and shot two of his officers whom he suspected were too pro-Japanese.

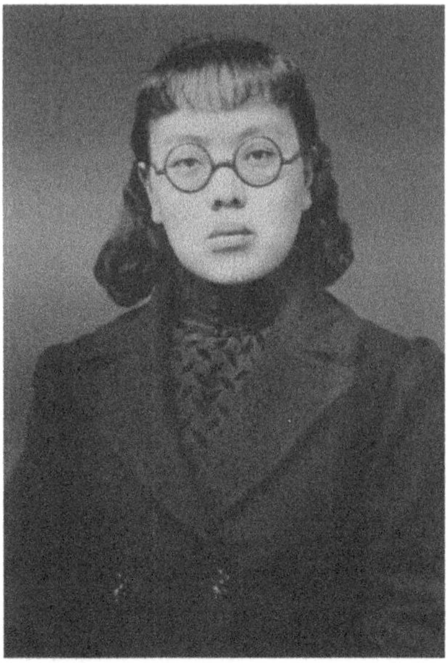

Li Yao's mother Li Yueheng as a young woman

Li Yao's father Li Tiren as a young man

In 1932, Li Yao's mother, Li Yueheng began her studies at the Women's Normal School in Hohhot, graduating four years later at the age of nineteen. Forming lasting friendships with the three girls in her dormitory, these years were the happiest of her life. Yet war drew closer. Inner Mongolia's province of Rehe (better known in the West as Jehol) was swallowed up by the puppet state of Manchukuo. Ignoring Western condemnation of this land grab, Japan left the League of Nations.

The Japanese advance brought new layers of complexity to life in northern China as competing forces jostled for power. Small potatoes could never be sure who to back. The old strategy of working away quietly while the bigwigs fought for the spoils grew more difficult as war destroyed homes, forced people to move and seriously disrupted daily life. Having captured Rehe, the Japanese began looking towards the adjacent Inner Mongolian provinces of Chahar and Suiyuan. Once these were taken, Japan could establish a useful buffer state, Kahoku Bunri Kesaku, lying between China, Outer Mongolia and Manchukuo.

Through 1934 and 1935 frequent armed clashes occurred. Alarm spread. Opposition to the Japanese advance came from the Chahar People's Anti-Japanese Army and a Mongol army led by Prince De (Demchugdongrub). But, while fighting the Japanese, Mongols continued to yearn for independence. Great plans were hatched in the Guangfu temple at Bailingmiao on the edge of the grasslands. The choices were never easy. The brutality of some Chinese warlords pushed some Mongols towards the Japanese. Others clearly preferred the Chinese, a known entity. But which Chinese? Under which warlord? One fighting for the Nationalists or one fighting for the Communists?

Prince De, becoming impatient for Mongol autonomy, set up a new military government at Bailingmiao, reorganising his army there with support from the Japanese and some Chinese collaborators. Plans were laid for a monarchical Mongol state stretching across Inner and Outer Mongolia. Chinese warlords had other ideas, wanting the Inner Mongolian provinces for themselves.

A warlord, Yan Xishan, governor of Shanxi province, sprang into action. In 1936, supported by Zhang Xueliang, Yan sent his army into the province of Suiyuan to wrest it from Prince De. In Yan's army were two Mongolian communists whose wives had been classmates of Li Yueheng. These two men were adamant, Yan's army should be fighting the Japanese. It was quite wrong to send them to fight against Chinese or Mongolian soldiers. Accordingly, on 21 February 1936, they led out some troops from Bailingmiao looking for Japanese soldiers to kill. Although their insubordinate action was quickly stopped by the army leadership, the incident was later celebrated as the first shot in Inner Mongolian resistance to Japan. Not long afterwards, Chinese warlords joined forces to fight the Japanese invader. Ethnic Mongolians, searching for independence, were conflicted, some fighting with Prince De and the Japanese, others joining Chinese armies.

For almost two hundred years, the Tibetan Buddhist temple at Bailingmiao has been an outstanding landmark, housing in its heyday 2000 monks and lamas. It is the 'Lark Temple' built in *Bailing Di*, the 'Land of larks'. No ordinary larks either but gifted creatures prized for their singing and artful mimicry. On the bend of a river, the temple stands at the crossroads of ancient caravan routes running east and west. We visit the site together in 2015. Passing lines of brass prayer wheels and a small, white-washed pagoda, we enter a warm dark room lit with rows of butter lamps. An old monk presses a blessing on David's forehead. In the main prayer room, brightly coloured flags hang from floor to ceiling, a cloth forest. Two rows of red-robed monks sit chanting in front of a large figure of the Buddha. They take no notice as the visitors move quietly around, intrigued by the bright frescoes bearing inscriptions in Tibetan, Mongolian and Chinese.

After her graduation in 1936, Li Yueheng returned to Fengzhen. As a primary school teacher, she earned 18 silver dollars a month. An ordinary labourer received no more than four, often less. Li Yueheng's good salary allowed her parents to buy a small courtyard house and a half hectare of farmland. For one short year the family lived together.

In November 1936, Prince De's army fought against warlord Yan Xishan's troops only to be beaten in one great battle, a battle that Chairman Mao himself was to celebrate. Li Yao's friend, Mr Wang from Jining, gathers together a group of local historians. Rowdy, cheerful fellows and dedicated smokers, they are keen to take the visitors to one of the small battle sites within this big campaign. The little village of Hong Ge Er Tu, way off the beaten track, is a collection of small houses surrounded by vegetable plots and high mud-brick walls. The dogs are barking but there are few other signs of life. Just outside the village is a shallow ravine, guarded by a crumbling watchtower at the edge of a wide plain. On the day of the battle the villagers hid behind their high walls as the Japanese army and Prince De's Mongol troops struggled towards them through severe wind and snow. The Japanese had the advantage of thick uniforms made from Australian wool. All hell broke loose when the enemy entered the ravine. Chinese machine guns in the watch tower mowed them down. Surprisingly, the villagers were led by a Catholic priest. What was he doing there? The local Party Secretary, himself a Catholic, takes the party into the little village church to see the priest's portrait, a stern dark-haired European man.

Adelaide papers ran stories about these large-scale hostilities between 'Mongols, backed by Japanese' and 'Chinese supported by Russia', while the Melbourne *Age* provided a small map to help its readers locate the province of Suiyuan. The *Age* reported that Japanese planes had dropped eighty bombs, 'some of them gas bombs', on the Chinese troops even though chemical weapons had been banned by the League of Nations. In Australia, World War II is said to begin in September 1939, but David argues that if Australia is to be an Asia-Pacific nation it might need to rethink this date—there is also 7 July 1937, the day when Japanese soldiers, trying to force their way into the walled town of Wanping, began fighting with Chinese around an ancient bridge, known to Marco Polo. Accordingly, this became known as the 'Marco Polo Bridge Incident'. From this place (Lugouqiao), fighting escalated. Very soon the Republic of China was fighting a full-scale war with the Empire of Japan. Had World War II begun?

On either side of the historic bridge at Lugouqiao, there is a long row of carved lion heads, each with a different expression. A very large Anti-Japanese War Museum stands nearby. When David was a university student, the 'Marco Polo Bridge Incident', just like the 'Mukden Incident', had seemed more mythical than real. Visiting Lugouqiao was a surprise. The bridge is just 20 kilometres from Beijing.

On 10 July 1937, the Adelaide *Advertiser* reported four battles at the Marco Polo Bridge, noting how washerwomen were 'returning to their laundry tubs' between intervals in the fighting. Gil and Glasson, fully occupied caring for their baby daughter Beverley, probably took little notice. As was customary, the Adelaide *News* sent reporters to meet arriving ships to gain eye-witness accounts of overseas events. Returning from his homeland, Mr Leone Wah, a prominent Sydney businessman, emphasised: 'China will fight to the last man and with the last ounce of energy.' Australian journalist Cecil Taylor, news editor of the Beijing-based English-language paper the *Peiping Chronicle*, supported this view, telling reporters that Chiang Kai-Shek 'is doing wonderful work'. Australians nonetheless were divided in their responses to the hostilities between China and Japan. Some thought it best to stay clear. There was too much to be gained from continued trade with Japan. Others were relieved that Japan's military effort was directed north towards China rather than south to their sparsely populated continent. A smaller number supported the campaign of articulate Nationalist Chinese diplomats led by Dr Pao Chun-jien in Canberra and Tsao Wenyen in Sydney who urged Australians to aid China in its hour of need.

Meanwhile, outright war drew ever closer to Fengzhen. September is traditionally the time for fighting in northern China, after the summer heat and before the brutal cold of a northern winter. In September 1937, Japanese troops took Datong with its large coal reserves. They then swung down towards Taiyuan, pillaging the city of Guoyang near Li Sanquan village as they went. Li Yao says that 2500 civilians were killed. Houses and temples were burned to the ground. In the nearby village of Nan Huaihua, people were cut open by *seppuku* or buried alive. Limbs and noses were hacked off. From this village of around one hundred families there were no survivors. By November 1937, Taiyuan had fallen. The devastation at Nan Huaihua is remembered today at a museum set in a large formal park. In the dark interior, visitors face confronting sculptures of the tortured and tormented.

While Shanxi suffered, the relentless Japanese were also pushing into Inner Mongolia. Moving into Suiyuan province, they soon took

Fengzhen. Suiyuan was to be ruled by Prince De as part of a new Japanese puppet state, Mengjiang. Li Yao's mother told him terrible stories about what took place when the Japanese took Fengzhen. All seventy-eight soldiers of the Citizen Training Corps were slaughtered. Small boys were bayonetted. Women were raped. Houses were set on fire. Li Yueheng and other girls hid in the cellar. One young girl, a close neighbour, was raped and killed. She was only seventeen. Among other victims was Teacher Qiao, the man who had encouraged Li Yueheng to continue her studies.

Life under Japanese occupation was very hard. Li Yueheng's parents lived on the outskirts of Fengzhen. Whenever they passed through the city gate they had to bow low to the Japanese soldiers. Li Yueheng's mother was an illiterate woman who did not know how to bow properly. Every time she entered the city, Japanese soldiers bashed her with a wooden club. It was soon too much for Li Yueheng. She fled to the countryside. Life was hard there for a woman who still had difficulty walking. Eventually she was forced to return to Fengzhen but many of her former classmates joined guerrilla groups led by the Communist Party. Li Yueheng would sometimes tell her son the story of how her classmate Jia Yuxiu was killed in battle.

At a Li family gathering in Hohhot, all the old people have stories to tell. Li Yao's brother-in-law Huan Zhong had been a small boy who stood watching as the Japanese marched in. When a man in front of him yelled at the soldiers, they beheaded him on the spot. Huan points to a scar on his forehead. He had been knocked to the ground by a Japanese boy, cutting his head badly as he fell. Walking back to the hotel, Li Yao tells David and Karen how he had divided his translation of *Gone with the Wind* with brother-in-law Huan Zhong, but Li Yueheng, ever loyal to her son, only ever read his half. We all laugh. It is a beautiful evening and the streets are now full of people enjoying themselves.

Li Yao's father, Li Tiren, had been a student at Zhangjiakou Agricultural College where he developed his progressive leanings. Called Kalgan by Europeans, Zhangjiakou was a strategically important city in Hebei, situated at a point where the river, mountains and grasslands converge and where the main caravan route from

Beijing to Inner Mongolia used to pass through the Great Wall. In 1937 this prized old city fell to the Japanese. By that time, Li Tiren was in Taiyuan, working for a newspaper called the *Zhong Bao*. A fragment of his writing survives: 'If the poor peasants are like hairs on the head; the soldiers of war-lords are like a comb; bandits are like a double-edged fine comb and local ruffians are like a razor.' Li Tiren married for the first time when he was only eighteen years old, according to the custom of the time. His wife was a peasant woman who gave him one son and one daughter, but she died when they were still small. Li Tiren then married his wife's cousin but she too died very young. Life was very hard in north China for women.

As the Japanese grew nearer, Li Tiren joined one of the many armed Guomindang groups springing up all over Suiyuan and Shanxi. Li Yao says that his father knew nothing about guns and fighting. Nonetheless, the group leader made him his lieutenant *aide-de-camp*. He didn't keep the position long. Just two days later, the Japanese overtook his unit and the men ran for their lives. Li Tiren set out for Li village, well away from the Japanese advance, but a very long way to go on foot with no belongings and very little food. He took byways and obscure tracks through the mountains. When he eventually arrived, he looked like a beggar. His family could not recognise him. His two-day career as a soldier for the Guomindang was over.

In these terrible times, it was still necessary to earn a living. Li Tiren searched hard for a job and reluctantly started teaching in occupied Fengzhen. Here he met his son's teacher, Li Yueheng, then aged twenty-four and rather old still to be single. She had turned down one proposal from a rich man. Wanting a husband who was well educated, she chose Li Tiren and soon they were married. But the young couple found teaching under Japanese occupation humiliating. They were ordered to learn Japanese and teach it to their students, something none of the local teachers wanted to do.

In September 1939, David's parents, Gil and Glasson Walker, heard the Australian prime minister Robert Menzies announce that Britain was at war with Germany. This meant that Australia too was now at war. Later, they would listen with alarm as radio bulletins reported the remorseless advance of German troops through the Netherlands, Belgium and France. Bombing raids on Britain began. As time passed, Australians grew increasingly concerned about Japan's intentions. Was war about to sweep over the Australian continent?

The Walker boys stepped up to do their bit. As a teacher with a pregnant wife and small daughter, Gilbert was not required to enlist but his younger brothers, Alan and Laurie, both single men, volunteered for the Royal Australian Air Force (RAAF). Soon they were dressed in smart blue uniforms, although at enlistment neither had ever been in a plane. Alan served with Bomber Command in Britain, flying missions over Germany. Laurie was the uncle that David never got to meet, a slight, dark-haired and very quiet young man who trained as a RAAF wireless operator.

In that difficult year of 1940, Li Yao's parents returned to Li village to be further away from the Japanese. Li Hai was pleased to welcome his new, well-educated daughter-in-law. His youngest son was there too, a new graduate from the Shanxi Polytechnical University. It was rare to have three graduates in such a small village. Li Yueheng suggested they should open a primary school. They could cover a range of subjects but they would not teach Japanese. There was no money in it, but with Li Hai's support and food from the farm, they would have enough to eat. Their house would be their classroom. Together, the three teachers opened the first primary school in the history of the Eighth Sumu. The news soon spread and poor peasants' children from distant villages began to arrive at this school where the teachers were well qualified, and tuition was free.

In June 1941, Laurie was sent to Darwin as a leading aircraftsman. Good to have the promotion but he was disappointed. He had wanted to follow his brother Alan to Britain where the action was. Darwin was a backwater where the men spent their time telling yarns, playing cards or walking to the little shop to collect their mail. Then suddenly everything changed. On 7 December 1941, the Japanese attacked Pearl Harbor, bringing the Americans into the war. On Boxing Day, as Gil and Glasson celebrated their fifth wedding anniversary, Hong Kong was taken by the Japanese. Within a month the town of Rabaul in Papua New Guinea had fallen and the Netherlands East Indies was in grave danger. No-one had news of Laurie. His squadron had flown north to engage the enemy.

Around this time, as the Japanese pushed into the centre of Inner Mongolia, a Japanese couple was posted to Li village to look after the railway. This was not too bad, Li Yao says, they were not military personnel and his mother liked the wife. Much more to be feared were the bands of Japanese soldiers who periodically swept through Li village. As soon as they heard about the little school that would not teach Japanese, they came to arrest Li Tiren. Luckily, he was off visiting his parents-in-law in Fengzhen, so the soldiers arrested another teacher called Li Xintang. Did they think he was Li Tiren, or did they not care who they arrested?

Some of Li Yueheng's colleagues were already in jail. Huddled together in the women's cell, they could hear the daily roll call, 'Li Tiren, Li Tiren'. 'Ah,' they thought, poor Li Yueheng's husband has been arrested. Every day, Li Xintang, not daring to argue with the guards, would shout out 'Yes. I am here!' Li Yueheng later learned how the Japanese tortured the prisoners in that jail by rolling heavy stones on their legs. Li Tiren was lucky to escape, but he had to go into hiding.

For several months, Li Yueheng did not know where her husband was. At the same time, Laurie's parents, May and Oswald, anxiously read the newspapers, wondering where their son might be. In February 1942, they read that a 'Battle for Ambon' was underway. Several days later a telegram arrived: Laurie was 'missing as a result of enemy action'. In 1946, a formal letter finally came from Casualty Section, Australian Armed Forces, stating that Laurence Douglas Walker had been killed at Laha on the island of Ambon. Not long after hearing this news, Oswald died, 'a broken man'. His wife, May, lived on to ninety-eight, a small, rather intimidating figure.

In October 1945, a couple of months after Australians had celebrated VJ Day and the end of the war with Japan, Li village was liberated by the Communist Eighth Route Army. The peace did not last long. By 1947 the Communists had gone, and Zhuozi County was occupied instead by soldiers of the Guomindang. A civil war between the Nationalists and the Communists had now begun. It was not until 1948 that Li village was once again liberated. Li Yao explains how, as an unborn child, he had welcomed the Eighth Route Army in the winter of 1945. Communist soldiers had often camped in the Li household but were not always ideal house-guests. One day, cold, tired and hungry, they demanded dumplings. Li Yueheng, heavily pregnant, went to the pantry to get some pork. Frozen solid, the meat slipped from her grasp, hitting the floor with a loud thud. The soldiers yelled, 'We drove away the Japanese devils and want to eat dumplings. You are a landlord's wife! Tomorrow, you must go with us!' Li Yueheng stood up to them: 'For eight long years we have longed for the Chinese army to liberate us. Now, you have arrived, and we welcome you warmly. You should not bully us!' The PLA leader snapped back, 'Shut up and do as I tell you! Tomorrow morning you will come with us!' Very worried, Li family members quietly warned Li Yueheng to escape. She replied: 'Don't worry, I am pregnant. I don't think they will take me to the front line.' Next morning, she told the group leader she was ready to be taken away. Looking her up and down he said, 'I know you are a teacher, but you are too outspoken. Don't forget you are a landlord's wife. Get a better head on your shoulders!' and they went away without her.

When David was growing up, his family seldom spoke of his uncle Laurie. It was only after his father Gil and his uncle Alan had died that David felt able to research what had happened. In 1997, he travelled to Ambon, a small, mountainous island in the Indonesian archipelago. In December 1941 around 1000 Australian troops had landed there to defend the island against the Japanese. Laurie and the RAAF men were stationed at the Laha airfield. Within a few weeks it was clear that the approaching Japanese had 'definite sea control as well as air superiority'. The RAAF squadron was told to return to Darwin. Nothing more could be done. Most of the men got away safely but the very last aircraft was badly damaged. The eleven remaining airmen were taken by the Japanese as prisoners of war.

In Ambon, David is told what happened next. An Ambonese worker, gathering coconuts watched through the palm fronds as Japanese soldiers brought Australians, tied up and blindfolded, to the edge of a deep air raid trench. One by one they were roughly beheaded by machete and thrown into the hole. The soldiers appeared to be in high spirits, laughing and joking as they went about their grisly work. At the end of the war, Australian troops discovered four mass graves at Laha holding the remains of around 340 men, Laurie and men from his RAAF squadron among them. Ninety-one Japanese were tried for these massacres. Some had previously served in China, where they had evidently honed their brutal craft.

By June 1946, as Australians enjoyed their first year of peace, the civil war in China continued. In liberated areas the Communists initiated a Reduce Rent and Interest Movement, where landlords were asked 'voluntarily' to reduce rents as a first step towards land reform. Although villagers still retained their land, a lot of their grain was taken away, given to the PLA or to those designated as poor peasants. Li Hai sat on a large stone overlooking Li village watching as the grain was removed from his barns and those of his six sons. A river of wheat, oats, and corn flowed out until all was gone. He could do nothing. That night he fell ill, dying soon afterwards, aged seventy-six. He left 15 hectares of farmland and 200 silver dollars to each of his six sons. Through this bequest, they received Landlord Caps that would weigh them down for decades to come.

Li Hai, as a filial son, had arranged for his Shanxi parents and grandparents to be reburied on the hill above Li village. Over time, twenty-six Li family graves appeared there. Li Hai planted a tree there. He often carried water up to that tree, hoping to see it grow tall and shady to create a place where his family could find rest and shelter. When Li Hai died in 1946, his sons buried him there as he had instructed, using the stones that he himself had carved and prepared for his grave.

CHAPTER 5

The birth of the little emperor

In the bone-chilling depths of a Li village winter, minimum temperatures fall to minus 30°C. 'It is cold enough to freeze your arm off,' the villagers say. Everything is under snow. Freer than the peasants toiling below, the swan geese have long since flown off to warmer climes. The sight of them flying tenaciously south, their blood-red beaks catching the dying sun, is nature's sign that winter is at hand. Chinese count down the eighty-one days to spring in nine groups of nine days:

> One, two, hands freeze outside
> Three, four, ice supports your weight,

Not until all of the 'nine nines' have passed will oxen once again 'fill the fields'. Winter had well and truly taken hold when Li Yao was born.

The poor who had migrated north from ravaged Shanxi knew what it was to be cold. In the growing Li family, money was always tight. It was a constant struggle to heat the house and provide warm clothes for their seven boys and three girls. Li Tiren never forgot the biting cold as he herded horses on the grasslands through the winter. He and his brothers always tried to stay close to the horses' warm bellies. When a new batch of steaming manure hit the snow they all raced to be the first to sink their bare feet into the comforting warmth.

All young girls were taught how to make shoes, but only for their fathers and brothers. Making shoes for a young man had to be done with care, it was a declaration of love. Li Yao's grandmother constantly struggled to make good winter shoes for her family. Each took several day's work. First, multiple layers of cloth were cut out to fit the shape of the foot, then glued together with a paste of sticky rice. When the sole was dry, it was reinforced with waxed thread. Night after night Li Yao's grandmother sat under a dim lamp sewing thousands of tiny stitches through the twenty layers of cloth that made up each sole. Only then would the top part of the shoe be constructed. Grandmother's shoes were plain and very practical. Only the rich could afford forty-layer *qiancengdi* shoes with embroidered uppers.

Inside the house a mother and her new baby stayed warm on the *kang*, a fixture in the homes of northern China. Mary Gaunt regarded the *kang* with some suspicion. She describes it as a stone sleeping platform, the length and height of a bed, covered with matting and warmed by flues carrying hot air from fires in the adjoining kitchen. During the day, a small, low table would be placed on the *kang* for serving food. Mary refused to get onto her first *kang* until she had doused the matting with borax disinfectant, followed by half a tin of Keating's Powders, a common Australian product which boasted that it 'Kills with Ease, Bugs & Beetles, Moths & Fleas'. Mary drew upon these experiences in north China for her later novel, *Wind from the Wilderness* (1919). Every house in Li village had a *kang*, the warmest and, in winter, the most sociable (but often smoke-filled) indoor area, especially for women and girls whose bound feet confined them to the house and courtyard.

Strict rules governed the conduct of new mothers in China. It still does today even among the overseas Chinese. But Inner Mongolia had its own way of doing things. Now in her seventies, Li Ruilian from Chifeng explains that for the first month after birth the new mother had to stay in bed, rest and feed her baby. To keep her warm she was wrapped in many layers of clothing. It was essential to avoid chills. Drinking or eating anything cold was an absolute no-no. There was to be no washing of the face, hands or feet and, most importantly, no washing of the hair. Why? Washing opened pores on the head allowing 'damp or evil air' to enter the mother's body.

Visitors were kept to a minimum. But it was believed that the first person other than the mother or the midwife to handle the newborn would have a long-term influence on its character. Li Ruilian's wisdom and good character were so highly thought of that she was frequently called upon to cradle new babies in the hope that they might grow up to be just as capable as she was.

There were many dos and don'ts about diet after delivery. Striking a happy medium between too much and too little food was a good start. But it had to be the right food served at the right time. It was never a good idea to eat raw, cold or spicy foods in that first month. For the first three days, millet porridge, boiled eggs and brown sugar were served. Plenty of protein was essential. Women could be given as many as ten eggs a day. Over the next three days, noodles and chicken soup were encouraged. Soup dumplings were introduced on day seven to help bones recover from the stress of childbirth. After twelve days it was time for green vegetables, a small amount of meat and some soft foods like steamed bread. Li Yao's mother had no choice but to follow this regime to the letter.

Things could hardly have been more different in progressive South Australia when David was born in November 1945. Glasson spent a week in hospital before returning home where she followed the most up-to-date instructions for scientific child-rearing. Out with the old and in with the new. There was nothing more up-to-date than the American authority Dr Spock and his influential manual, *The Commonsense Book of Baby and Child Care*. Glasson was a modern woman who took pride in feeding her baby by bottle at strict three-hour intervals. There was to be no breastfeeding on demand.

In South Australia, heat rather than cold was the problem. By early November 1945, Adelaide had already recorded its first day over 38°C. As they tried to keep baby David cool, Gil and Glasson worried about bushfires. Wet towels were placed around the crib, and after sunset, doors and windows were thrown wide open to catch any fleeting breeze. They had almost lost their first child, Beverley, as brutal temperatures scorched the state for days on end. Birds had fallen stone dead from the sky. At night, Gil would slip into the back garden, refill the bird bath and bury any dead birds he could find.

Chinese names with their sing-song tones seemed strange to Australians. Although contemporary Australia would consider them offensive, up until the 1940s, jokes about 'Ching Chong Chinaman' were thought to be funny. And which was the family name and which was the given name? Moreover, why didn't Chinese wives take their husband's name? Li Yueheng was a Li by descent not by marriage. Her given name 'Yueheng', 'eternal moon', evokes gentleness, femininity and silent yearning for a distant and mysterious world which has long fascinated Chinese poets, lovers and dreamers. Other given names referred to Confucian virtues or to aspects of nature (sea, forest and flowers). Some names had patriotic associations. During the Cultural Revolution, 'Guarding Chairman Mao' ('Weidong') was a popular choice.

On a trip to Australia in 2014, Li Yao visited Melbourne's Chinatown where he saw an arch decorated with sayings from the ancient *Book of Songs*. On one side of the arch are the words *Ri Sheng* (rising sun) and on the other, *Yue Heng* (eternal moon). 'I felt it is my mother waiting for me there,' he says. 'I took a photo of the arch and from then on the first thing I do whenever I visit Melbourne is to go to Chinatown to see it. I feel my mother's guiding presence there.' Li Yao sends a photograph of himself in front of the arch. A formal pose, no smile. The posed photograph is a Chinese institution. To capture just the right look, several photographs are often taken. Li Yao constantly checks his smartphone, removing his glasses to scrutinise each new image. He posts his best photos to WeChat where they are shared by who knows how many people.

Li Yueheng died in November 2012 at the great age of ninety-six. Her life spanned immense changes. This young girl whose feet had once been bound lived to see China become a world power with opportunities for ordinary people and many new technologies, computers, high-speed trains, mobile phones—unimaginable in her childhood. In her lifetime, China has moved from the countryside to the city, from rural communities to towering rows of apartment buildings.

The first ceremony after Lunar New Year is 'Tomb Sweeping Day', a time for families to pray for their ancestors, clean their graves and burn joss sticks and paper money. There are two remarkable burning towers, each about 5 metres high, at the Chinese cemetery in Beechworth, a former goldmining town in country Victoria. They were erected in the 1850s when there were over 7000 Chinese seeking gold at the nearby diggings. Mary Gaunt was born in February 1861, only a 'stone's throw' away, soon after her father had been appointed as 'Protector of the Chinese'. Mary remembered Chinese miners coming to their door to seek protection after acts of vandalism or violence. 'Vegetable John', a Chinese market gardener, was another regular visitor.

One day in 2015, Li Yao and his elder sister decide it is the right time to visit their mother's grave near Jining. Li Yueheng had chosen this particular cemetery herself. Li Yao suspected there were too many bitter memories in Li village for her to want to return there. The cemetery spreads out across a sloping hillside, facing the rising sun. The little party finds Li Yueheng's grave. Its white marble headstone gives the dates of her birth and death and displays a photograph of her and her husband although Li Tiren, who died in 1969, does not lie here. He is buried in the Li family grave above Li village. All that Li Yueheng still had of him was a pair of his reading glasses. These and a small photograph of him are buried with her.

Li Yao builds a small fire. David looks across to the graves on either side. There have been fires there too. Li Yao and his sister burn funerary money and make small offerings. On hands and knees, they pray to their mother, not quietly as Australians might do, but openly and emotionally, calling out her name, telling her how much they love and honour her, asking for her forgiveness, her blessings, her support. They are her children. Li Yao explains to his mother that the strangers are friends from Australia who will help him write a book about the Li family. He tells his mother how he has taken these friends to visit Li village. They have seen her tiny home and the school where she had taught. As the children talk to their mother, tears run down their faces. Li Yao nods as Karen places a small stone on the grave as a mark of respect. David stands to one side, watching quietly. He was taught to avoid emotional display. Yet, standing on that hillside, he thinks of his own mother's protracted and terrible death.

He visited her grave in Adelaide once only, in silence. Glasson had been cremated and had no headstone, just a simple plaque. She was a difficult, quirky, but often funny woman who never really embraced the role of mother and housewife, never hiding her belief that having children was overrated. After the birth of her first grandchild, she told her daughter Beverley that one was enough. Glasson's own one child policy.

Glasson did not want to die destitute or demented. She avoided destitution but not dementia. In her late 60s, Alzheimer's disease took hold. Her death forms the final chapter of *Not Dark Yet*. Li Yao says, 'I always cried when I read that chapter.' David imagines Glasson's death as a slow drowning as she was drawn ever deeper into the inaccessible depths of a dark ocean, a soul lost to family, friends and the world:

> The tide goes over, the waves ride over you
> And let their shadows down like shining hair

Long before she died, Glasson had gone.

Who are we when names with all their associations and history disappear? Who are we then? Recently, dementia struck David's sister, Beverley. Names retreated beyond her reach. She began to refer to 'your lovely wife' or 'my other brother'. Gaps in her memory grew wider. In the terrible year of 2020 when David and Karen were locked down in Melbourne, Beverley died suddenly in Adelaide.

Let us take stock of names. Li Yao's father was named Tiren, perhaps a quiet reminder to be kind to others? But for a boy born in 1905 to parents who had lived through the great northern famine, the name may have carried a more historically resonant plea to be merciful to those experiencing misfortune. On the night before his first child (Li Yao's older sister) was born, Li Tiren dreamed that a strange figure holding a lotus flower barred his way. The man told him that if he took good care of this flower the family would enjoy a happy life. So Li Tiren named his baby girl *meng* (dream) and *lian* (lotus). Clever Li Menglian became the apple of her father's eye, but happiness was to elude this family.

Li Yao (right) with his brother Li Xin

In a society that knew terrible famine and privation, all parents wanted their children to prosper, to have food on the table, clothes on their backs and a safe place to call their own. Grandfather Li Hai had always told his family that money made the difference between having an education and missing out. He never forgot how he had lost a court case to a wealthier and better educated neighbour. Li Yao's younger brother was named 'Xin', for prosperity. How did that one turn out? Li Yao shakes his head. 'Not so well,' he replies, 'not so well.'

As the first son, Li Yao was a welcome addition to a family where extra hands and strong backs were always in demand. In *The Good Earth*, her famous account of village life in rural China, the American author Pearl Buck describes the fanfare that greeted the arrival of a boy: festive drinks and baskets of painted red eggs. Then after the first month, a feast of noodles to wish the baby a long life. David is puzzled. What is the connection between noodles and longevity? 'Look here brother,' Li Yao explains, 'noodles are long.' He holds out his arms. Long noodles, long life. But Li Yao is having none of this Pearl Buck nonsense. 'No, no,' he says, 'Li village is in north China and that story is set in the south.' He is an Inner Mongolian patriot who thinks southerners are different and a bit suspect. What southerners did was their business. In down-to-earth north China, having a boy was good news, but there was no silly carry-on with painted eggs and the like. Besides, in the Li household, Menglian was the special one.

Even so, the little fellow was given a big name to live up to. Seven thousand years earlier, on the fluid borderland between myth and recorded history, the sagacious leader, Emperor Yao, established his kingdom in Shanxi. Confucius sang Yao's praises: 'It is only Heaven that is grand, and only Yao corresponded to it. How vast was his virtue! The people could find no name for it.' Emperor Yao came to power at the age of twenty, dying according to the ancient dynastic histories at the ripe old age of 119.

Chinese archaeologists working in the Shanxi city of Taosi have excavated the oldest observatory in East Asia, dating from Yao's reign. Their discovery supports claims that Emperor Yao created the 366-day calendar, a brilliant achievement for an agricultural society governed by the seasons.

Science had its place but so did magical thinking. Portents, sacrificial offerings, good luck charms and prayers were a part of daily life. Evil spirits are crafty and hard to outwit but they move in straight lines and are not good at turning corners. To deceive them, bridges must have sharp turns and deceptive angles. Entrances should present a blank wall to confuse ghosts. Doorways should have a raised step to trip up demons. Auspicious names were useful. Did Li Tiren expect his new son to emulate the great Yao? Strenuous denial from Li Yao. Nothing of the kind. His parents just wanted him to grow up to be a good and useful man. He is both.

Li Yao picked an auspicious day in the lunar calendar to enter the world, 8 December 1945. In Chinese, eight is a lucky number, *ba*. Four (*si*) is not so lucky, sounding very like the word for death. Sound matters a great deal to the Chinese. Best keep well clear of the number four. Never order four dishes at a restaurant. It could end badly. As the twelfth lunar month is *la*, our tiny celebrity arrived at *La-Ba*, a festival observed for over two thousand years. In the Buddhist calendar, it marks the date of Buddha's enlightenment. At *La-Ba*, prayers are offered for a bountiful harvest.

An overnight snowfall has painted Beijing white as David and Karen travel on Metro Line Four to Li Yao's apartment for their first *La-Ba* celebration. Trains come every two minutes. The journey starts in the Haidian district where all the universities are located, so fellow commuters are mainly young students glued to their smart phones. Old folks more commonly travel by bus. Li Yao is waiting on the platform to take his guests by electric bus to his apartment block. The building follows a familiar Chinese pattern, a thickly padded curtain at the entrance keeping the cold at bay. The public spaces—stairs and lifts—are dark and poorly maintained. At his door, the foreigners totter about, awkwardly removing their winter boots. Once inside, they find a small, comfortable, brightly lit apartment. Neatly shelved books line the walls, including all Li Yao's translations. There is a photograph of him receiving his honorary doctorate from the University of Sydney. Something Li Yueheng would have been so proud to see.

The day is uncertain about whether to snow or not. Sitting at the little table set by the second floor window, one can see rows of other apartments. Between them are neatly maintained gardens. There is a little flurry of snow. No festival could be properly celebrated without a distinctive dish. At *La-Ba* it is rice porridge or congee. Tradition and the law of numbers dictate that the rice porridge has eight ingredients (of course), including glutinous rice, red beans, millet, sorghum, peas, dried lotus seeds and, depending on what is available, dried dates, chestnuts, walnuts, almonds or peanuts.

In the old days, the porridge was boiled for several hours, then presented as an offering to the ancestors. All had to be done before noon. Family members then gathered to share the porridge and local gossip, always leaving something behind in the bowl, the kind of thoughtful gesture that might help secure a good harvest. During *La-Ba,* cloves of garlic are soaked in vinegar and left to pickle for twenty days to be served as a garnish for the dumplings essential to the biggest festival of them all, the Lunar New Year. At this time, the first full moon of the year makes its appearance, bearing the outline of Lord Hare, a severe god busy mixing medicine to save people from plagues.

Li Yao's modern apartment is a long way from the Li village of the 1940s. There at *La-Ba,* frozen hands gripped bowls of hot porridge, grateful for the nourishment and warmth. When the harvest failed, the porridge was thin and watery. The men always ate first, talking of how the cold wind coming off the grassland cut through them like a knife. On the day before *La-Ba,* Li Yueheng had begun preparing the porridge, sorting out beans under the watchful eye of the midwife, Auntie Di, Li Tiren's cousin. After a time Auntie jokingly observed that Li Yueheng did not appear to be putting her heart into the preparations: 'It seems that you don't want to eat *La-Ba* porridge? Soon we might be far too busy for you to worry about *La-Ba*?' When labour began, Auntie Di was very pleased to be proven right. Everyone heard her tell the story of those half-hearted *La-Ba* preparations, some heard her tell it more than once.

When Li Yao was a small boy, he loved sitting on the *kang* listening to his mother's stories. 'On the night before you were born,' she would tell him, 'I dreamt of entering a magnificent palace full of fine jewels, sparkling pearls and precious gems—jade, diamonds, agate, cinnabar and amber.' There was gold and silver everywhere. Shimmering silk fabrics adorned the walls and windows. Hand-woven carpets lay on the floors. A new world was coming. She might not live to see it but surely her little boy would.

She told another story. On the day Li Yao was born, a magpie flew over the compound, a very rare sight at that time of year especially in a village with no welcoming trees for birds. The little songster perched on the Li family roof, singing its heart out. It was the talk of the village. Everyone knew that magpies were a good omen. The pleased parents gave their son a pet name, *Zhao-lin, zhao* for omen and *lin*? That was short for *Qi-lin,* an imaginary unicorn-like animal with a horn growing in the centre of its forehead, a portent of good luck and happiness in a society that too often knew neither. But the name *Qi-lin* also spoke to a high moral purpose and the selfless pursuit of wisdom. Farmyard roosters were two a penny, but not this one. He was a Rooster born at *La-Ba* and escorted into the world by the magical *Qi-lin*.

David as a young boy in Cadell

These beautiful stories highlight differences between Chinese and Australian naming. The Chinese choose a name with a body of cultural associations, legends and auguries that they hope will ease the baby's journey through life. They say: 'a well-chosen name can turn a beggar into an emperor'. A good name is a talisman given by the parent to the child. In Australian Anglo-Celtic families, names carry a lighter burden. The child has to make the name their own, the name does not mould them.

Gil and Glasson told no stories about naming. They could have told little David quite a tale. In the Old Testament, David is a shepherd, who grew into 'a man skilful on the lyre, wise in speech, and brave in battle'. Few biblical stories are more popular than that of David and the giant Goliath. Michelangelo must have loved the story. He painted it on the ceiling of the Sistine Chapel in Rome and his 'David' in Florence is the most famous of all sculptures. Plenty to work with there. In truth, the choice of name was much simpler. The new baby's uncle, Alan David, had just returned to Adelaide from war-torn Britain. Baby David was given his uncle's name and he still carries it with pride.

A settler society told many stories of home. May, David's grandmother, was the family matriarch. Her maiden name MacLaren made the association with Scotland clear. Like people from Shanxi, the Scots were known as honest and famously frugal people. David knew little of the McLaren clan's thousand-year history but down to the 1920s, the Walkers identified more with those Scottish MacLarens than with anything Australian. When COVID-19 passes, it might be time for David to visit the small town of Comrie near Edinburgh, the MacLaren family 'home', their Li Sanquan.

Unlike David, Li Yao's infancy was touched by war. When he was only twenty days old, PLA soldiers once again camped in their courtyard house, joining the Li family to sleep on their very big *kang*. Sitting there wrapped in quilts, one of the soldiers began cleaning his rifle. His gun suddenly went off with a flash and a mighty bang, a bullet burning a hole in the ceiling. Li Yueheng feared for her new baby. Had his brain been shaken inside his skull? Would her little Rooster turn out to be a fool? But Li Yao thinks he was lucky. The mighty bang surely sent him wisdom and made him cleverer. He began to learn characters when he was only three years old.

When Li Yao was small, it was common for farmers to find old bullet cases, even live bullets, shell casings and grenades in the fields. War had swept over the area so many times. The peasants prized these objects, turning copper shell casings into pipes. One day Li Yueheng took her two-year-old boy to his uncle's house. As she sat there chatting with her sister-in-law, Li Yao explored the floor, and was delighted to come across the copper casing of a long bullet. Putting it in his mouth like a cigarette, he ran to the *kang* to show off his great find, only to fall over. The sharp edges of the bullet casing cut deeply into his soft palate sending blood everywhere. His terrified mother had no idea what to do. Li village had no doctor, they were in the middle of a civil war and the railway line was cut. There was no way to get to a hospital. All they could do was pray. Li Yao remembers his wound hurt badly. Every day his anxious father would put him on the back of a cow, and amble off towards the hills, believing that fresh air would promote healing. Unable to eat any solid food, Li Yao was fed goat's milk. Miraculously, two weeks later, his wound closed over completely.

CHAPTER 6

The sweet tangerine

After Liberation it soon became clear that throughout China, even in remote Li village, there would be great change. Old social rankings would go. CCP members travelled far and wide to reclassify people as landlord, rich peasant, middle peasant, poor peasant or bad element (rent collectors, bullies or criminals), labels that they would carry with them for decades. In the winter of 1950 when Li Yao was five, a new law for the Land Reform Movement was passed, stating that 'the feudal exploitative system of landownership by the landlord class shall be abolished'. In Zhuozi County, Li Tiren and Li Yueheng were respected teachers, but both gained a new label. Now they were Open-minded Landlords. How was this better than being just a landlord? It meant they were less likely to be harshly criticised by zealous local cadres. Landlords had to attend 'struggle sessions', submitting to criticism and self-criticism until their minds were clear of bourgeois Western ideas and they accepted and approved the CCP and the Soviet Union.

Worlds turned upside down have intrigued many writers. Few were more original than that curious man, Lewis Carroll. In his great classic, *Alice in Wonderland,* cleverly masquerading as a children's story, Carroll created an absurd, amusing and often frightening world where things are never quite what they seem. Alice is extremely tall one moment, tiny the next. Turning around and around as she falls down the rabbit hole, she wonders where she will end up. 'How funny it'll seem to come out among the people that walk with their heads downward! The Antipathies, I think . . .'

Growing up, Li Yao learned that while words were exciting and beautiful, they could also be extremely dangerous. He encountered *Alice* at a time when a whispered word could very publicly turn a big potato into a disconcertingly small one. Li Yao and David both started reading in the late 1940s and neither would ever want to leave the world of words.

Although David's father Gil expressed great respect for reading, he did not do much of it himself. All he needed were the financial and sporting pages of the *Advertiser*, where he could follow the cricket scores and the latest movements on the stock exchange. As a boy, Gil had watched his father emptying the till each evening, recording the takings in his big ledger. Here was a simple plot, that of profit and loss. Accurate book-keeping was the measure of a well-managed business. Gil had heard many 'get rich quick' stories. Burra was not far from Broken Hill, a town where huge deposits of iron ore and silver sustained one of the richest mining companies in the world. Gil was only twenty when he bought his first parcel of Broken Hill Proprietary (BHP) shares. He dreamed of becoming a banker.

The very next year, the Great Depression hit Australia. Now the only job Gil could find was chopping wood. After six months swinging his axe, he grabbed the opportunity to become a primary school teacher, a secure job which would give him the opportunity to go to university, the first in his family to do so. Gil slowly completed his degree part-time while he worked as a teacher with a young family. Much of it seemed a chore, especially Latin. The only subject that excited him was Geology, an enthusiasm partly explained by his share portfolio. The rest can be safely attributed to the professor of geology, the world famous Antarctic explorer, Sir Douglas Mawson.

When he entered the ranks of the South Australian Education Department in the early 1930s, Gil knew he would retire on 10 November 1973 at the age of sixty-five, which is exactly what he did. Throughout Gil's teaching career, South Australia remained one of the most stable places on earth. In 1938, the shrewd, non-drinking Methodist and man of the land, Thomas Playford, became premier, a position he held until 1965, an Australian record for political longevity.

Things were very different for the Li family in China. After invasion and then civil war, they had to face the consequences of their classification as landlords. Li Yao concedes that strictly speaking, this classification was correct. Most of the farmland around Li village belonged to his extended family. So during the Land Reform Movement, all their land was redistributed to poor peasants. Not only their land but their cattle, their horses, sheep, houses, money and furniture, everything had to be divided up. Li Tiren had to move away to teach in the city of Jining, while Li Yueheng and her children were crammed into a single room in the west wing of an old courtyard house in Li village which they had previously rented out to a tenant named Zhou. Meanwhile, Zhou moved into the Li family home, three principal rooms around a south-facing courtyard. He also took the family furniture.

Before land reform, the Li family had got on well with the Zhou family. Old Zhou was also from Shanxi. His two sons were good farm hands, so his family always had enough to eat. They had the same food as the Li family. Every year Li Yueheng would buy a piglet for Zhou's wife to raise. At Spring Festival, the two families shared the pig, half in half. Li Yao accepts that there was still some exploitation because the Li family did not have to do farm work.

Li Yao does not know how much land his family retained after land reform but remembers they had 'one limb of an ox' left for farm work. How did that work? It meant the ox was shared among four families. The village people still remained outwardly friendly. Li Yueheng was a respected teacher who taught their children, some of whom later became minor local officials. Even so, acts of kindness were risky. In 1950, on the night before Spring Festival, peasant Fan had slipped into the Li house with some paper to cover the window in Li Yueheng's little room. It had no glass to keep out the bitter cold. Knowing the Lis had no money, Fan wanted to help even though helping a landlord family had become a dangerous counter-revolutionary act. Li Yao has not forgotten Fan's kind gesture.

Li Yueheng practised the virtues of modesty, generosity and politeness which she sought to instil in her children. In very difficult circumstances, she tried to remain optimistic. Life was not unbearable.

The Li family was not suffering so very much. They had lost their land, their house and nearly everything they owned, but they were not beaten, had not been put into prison or killed. Landlords had become fair game and there were many stories of beatings and murders.

One day Li Yao's mother took him to a big village fair, 10 kilometres away, a long walk for a small boy. The road was rough and his feet grew very sore. Li Yueheng was determined to see a famous film, *The White Haired Girl*, the harrowing story of a poor peasant who falls so heavily into debt that he has to sell his daughter to a brutal landlord. Consumed by shame, the grieving father kills himself. His terrified daughter runs away, hiding deep in the mountains until her hair turns completely white. She is found there by a young farmer, whom she has always loved. Together they take revenge on the hated landlord. The film sent a message: the old society turned a person into a ghost whereas New China turned ghosts back into people. Had Glasson been so inclined, she could have taken young David to see this film when it was shown at Adelaide's Curzon Theatrette, in August 1952.

At the fair, Li Yao's mother bought him a rubber ball, the only toy she could afford during the years of land reform. Memories are coming back to him now. They say that as we grow older what we did yesterday can disappear overnight, while scenes from our distant childhood return to pay us a visit. And there he is, lying at his mother's side on the *kang*. As soon as everyone else was asleep, his mother pops a little piece of tangerine in his mouth, a sweet, unexpected burst of pleasure. Tangerines were very difficult to obtain in north China, let alone in Li village. Someone must have sent his mother one. She had saved it for him. With so many other children around she could not risk the commotion that would arise if anyone saw her giving Li Yao this treat during the day. She waited and gave him little pieces at night. She loved her son very much.

When David was little, the Walker family lived in the small fruit-growing town of Cadell on the River Murray, named after the dashing Captain Francis Cadell, the first to run paddle steamers up and down the river from the early 1850s. There was still an occasional paddle steamer to be seen on the Murray. David remembers going with his mother onto a boat anchored at the river's edge. The magnificent wheel made a great impression. Women were everywhere in hats and their best dresses, perfumed and chatty, balancing cups of tea and little cakes. The memory is sharp, like a brief film clip, but what were they there for? The answer is long gone.

In Cadell, the Walkers lived in a small, three-bedroomed weatherboard house owned by the South Australian Education Department and just across the street from the primary school where Gilbert was now 'Headmaster'. A veranda ran around the house on three sides, a good place to play on hot summer days. Local orchardists grew oranges, apricots, peaches and nectarines. A half-case of fruit was often left at the back door, a gift for the teacher. David still eats vast amounts of fruit. Li Yao orders plenty of watermelon for him as they travel around China.

Although Gil and Glasson were quite strict with their children, they faced small episodes of rebellion. One day, David's sister Beverley took her father's false teeth and buried them in the garden. As she stubbornly refused to reveal their whereabouts, it was some time before Gil retrieved them, soiled and rather gritty. David also had his moments. One afternoon, when he was aged four, he set off down the road to begin a new life away from his annoying family. He was off to see his friend Glenda Coxall. The diminutive traveller was spotted by a local farmer and returned to his parents.

During the time of land reform, Li Tiren began teaching in the Fourth Primary School in Jining about 30 kilometres from Li village. Jining is an ancient city with a history going back thousands of years to the Shang dynasty (1600–1046 BCE). There are stories, always stories. One tells how a royal wife swallowed an egg dropped by a black bird, before miraculously giving birth to the first Shang ancestor. One wintry day in Beijing, Karen and David visit the National Museum where they see early Shang writing on turtle shells. Depending on how the shells cracked in a fire you could determine the future. Useful. Now Jining is a modern city just two hours from Beijing by fast train.

Li Yao missed Li Tiren greatly while he was away in Jining. But one day, his mother allowed him to go with an older cousin to visit his father. Li Yao felt very important. He had been told to deliver a message: Li Tiren was to buy two bolts of cloth, compensation for the poor peasants of Li village. Li Yueheng had already given them everything she had of any value—her watch, her ring, her bracelet, her silk clothing. It was not enough. They still required another two bolts of good cloth.

When Li Yao stepped off the train, his father embraced him warmly, explaining that now they were going off to buy a sticky rice ball. Li Yao asked him, 'What is a sticky rice ball?' 'A small white ball,' Li Tiren explained. Li Yao was perplexed. 'A white ball?' All that he could think of were the woollen balls dangling from the masks used by actors in Chinese opera. Amused, Li Tiren, said, 'No, it is a kind of food', and he heated rice balls up in a little tin mug. His small room contained only a narrow bed, a tiny stove, an earthenware pot, one bowl, one mug, one spoon and a pair of chopsticks. Li Yao remembers how sticky the rice ball was and how sweet. That night, he slept very soundly alongside his father in the narrow bed, the happiest he had been for a long while.

The next day, Li Tiren bought two bolts of cloth with money from his slender salary before saying goodbye to Li Yao and his cousin at Jining Station. Li Yao cried, not knowing when he would see his father again. Waving as the train moved off, he saw his father was crying too. Li Tiren was well aware that his wife and children were having a hard time in Li village. But he could not go home. As a landlord, the best choice for him was to stay away.

After school in Cadell, Gil would play ball games with his children. Sharp catches taken inches from the ground were applauded. Catching and throwing were highly prized skills in a community where people's leisure time was spent playing cricket and tennis. In summer, Gil would take the children down to the river to teach them to swim. That was fun, but the River Murray was dangerous, full of treacherous underwater snags. Every summer there were drownings. Even so, David loved to wander there on his own, peeling away long strips of bark from the tree trunks looking for spiders and lizards.

Along this river bank, the Ngaiawang people had lived for 30 000 years, catching fish in stone and net traps and making canoes from the bark of the mighty river red gums. The river was their source of food, their playground and their connection to country. But there were no stories about the songs, dances and rituals of these people. They were no longer there. David would have liked their Dreaming stories telling how a huge Murray cod had been chased by a mighty hunter down the river. Trying to escape, the great fish had thrashed along the channel, forming bends, reaches and billabongs as it went.

Travelling down the Murrumbidgee River towards its junction with the Murray in 1829, the explorer Charles Sturt saw young Aboriginal men with 'smooth hair and an almost Asiatic cast of countenance' and older men with 'lofty foreheads' standing 'exceedingly erect'. Sturt also saw 'dreadfully emaciated' children and commented that the women were quite unappealing. Entering the River Murray, and navigating its reaches near Cadell, Sturt came upon 'a vast concourse of natives'. He thought some, daubed with 'white pigment', looked like skeletons, others were covered in 'red and yellow ochre'. A confrontation seemed likely until a second group arrived on the opposite bank. A commanding figure 'threw himself from a considerable height' off the cliffs and into the water. Confronting the first group, he forced them to withdraw with an authority that astonished Sturt.

The cliffs on the River Murray at Cadell are majestic. Closing his eyes, David can see them still. As a small boy he sensed their grandeur as something ancient and powerful. He liked to watch the play of light across them as they changed within minutes from a shining kingdom of golden light to a world of moody shadows. He would run home then, to the safety of his bedroom to play with Marmalade, his clever ginger cat. In the middle of World War I, the South Australian artist Hans Heysen painted *The Murray River Cliffs* near Blanchetown not far from Cadell. In that grim year of 1916, it was a quiet, contemplative place for a painter with a German name.

Everywhere you look, the cliffs at Cadell are layered with shells from a lost marine world. For Sturt, this was evidence that the biblical story of the Great Flood was true; God in His wrath had decided to wipe corrupted humanity from the earth. A real clean-up campaign. Everyone except righteous Noah had to go. Pre-warned, Noah spent 100 years building the Ark. He and his immediate family were the only humans to survive, just eight of them along with all those animals. David was at best a fitful and inattentive biblical scholar, but as a child he often wondered how Noah had managed to get all those animals onto the Ark. And how was it that the fierce animals did not bite the gentle ones?

Following the Land Reform Movement, a decision was made to change the name of Li village. Wanting to erase the memory of their landlords, the peasants wanted the village to become 'Fanshen village', revolutionary village, village turned upside down or perhaps 'Happy village'. The new names did not stick. Today it remains Li village. Nevertheless, Li Yao emphasises that land reform had a big impact on the lives of poor peasants. He sings a song from those times:

> Three teams of oxen and a horse,
> Have made me very happy
> In the past, these things could not happen to the poor.
> But this year, rolling wheels have brought them to my door . . .

Soon after land reform, Li Yueheng returned to Jining where she rented a shabby little house. On a clear night you could see the stars through holes in the roof. When the roof leaked, the children put out bowls to catch the water. In winter it was extremely cold. Although this was a difficult time, it was now possible for Li Yao and his two elder sisters to attend the nearby primary school.

In 1951, the Suppression of Counter-revolutionaries Movement swept over China, a campaign to round up bandits, secret agents, bullies, reactionary leaders and members of the Guomindang. According to official Chinese sources, by 1952 at the end of this movement 1.27 million people had been detained and 710 000 had been killed. Li Yao's third uncle, Li Deren, was one of those targeted. As a captain of the local Guomindang Home Guard during the Civil War, he was viewed as a reactionary leader. But in truth, Li Yao says, his uncle had simply inherited his landlord status and knew next to nothing about politics.

One night an old tenant, Lao Geng, slipped into Li Deren's house to warn him that he was about to be arrested. Why would he do this?

Many years earlier, Lao Geng had collapsed in distress on Li Deren's doorstep. After being nursed back to good health, he stayed on to work for his kindly benefactor and in time, accumulated enough money to buy some farmland and his own little courtyard house. Now Li Deren was in trouble, Lao Geng was determined to save him. Very afraid, Li Deren grabbed a few small items and fled into the night. No-one in Li village knew where he had gone. A rumour did the rounds that he had escaped to Taiwan. Li Yao says this was absurd. There was just no way in 1951 that a landlord of few means could escape from remote Inner Mongolia to Taiwan. In fact, Li Deren hid in Hebei for a time, working for Lao Geng's relatives. But there was no escaping the all-seeing Suppression of Counter-revolutionaries Movement. Li Deren took to the road again, this time to Xinghe, the border town where Li Yao's great-grandfather Li Dabao had lived many years earlier. Here, Li Deren changed his name and lived a fugitive existence, but his life was over. He hanged himself in 1958 and is buried by the canal. When his son (Li Yao's cousin) looked for his grave, no-one knew where it was. Li Deren is the only member of the immediate Li family whose body did not come back to Li village to be buried alongside Li Hai.

Li Tiren continued to work at the primary school in Jining. Some of his colleagues were arrested at night because they had been Guomindang officials. Others had been secret agents who had moved from Shanxi, Hebei and other places to Inner Mongolia in order to avoid punishment. These arrests made Li Tiren very anxious. He too had joined the Guomindang when he was an idealistic student. This was in 1925 when the Guomindang was cooperating with the Communists. At that stage, under the leadership of Sun Yat-Sen, it was still a progressive party. As a young man filling in forms, Li Yao always stressed this date. Naively, he thought it showed that his father was a good man because in 1925, the Guomindang had cooperated with the CCP. But only two years later, the Guomindang and the CCP had gone their separate ways as enemies.

After graduation, while working for the *Zhong Bao* newspaper, Li Tiren was just an ordinary Guomindang party member who didn't attend many party activities. Then shortly before the beginning of the anti-Japanese War in 1937, Li Tiren met a former acquaintance, Zhang Wanren, who told him that he had been expelled from Suiyuan province for organising a student movement and now had nowhere to stay. Could Li Tiren take him in for a few days? Although Li Tiren barely knew Zhang, he welcomed him into his home. A month later, Zhang at last moved on. For a long time Li Tiren heard no further news of him, although there were reports he had joined the Communists in Yan'an.

Ten years later in 1947, Li Tiren heard someone calling out to him: 'Old Li !' Turning around, he was very surprised to see Zhang and even more surprised to learn that Zhang was now secretary of the Guomindang at Fengzhen. The last Li Tiren had heard, Zhang was a Communist, a man on the run. How could he now be with the Guomindang? Zhang did not explain but simply asked where Li Tiren was working? Hearing that he was the director of the Fengzhen Mass Education Museum, Zhang was delighted. 'Very good,' he said, 'now my old friend, I can appoint you officer in charge of propaganda and secretary of the Party Branch in the city district.' Li Yao does not know if his father was happy to have been made a Guomindang official, all because of the help given to Zhang ten years earlier.

The new promotion held the seeds of disaster. In the 1950s it made Li Tiren a target for the Suppression of Counter-revolutionaries Movement. He and Li Yueheng worried a lot, especially after Li Deren's sudden flight. Li Tiren carefully explained his circumstances and history to CCP officials, then waited for the day when he too would be arrested. Li Yao remembers how each night he would stand with his mother at the gate of their little house, waiting for his father to return from work. It was winter. The cold wind messed up his mother's hair as Li Yao clung to her. One time, it grew very late and Li Tiren had still not returned. His wife, wild with anxiety, started walking towards the school. Seeing Li Tiren coming towards them at last, Li Yao flew into his arms. His father reassured him, 'Don't worry, my little man! There was just a meeting in the school tonight.'

It was common for people in work units to act on old grudges, denouncing unpopular workmates. Perhaps because Li Tiren worked very hard and was on good terms with his colleagues, he did not get into too much trouble. He was even elected an Advanced Education Worker of Jining, with a salary of 66 yuan per month, the highest paid to primary school teachers. But 'good times don't last long'. Between 1953 and the beginning of 1958, the government began to scrutinise personal histories. This time Li Tiren did not escape. He was classified as a historical counter-revolutionary because for that brief time he had been the officer in charge of propaganda and secretary of the Guomindang Party Branch in Fengzhen. His salary was reduced to 47 yuan per month.

Li Tiren and Li Yueheng never talked openly in front of their children about the government and the CCP, fearing they might repeat something and get into trouble. But on one occasion they did talk about Zhang Wanren, a really lucky man! Shortly before Fengzhen was liberated in September 1948, he had been transferred to Hohhot which then surrendered peacefully to the PLA one year later, in September 1949. In the spirit of letting bygones be bygones, all Guomindang officials in Hohhot were exonerated. Zhang suffered no penalty and went on to become the director of the Inner Mongolia Library. Si Yange, the man who had replaced Zhang Wanren as secretary of the Guomindang Headquarters in Fengzhen, was not so lucky. Fengzhen had to be liberated by the PLA with force, so during the Suppression of Counter-revolutionaries Movement, its Guomindang officials were condemned. Li Yao can still remember how his mother went to Si Yange's house to console his widow after his execution.

In China in the early 1950s it was not a good idea to be a landlord or to have links with the Guomindang. In Australia it was not at all a good idea to be a Communist. In 1950, the *Advertiser* warned that Communism pursues its 'sinister purpose' with 'furious zeal' and 'limitless opportunism'. Archbishop Mannix, the head of the Catholic church in Australia at the time, told his flock that 'too many people were slow to realise the menace'. Communism he said was 'like a bushfire' threatening to 'sweep over Europe, Asia and the world'. Malcolm MacDonald, British Commissioner General for South-East Asia, came out from London to tell Prime Minister Menzies and his Cabinet that 'Australia faces the gravest danger'. Even so, these warnings were less concerned about what Communists might be doing in China than what they might get up to in Australia.

Gil and Glasson no doubt had their concerns about the spread of Communism, but there was a much more immediate danger, the spread of poliomyelitis. In December 1949, the Adelaide *Chronicle* reported, 'Sharp rise in polio cases'. In the preceding week, fifty-four patients had been admitted to Northfield's Infectious Diseases Hospital. Children with polio could spend six months in iron and plaster frames designed to relax their muscles. Many became crippled for life. Worse still was the 'iron lung'. Some children died of inflammation of the brain and encephalitis. Doctors were inundated with calls from anxious parents. Many schools, including Cadell Primary, closed early for the Christmas break. End of year celebrations were cancelled. No-one knew what had caused the polio outbreak, but low-lying Cadell was thought to be particularly susceptible.

In 1953, the Soviet film *A Village Schoolteacher* was very popular in China. It tells how a young woman leaves her bourgeois life to teach peasant children in Siberia. The film's stirring music and theme of socialism and education changing lives impressed Li Yueheng. She was no longer young but she was idealistic. Responding to the government's call, she volunteered to become sole teacher at a little school in Bolitu, a village about 4 kilometres from Jining. To go there required considerable family reorganisation. Her two elder daughters went to live with their father, her youngest son went to his grandparents in Fengzhen, while Li Yao's young sister went to a sister-in-law in Li village. Only Li Yao accompanied his mother to Bolitu.

Bolitu had never had a primary school. Li Yueheng was the first teacher the villagers had ever met. A barn belonging to a landlord was used as a classroom, 'desks' and 'chairs' were made out of packed clay. The school had twenty-five pupils who were taught Chinese, mathematics, music and physical education by Li Yueheng. The barn had only one paper window, soon torn open by a harsh gust of wind.

We make the trip to Bolitu to see the building where Li Yao and his mother had lived. Opening a rickety gate to enter a small courtyard where some runner beans straggle up a line of sticks, a very old woman peers out of her doorway and beckons the visitors in. She and her husband live in two very small rooms—just the *kang,* a cupboard and a place to cook. But there is a satellite dish on the roof and a small TV set. The floor is beaten earth. The old woman has a beautiful smile for these visitors who want to take her photograph. She is happy here and does not want to move into the new high-rise apartments the local government is building.

Li Yao remembers how during their stay in Bolitu, his mother would sometimes take him with her to visit pupils from surrounding villages. If it grew late, they would stay overnight in a peasant's house. Li Yueheng got along very well with these people. When they butchered pigs or sheep, they would often invite her and her boy in for a meal. But life in the countryside at last took a toll. One day, after a physical education class, a severe miscarriage almost claimed Li Yueheng's life. By the end of 1954, she was transferred to a primary school back in Jining. Saying goodbye was hard as the peasants were unwilling to part with her. But the change allowed the Li family to be reunited at last.

In 2009, when David was writing *Not Dark Yet,* he went back to Cadell. The old house was still there looking much the same although the trees around it had grown. Additions had been made to the primary school across the way. But the greatest change was to the orchards. The fruit trees were dead or dying from salination. It seemed there was nothing for it but to rip them all out. 'This lot will all be gone by next week,' he was told by one farmer. The only thing doing well in Cadell was the newly built Correctional Facility, housing a disproportionate number of Aboriginal inmates. Back then that was called a jail.

CHAPTER 7

The little literary giant

The two Roosters, as children of primary school teachers, were taught early in life by their parents. For them, coping at school on their own came later than for most children. Both were shaped by ethical codes (Methodism and Confucianism) that emphasised correct behaviour. They had to be good boys who would not embarrass their families. While David knew his parents were well respected, Li Yao soon discovered that his were bad elements, people from the wrong family background. China was undergoing revolutionary change while Australia was a stable settler society. In the 1950s, China's 'big brother' and source of inspiration was the Soviet Union. Australians at that time saw Russia as a distinctly sinister communist power. While drawing nearer to the United States, Australians continued to emphasise their cultural connections with the democratic traditions, sporting prowess and splendid history of Great Britain.

Li Yueheng started to teach her clever little boy his characters when he was only three. She was proud of his excellent memory. Li Yao says his parents were not too strict, rare at that time in China. In the 1930s, the great writer Lu Xun noted that there were two common ways to bring up children. First, 'Let them run wild without any control' so they could swear and fight. He thought this approach made them 'petty tyrants' at home, but as lost as 'spiders without a web' outside it. Alternatively, treat them so harshly that they turned into obedient marionettes. But then, when set free, they were like little birds who could 'neither fly, sing, nor hop'.

When Li Yao started school, one of his parents was always there. From Grades 1 to 4 his mother taught him, from Grades 5 to 6 it was his father. In those early years after Liberation, most of the village families were illiterate and the school kids were much older than Li Yao. To these older children, he seemed like a little doll, someone to play games with. He says they were always very kind to him. As he listens to this, David grows impatient. He knows that Li Yao owns an old-fashioned pair of rose-coloured glasses. He must be wearing them again. David remembers having teachers as parents very differently. You couldn't win. If you did well it was because your parents had fiddled the books to get you a good result. If your grades were poor it meant you were so dim-witted that even your parents could do nothing for you.

Li Tiren often brought books home for his son. One of Li Yao's favourites was *The Secret of the Magic Gourd*. A young schoolboy finds a magical gourd that grants his every wish. The little rotter lies, cheats and behaves like a spoilt brat before he learns a powerful lesson. The only way to succeed is through hard work. Li Yao seems to have taken this message to heart. Another favourite was *Zoya and Shura*, based on the true story of Zoya Anatoleyevna Kosmodemyanskaya and her brother. During World War II, Zoya joined a partisan group. As the German army approached Moscow, she was caught behind enemy lines. When tortured she refused to give anyone away. The Germans hanged her. But Stalin named her a 'Soviet hero'. Russian soldiers would cry, 'Revenge for Zoya!' as they went into battle.

It had taken some time for Chinese readers to become aware of Russian writers. It was only when translations began to appear in English that Russian writing became accessible to them. Lu Xun observed that once Chinese people started reading these works, Russian literature became their 'guide and friend'. Every branch of Chinese literature was influenced by the Russians, including books for children. From the nineteenth century, Russian educators believed that children's literature was important for their moral education. Maxim Gorky, an early pioneer of children's writing, hoped his work would stir their interest in intellectual and scientific matters. Lenin's widow, Nadezhda Krupskaya, took this further, seeing children's books as 'one of the mightiest weapons in socialist education of the new generation'.

When the teacher and committed socialist Helen Palmer visited Beijing in 1952 as a member of an Australian delegation to the Asian and Pacific Peace Conference, she was impressed by the availability of children's books. At a bookshop in Morrison Street (now Wangfujing), she saw hordes of children poring over books and settling down in corners to read, not at all distracted by the sight of foreigners. She looked at three books: one was about raising chickens, one was a life of Darwin and the third was a fantasy tale. Liking these 'bright little books', she made several purchases.

Li Tiren subscribed to several children's magazines for his son. Li Yao was particularly fond of *Children's Literature, Boyhood,* and *Chinese Juveniles*. He was not at all interested in calculating things; he didn't like physics or maths and was no good at games. He only liked reading. And it was his father who first taught him to love literature.

David was not such a bookish boy. He liked riding his bike, first at Cadell and then, as his father moved from school to school around the state, he perfected his skills: at Northfield on the outskirts of Adelaide, in Freeling near the wine-growing Barossa Valley, at Ardrossan on the Yorke Peninsula over to the west, and at the once volcanic Mount Gambier in the south-east. In Ardrossan, he was given a small device that measured distance. After attaching it to the front wheel of his bike, he pedalled away for days on end trying to push his mileage higher and higher. He loved that bike. When he finally came inside just before five o'clock, he would grab a piece of fruit and sit down to listen to the 'Argonauts Club' on ABC Radio. It opened with a catchy theme song:

> . . . come with a hop, a skip and a run,
> It's time for the session, it's time for the fun.

The program was based on the legend of the Argonauts. In the years before the Trojan War, the Greek hero Jason leaves Thessaly on his good ship *Argo*, accompanied by forty-nine strong rowers or Argonauts. His mission is to steal the Golden Fleece hanging on a tree in a sacred grove in Colchis, guarded by a dragon that never sleeps.

In 1950, there were over 50 000 members of the 'Argonauts Club', each of whom received a ship name and a number. David was Sestus-26. He found no contradiction between this distant world of Greek mythology and the world around him. He laughed loudly listening to the adventures and mishaps of *The Muddle-headed Wombat*, based on Ruth Park's children's classic. Wombat's bicycle had red wheels. He had a lot of fun with his friends Mouse and Tabby the Cat. There were songs, pranks, jokes and byplay. 'Mac' the presenter was a little bit like the Headmaster keeping order (or trying to) while 'Jimmy' his assistant was a naughty fellow whose jokes always landed him in hot water.

By sending in contributions to the program, children won points. Another song urged them on:

Fifty mighty Argonauts, bending to the oars,
Today will go adventuring to yet uncharted shores,
Fifty young adventurers today set forth and so,
We cry with Jason 'Man the boats', and Row! Row! Row!

Sestus-26 adopted 'man the boats' as a brilliant rallying cry for family and friends while 'Jason' became one of the most popular names for boys in Australia. Brian, David's elder brother, a very diligent Argonaut, achieved an Order of the Golden Fleece (400 points). Sestus-26, a rather more erratic 'rower' only got as far as the Order of the Dragon's Tooth (150 points). If David was a fitful rower, he was a keen listener. He loved the radio and was sometimes allowed to turn it on himself. There was a crisp click, a small light lit up the dial and after a crackle or two out came the familiar theme song, comfort, security and excitement all bundled into one.

Through the week, different personalities gave short talks. On Monday, 'Tom the Naturalist' introduced Australian plants, birds and animals. Although they frightened him, Sestus-26 was keen to hear about snakes and lizards. There had been a lot of lizards in his short life and quite a few snakes. But one memory still jars. He once joined boys throwing stones at a harmless blue-tongue lizard. Why had he done this? Certainly, he grew up in a world where humans felt that it was their right to decide the fate of animals. His father shot snakes because they were dangerous and rabbits because they were a pest. David had seen the bodies of magnificent wedge-tailed eagles, wings outstretched, nailed to fences. Later he learned that George 'Chinese' Morrison', who became the well-known *Times* correspondent in Peking, had once set out from Geelong in the late nineteenth century, rifle in hand on one of his walks, and shot eighty koalas on his way.

On Tuesday, 'Phidias' talked about painting. Unknown to Sestus-26, this was the Adelaide-born painter Jeffrey Smart, a very fine artist. Phidias his *nom-de-plume* was a Greek sculptor famous for his gigantic figure of Zeus at Olympia, one of the Seven Wonders of the Ancient World. Some of Smart's early works were painted near Burra during a trip with Hans Heysen. Later in the week, 'Icarus' spoke about writing and literature and 'Mr Melody Man' played classical music.

The accents David and his family heard on the radio were mainly British, not typical Australian voices. The BBC was the gold standard. In those days, the English liked to compliment colonials who had mastered a 'proper' accent. 'Oh!' they would say, on hearing that a visitor was Australian, 'I should never have thought so', thereby delivering, as novelist Martin Boyd noted, not the worthy compliment they imagined but a 'frightful insult'. While David was attracted to words, he was intrigued and troubled by speech, unsure not only of accent but also of vocabulary. In a household of teachers, he soon found there were forbidden words. Swearing was extremely bad, but some colloquial words were also prohibited. He was once told off for using the word 'bloke' when Gil thought 'man' was a better choice. His father was too much of a gentleman to ever be referred to as a 'bloke'. The female equivalent to a 'good bloke' was a 'good sort'. Glasson Maude Wallace Bourne Walker was on no account to be thought of as a 'good sort' and never as a 'sheila'.

Mixed in with the range of BBC voices brought into the house by the radio were occasional accents from European migrants as well as diverse regional accents from across the British Isles. As a country boy, Gil was keen on cricket. Every kind of English accent could be heard from commentators as Australia battled for supremacy over England in competition for the Ashes. Among the specialists dissecting the finer points of the game, the South Australian former player Johnny Moyes was a favourite. There was nothing BBC about his voice, but his wit and love of words was magical for a small boy. Cricket commentary was one of the few fields where Australian men were permitted to play with words.

When David was eight, the young Queen Elizabeth ascended the throne. The royal wedding and the coronation were brilliant affairs. Magazines were full of pictures of carriages, crowns and pageantry. There were a lot of colouring-in books with royal themes, requiring yellow pencils for all that gold. There were scrapbooks, scissors and bottles of glue. In 1954, the Queen became the first reigning monarch to visit Australia. If the Royal Visit presented a rather feminine world of dresses, hats and floral displays, a different side to the British character was on display when David was taken to see the film, *Conquest of Everest*. On this special occasion, Glasson fussed over his curly hair. As the Headmaster's son he had to look his best, with tie, blazer, neat short pants and polished lace-up leather shoes. Gil wore a smart, three-piece suit, with tie and hat while Glasson had a hat and gloves to go with her best frock.

The *Conquest of Everest* was filmed in 1953, but probably reached Ardrossan the following year. The hall was packed, people had come from miles around to see this account of the British mountaineering expedition, the first to conquer Everest. Before the film started, all stood for the national anthem:

> Send her victorious, happy and glorious,
> Long to reign over us,
> God Save the Queen

Then came a stirring soundtrack and remarkable aerial photography courtesy of the Indian Air Force. This was a world of courage and robust British manhood. The documentary told the thrilling story of how Edmund Hillary, a bee-keeper from New Zealand and Tenzing Norgay, a Sherpa from Nepal, were the first to reach the summit of the world's highest peak. There, as citizens of the British Commonwealth, they planted the Union Jack. The film went on to show 'hero-worshipping natives' celebrating the occasion in Kathmandu before cutting away to London where the young Queen honoured the men who had stood 'where no man had stood before'.

When he was ten, Li Yao registered to enter the First Middle School of Jining, one of the best in Inner Mongolia. The School President objected. Li Yao was too young. They only took pupils aged twelve years and over. Li Yueheng marched off to see the Director of the City Board of Education, a man she knew well. Patting him on the head, the Director looked at Li Yao and said, 'No problem, let him try.' It would not matter if Li Yao failed to get in, he could always register to sit again the next year. Li Yueheng was happy with this ruling but very determined. She looked sternly at her son and said, 'You must study hard. You must pass the entrance examination. Don't make me lose face!' Li Yao was not at all sure why she would lose face if he failed the exam, but he looked back at her and replied, 'it will be all right. I will not make you lose face!'

There were only two papers for the middle school examination. Li Yao explains how he planned to pass. He had it all worked out. He was poor at mathematics but he knew how to add, subtract, multiply and divide. He thought that even if he only got 50 out of 100 for his mathematics paper, it would not matter. He was so good at Chinese. In Chinese he would get 90 out of 100. This would mean that his average mark would be 75, a pass, no problem! (David, who is somewhat better at maths, notices that this average is incorrect, a clear demonstration that Li Yao is still no mathematician!) But, having thought it all out, Li Yao continued reading his stories as keenly as ever and didn't worry himself with the dreadful mathematics textbook. The day of the Chinese examination came round. The set topic was 'My Motherland'. Li Yao wrote and wrote. When he later told his mother what he had written, she smiled and said nothing. But it was clear that she thought he had done very well. She knew that her little son was not going to make her lose face. From then on, Li Yao says, he was determined that he would never do this to his parents. 'Don't lose face for the Li Family' became his motto for the rest of his life.

On 1 September 1956, Li Yao became a student in the First Middle School of Jining, in the same class as his second eldest sister, Li

Mengqi. The little Rooster came out from under his parents' wing, to be supported and protected by his sister in this new environment. He went back and forth to school with her each day. Li Yao liked Chinese literature but was not so taken with Chinese grammar. When literature classes started, he was excited. His textbook had a hard cover, the first he had ever had! All the other textbooks were inferior paperbacks. He read so many beautiful stories in his new textbook. Li Yao recalls, 'Oh my *Chinese Literature*! How much you meant to me!'

Some of the stories were Chinese classics like *The Book of Songs*, a collection of ancient Chinese poetry; *Analects of Confucius*, the thoughts and teachings of the great philosopher; and *The Water Margin* (or *Outlaws of the Marsh*), lively tales about a group of heroic bandits. Li Yao liked Lu Zhisen, 'the Flowery Monk' in *The Water Margin* who sports a full-body tattoo and belts his enemies with a heavy iron staff. From their stronghold on Mount Liang, in the middle of an extensive marsh, bandits conduct raids on local villains and corrupt officials.

The author Lu Xun, woodcut by Li Yitai (1954)
Sydney University Art Gallery

Li Yao's textbook, *Chinese Literature*, contained some stories by Lu Xun. After returning from medical school in Japan, Lu Xun had worked as a teacher while starting to write. In 1929 he outlined his views at a lecture at Yenching University (now Peking University):

> . . . although devotees of art like to claim that literature can sway the course of world affairs, the truth is that politics comes first and art changes accordingly . . . Events are seldom what men of letters expect.

Lu Xun, who died in 1936, was highly acclaimed during the first years of the People's Republic of China, when quotations from his writings were frequently used and misused. Mao Zedong was a lifelong admirer of his work.

Li Yao's literature textbook also introduced him to Russian writing. He loved Pushkin's poem *The Tale of the Fisherman*. A poor fisherman catches a golden fish that will grant wishes, but lets it go. This makes his old wife very angry. She tells her husband to go back to ask for a new trough to replace her broken one. Her wish is granted. The next day the wife sends her husband back to ask for a new house. This wish too is granted. The wife becomes insatiable. She wants a palace, to be a noblewoman, to rule the province, to be Tsarina. When she finally asks to become Ruler of the Red Sea, the fish returns everything to its original state including the broken trough.

David was not such a bookworm as the young Li Yao, though he did love the outrageous Mr Toad in *The Wind in the Willows*. Even better was the Australian classic *Bush Christmas*. He would listen intently whenever his mother read it aloud. Glasson was an expressive reader with theatrical tendencies, making the most of a story in which five children from an outback station recover prized family horses stolen by two unsavoury thieves.

Every night after class, Li Yao would read his Chinese literature textbook. Very soon he had finished half of it. His parents were happy to see him reading so voraciously but warned, 'You must study mathematics too! Otherwise, you won't be able to graduate from middle school and you won't be able to study at university!' Li Yao was quite taken aback. He really wanted to go to university. He had to make it happen! He made up his mind to study mathematics.

Due to his inattention, Li Yao found that his basic skills in mathematics were very poor. His teacher was an old man with a lisp and Li Yao could not understand what he was saying. He did not like this teacher at all. One day there was a class on linear equations. The teacher set a problem: there are chickens and rabbits held together in a cage. In total there are eighty legs in that cage. 'Now', he asked, 'who can tell me how many chickens and how many rabbits there are?' Li Yao looked around. It seemed that all his classmates knew the answer. The old teacher asked, 'Li Yao, do you know how many rabbits and how many chickens there are in the cage?' Li Yao was at a complete loss. Very perplexed, he asked, 'Why would you want to put chickens and rabbits together? It sounds very impractical.' His classmates burst out laughing and his teacher was annoyed. Li Yao's resolution to learn mathematics evaporated. He stopped doing his homework and simply copied from his sister. Li Mengqi was good at maths. Somehow, he still managed to scrape through the maths examination every term.

Li Yao's teacher for Chinese, Guan Shulan, was a recent graduate from Inner Mongolia Normal University (IMNU), a university that trained teachers. This is indicated by the word 'Normal', derived from the French system of *École Normale*. Very tall, beautiful and slender, her hair fell in two long plaits down her back. Li Yao was smitten. At that time, he and his classmates spoke Chinese with a heavy local accent. Teacher Guan's accent was much better. She read poems by Pushkin to the class. She let them listen to the gramophone, then a rare object in Jining. One record she played was *The Little Match Girl*, by Hans Christian Andersen. Did she know that Andersen was fascinated by China? In one of his most famous fairy tales *The Nightingale*, the story takes place at the Chinese emperor's palace: 'the finest palace in the world, made entirely of porcelain . . . The garden was full of the rarest flowers and the loveliest of these had little silver bells tied to them which tinkled so that no one should go by without noticing them.' But Teacher Guan was soon transferred to another school. When the class monitor received a letter from her, the other pupils were very envious.

Karen first heard the sonorous tones of Russian when her father took her into Wellington, New Zealand, to see *Eugene Onegin*, a Soviet film from 1959 based on Tchaikovsky's opera, itself adapted from Pushkin's famous verse novel. On Sun Island in the majestic Songhua River near Harbin she thinks back to this excursion. Harbin is a Chinese city with a rich Russian and Jewish heritage. Exploring the island, Karen and David meander through avenues bright with spring blossom. Deep in conversation with Li Yao and his friend Yujia, no-one notices the massed grey clouds and darkening sky. Within moments a storm descends. Sheltering in a little kiosk, Yujia bursts into fluent Russian, giving a moving recital from *Eugene Onegin* as the party waits for the storm to pass.

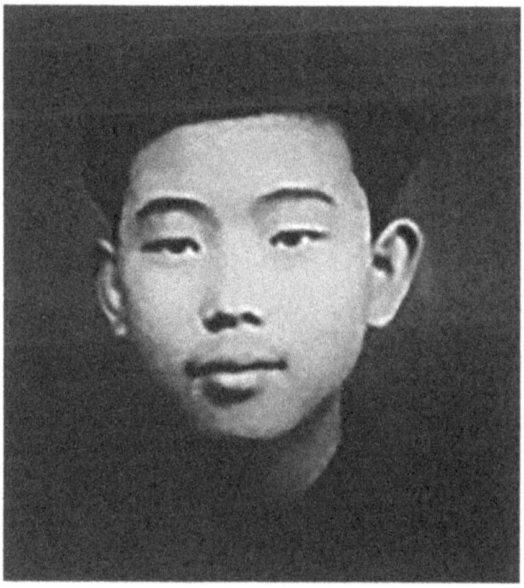

Li Yao as a Little Literary Giant,
at First Middle School, Jining

There were over 2000 pupils at Jining Middle School. Every year it held a poetry competition where pupils would read their work aloud in the large auditorium. When Li Yao was only eleven, he entered this competition with a poem describing his classmates doing their morning exercises. It hit the mark, gaining him a creditable second place. His classmates began calling him 'Little Literary Giant'. His parents were very proud. He now practised writing poems every day, aspiring one day to be a writer and a real Literary Giant.

By 1959, Li Yao had acquired a small library. Magazines arrived monthly, including *Renmin Wenxue* (People's Literature), *Wenyi Bao*

(Literature and Art Magazine) and *Russian Study*. *Renmin Wenxue* was the first literary magazine published in China. One poem in it is about Beijing, recounting the city's troubled history: the foreign invasions, the oppression by landlords, the student protests on May Fourth and the irony that the city was called Beiping (Northern Peace) under the Guomindang. At last, in the newly liberated city, groups of workers in their blue uniforms build sewerage systems and lay electrical cables. To this city the poet cries:

> You should use an even stronger voice
> To answer China
> To answer the world
> And say 'Beijing is for the people!'
> Beijing is for the people.

Every summer Li Yao went to Fengzhen to stay with his maternal grandparents. Here he discovered a trove of rather different books belonging to his mother. One was the classic *Dream of Red Mansions*, by Cao Xueqin. With a complex plot and a cast of hundreds, it explores relationships between the sensitive male heir of the wealthy Jia clan and the twelve beautiful girls who live in the wings of his family mansion. The Cao Xueqin Memorial Hall can be found in Beijing's expansive Botanical Gardens. A modest courtyard house hidden behind high walls, it marks the place where the writer completed his masterpiece. In front of the gate are three ancient trees. One day, the two Australians join 'foreign experts' from Peking University on a trip to the Grand View Garden (*Daguanyuan*), a sprawling film set created in the 1980s as the setting for the popular television version of this classic tale. Each of the twelve beauties had her own little courtyard house with a day room and curtained bedroom. Three enormous plum trees stand nearby, covered in blossom.

In the summer vacations, Li Yao drew closer to his rather feckless maternal grandfather. He was a wonderful storyteller. This lazy fellow loved drinking and Peking Opera. He would sit with Li Yao on the *kang* and tell him folk tales from *Xue Rengui's Expedition to the East*, based on the adventures of a great Tang General. He told him about the *Legend of the White Snake*, an ancient story in which a snake spirit becomes a beautiful woman. As he grew older, Li Yueheng encouraged her son to borrow books from the library. She was trying to save money and even criticised her husband for buying too many books. Li Yao, taking this frugality to heart, started visiting the library. The librarians came to know him very well and recommended books he might like. In the seventeen years before the Cultural Revolution, 377 novels were published in China. Li Yao managed to read a large number of them. Had this little bookworm been Glasson's son, he would have been marched out of the house to play in the garden.

Before Li Yao graduated from Jining First Middle School in 1962 he had become well known for his writing. In the yearly literary competition, he would often win first or second prize. His teacher, Gao Rongting, was in charge of propaganda. He came to like his talented student very much, appointing him editor-in-chief of the school's blackboard newspaper. The 'Little Literary Giant' was then only fifteen but took his responsibilities very seriously.

CHAPTER 8

Leaping forward

In April 1956, Mao Zedong chaired an enlarged meeting of the Political Bureau of the CCP Central Committee and proposed that 'letting a hundred flowers blossom and a hundred schools of thought contend should become the policy for developing science and flourishing literature and art in China'. Accordingly, party committees at all levels invited people to openly critique the communist regime. In a spirit of helpfulness, people stepped forward to identify CCP mistakes: over-centralisation, over-reliance on Moscow, suppression of critical thought in universities, censorship of the media and art, neglect of rural poverty. Few suspected the campaign was a clever trap, designed by Mao to 'lure the snakes away from their hideouts so that we can kill them'. The Anti-Rightist Movement had begun. By the end of the summer of 1958, some 550 000 intellectuals were labelled Reactionary Rightists and vigorously denounced. Hundreds of thousands were sent to rural regions and consigned to years of drudgery.

In Inner Mongolia, the Anti-Rightist Movement was prosecuted with great vigour. Although the leader of the Inner Mongolia Autonomous Region, an ethnic Mongolian called Ulaanhu, was still too powerful to be denounced, the CCP successfully identified many elitist targets. By June 1957, many thousands of cadres had been marched off to the countryside for compulsory re-education. Li Yao's middle school suddenly became a nightmarish place. Some of his teachers were targeted because they had worked for the Guomindang or had fought in the Nationalist army. One by one, people with poor histories were removed from the teaching body.

The eleven-year-old Li Yao did not understand what was happening, although he knew it was something terrible. His parents went off to meetings every day, always returning home very late. Nothing was said in front of their children. But one night in the dark, Li Yao heard his mother asking softly, 'Who spoke at your meeting today?' When Li Tiren whispered back, 'Zhao' she quickly warned, 'Interesting. But remember to be careful when you mention names! Disaster comes from careless talk.' Li Yao lay there wondering what kind of disaster comes from careless talk?

In 1959, David entered Enfield High School, the first secondary school to be built in Adelaide's northern suburbs. When it opened in 1953, there were only ninety-five pupils and a staff of six. But the school had promising British trappings including a uniform in maroon and gold and a school crest with an emblem of the rising sun above the Latin motto *Pactum Serva*. Six years on, there were over 1500 students. Many of them were children of post-war immigrants, part of Australia's plan to 'populate' rather than 'perish'. David sometimes visited friends among these new arrivals who lived in a crowded migrant camp across the road from the school. They were temporarily housed in Nissen huts made from a half cylinder of corrugated iron. In summer these huts became dreadfully hot.

In the poorer northern suburbs, city planners had located an infectious diseases hospital, a mental asylum and a prison. Enfield High students sometimes joked that their school shared characteristics with all three institutions. David soon gained a diverse circle of friends; no-one much cared where anyone came from. Mitko, a tall, dark, handsome fellow, hailed from somewhere in Eastern Europe. 'Biggles', a very dark young boy, probably Indigenous, may have been a member of the 'Stolen Generation' since the rest of his family were fair-haired and blue-eyed. John had an impossible Polish surname and was probably Jewish. Walter had just arrived from Ireland and was living in the migrant camp. 'Bog-o' was native-born Australian. No-one came from Asia. These lads did a lot of fooling around and would have been hell to teach!

Enfield High had a well-earned reputation as a rough school. Other Adelaide high schools generally were well-established seats of learning of strong academic standing. The larger private schools were in the wealthier eastern suburbs, set in handsome grounds with expensive facilities. They charged high fees, catering to parents who wanted their children to enter professions like law or medicine. The Walkers were not a private school kind of family. Even though they were teachers, Gil and Glasson seemed to doubt that their children had the brain power and the discipline to scale those giddy professional heights. Gil once took his younger son to an 'aptitude test', hoping it would reveal something he was able to do. The answer came back, 'wool-classer', but the night-school instructor who taught wool classing quickly singled David out as a hopeless case.

When David first arrived at Enfield High the facilities were minimal: two brick buildings and some temporary pre-fabricated 'portables'. The school was bulging at the seams. But a new building was completed that year, praised by the local mayor as a 'very fine structure with all modern conveniences'. It may have been a 'credit to the district', but David and his classmates remained in the portables. A new 'beautiful library' attracted very favourable comment but suffered from the drawback that it was 'sadly lacking in books'. The parents and friends' association was told that their main project for 1960 would be to 'raise money to supply the library with suitable reading for scholars'. No Enfield High students thought of themselves in these terms.

At that time, David's main reading was the 'One-Eyed Barracker' in the *Sunday Mail*, a commentary on the Australian Rules football games played the previous day. The 'Barracker' had a sweeping disregard for good sportsmanship. He ridiculed the umpires, gloated over victories and was full of sour grapes about defeats, breaking every rule of the sporting code. Looking back, David thinks that it was sport rather than religion or parental instruction that taught him how to behave. Sporting codes were an imperial legacy, imported from the playing fields of Rugby and Eton in the nineteenth century and surviving more or less intact in 1950s Australia. Being of British stock, and with the advantage of a sunny climate, Australians were expected to be very sporty. Sportsmen must be manly and control their emotions at all times and never acknowledge pain when injured. They must shake hands with their opponents after a match. Handshakes really mattered. A firm handshake signalled manliness, confidence and decisiveness. It sorted out the men from the boys. Sport and its disciplines were indeed only for boys. Girls played games.

Two new bitumen tennis courts appeared at Enfield High in 1958. After playing on them as often as he could, David made it into the school's top tennis team which played in an inter-school competition every weekend. This educated him in the intricate workings of the class system in a society that prided itself on not having one. When his team of four visited the big private colleges, they entered a world of comfortable changing rooms, hot showers and expensive facilities. Some schools even had tennis coaches who had been fine players in their day. Other coaches, it is now clear, had a troubling fascination with young boys. Most remarkable to the Enfield High team were the rows of beautifully manicured lawn tennis courts. They noticed the difference.

At Middle School, Li Yao's teacher of Chinese was Liu Yun, a very humorous and well-liked man. His students loved him for his jokes and good humour, even tolerating his banal verses about Jining's weather:

> Jining is cold, Jining is very cold!
> The ice on Overlord River is thick,
> The wind on Tiger Mountain howls.

At the start of the new term, all the students were very upset when this amusing man simply disappeared. What had happened to him? The rumour mill said he had been picked off as a former Guomindang county magistrate. If that could happen to him, who would be next? Everyone became very nervous. Knowing his father's incriminating history, Li Yao grew afraid of anything to do with politics.

One day, when the students were assembled in the playground, the school president announced that Teacher Zhang Jian was a historical counter-revolutionary. Police arrested him on the spot. Sitting in the front row, Li Yao could see everything. Teacher Zhang grew very pale and trembled all over. When Li Yao glanced over to Zhang's wife, standing nearby, he saw how controlled she was. As a CCP member, she must not cry but must make a clean break from her husband. Li Yao thought of his mother, running along the road at night to look for his father, the harsh wind messing up her hair. He never saw Teacher Zhang again but once he encountered Zhang's wife, who had grown very thin. Li Yao remembered her kindness to him when she was school librarian, recommending books like Gorky's *Childhood* and *My University*.

One night, Li Yao's parents did not return home. All the teachers had been gathered together for a meeting concerning the Anti-Rightist Campaign and were not allowed to leave. Li Yao and his second sister, aged fifteen, found themselves alone in the little room where they lived, attached to his mother's school. Frightened, they asked an older classmate to stay. She understood and came at once. It was winter. The wind howled. Not a soul was about. The children huddled together on the *kang* very much afraid.

As the Anti-Rightist Movement got into full swing, large posters and slogans began to appear on the school walls. Attention turned to the director of teaching and discipline, Qiao Xiangheng, a man in his fifties. Li Yueheng had known him from the days when he led the Land Reform Work Team in Li village. She told Li Yao that Qiao was an old revolutionary and not a Rightist. The trouble was that Qiao liked to dabble at painting, always in the traditional style. But as a remnant of the old order, traditional painting had become suspect. Critics seized upon one of Qiao's paintings depicting two gourds. In the past, two gourds had symbolised a long harmonious union. But the CCP Branch Secretary and his colleagues saw more in it than that. Clearly, the large gourd represented the Soviet Union while the small one was China. It meant that the small gourd always needed to learn from the big one. His secret was out! Qiao was mocking the CCP for following the Soviet Union. Qiao could not rebut this accusation, even if 'he had one hundred mouths'. He was arrested as an extreme Rightist. A year later, he was brought back to the school to stand trial, now a frail old man in handcuffs. The judge sentenced him to fifteen years in prison. Li Yao dared not look at Qiao as he was escorted by police to the waiting prison van. He raced home to tell his parents the dreadful news. They remained silent. Li Yao thinks his parents were lucky not to be classified as Rightist. Three relatives were denounced, including his cousin Li Zhang, the singer and storyteller who looked for the family village back in Shanxi.

Not long afterwards, Zhao Yongsen was uncovered as a Rightist at Li Tiren's school. This was the man whose name Li Tiren had once whispered to his wife during the night. His colleagues had charged him with 'digging up the corners of socialism' because of a story he had written about a bank robber. Although this story was never published, he was arrested and sentenced to eight years in prison. Not long after, two teachers in Li Yueheng's school were classified as Rightists. One was Teacher Xiao Yuwan, a vibrant woman from Fengzhen who liked singing and playing basketball. The Li family knew her family very well. Xiao was sacked and had a miserable time for many years. She must have fully comprehended that 'disaster comes from careless talk' because she pretended to be dumb and witless until the end of the Cultural Revolution.

Three more Rightists were then found in Jining First Middle School. One was the biology teacher. He liked Li Yao, telling him interesting facts about fruit and vegetables. Another was the school doctor, a Mongolian war veteran. When Li Yao developed a painful corn on his foot, the school doctor had offered to remove it. He reassured his apprehensive patient and the small operation went well. Over sixty years later, whenever Li Yao sees the small scar he wonders what became of this kind man.

The Anti-Rightist Movement made all the adults Li Yao knew more fearful, especially the teachers. His parents worked harder than ever, getting up very early for school meetings and staying behind in the evenings for political study. Supper became a very late meal after which everyone went straight to bed, worn out. Li Yao's parents had no time to look after their children. They never found out that Li Yao was copying his sister's maths homework.

Soon after this, the Great Leap Forward began. In May 1958, the Eighth National Congress heard Chairman Mao deliver a new message: 'Work hard to get ahead, to build socialism better, faster and more economically'. They were told that China must surge ahead of the West and create a true communist society. In July, the first large *Renmin Gongshe* or People's Commune was established in Henan province. By the end of the year nearly all of China's rural population had been gathered into communes. This also happened in Inner Mongolia.

Li Yao and his classmates took to the streets to promote Mao's new directive. They stopped people at random, asking them to recite the new doctrine. If they could not do so, the students repeated the General Party Line to them word for word until they got it right. They also performed small plays. In one, Li Yao was a Chinese worker and his classmate was an 'English Capitalist'. The plot was simple. Li Yao announced, 'We are Chinese workers. Under the leadership of our great party, we will surpass the United Kingdom within fifteen years!' Loud applause. Li Yao then kicked his classmate on the bottom, whereupon the terrified 'English Capitalist' fled. Li Yao says he was very proud of his performance.

Leaping forward required steel. In 1958 Mao mandated a doubling of steel output. Small backyard furnaces sprung up all over China. Soon after National Day, Li Yao's class joined in. Although they knew nothing about steelmaking, all the boys were very excited because classes were suspended. Instructed by the head teacher and class monitors, they built two small brick blast furnaces. In went iron ore and coal. When the fire was lit and bright flames appeared, everyone shouted. With similar furnaces dotted around the school grounds, there was fire and smoke everywhere. It felt like the eve of Spring Festival, when fires were lit to welcome in the God of Wealth. Pupils ran about, laughing and joking. At midnight, when some fiery-red molten iron finally emerged, teachers and students cheered. Success! Everyone sang:

> Let us join hands and dedicate our youth to the development of the Motherland!
> Let us compose an even more brilliant chapter for the future of the Motherland!

As dawn approached the sky grew lighter. Li Yao's classmates carried their treasure to the CCP Branch Office where a very pleased Branch Secretary was collecting steel from all the classes at Jining First Middle School. Noticing the chemistry teacher frowning, the Party Secretary asked: 'What is it, Teacher Bai?' Teacher Bai seemed unable to say anything. 'What's wrong?' demanded the Secretary. Teacher Bai murmured: 'It doesn't look like steel.' Looking around quickly, the Party Secretary snapped: 'Shut up! Of course it is steel, no problem.' The chemistry teacher nodded his head like a chicken pecking at rice. 'Yes, yes, no problem,' he said, 'it is steel.' The Party Secretary was mollified. 'Very good!' he said as he touched the teacher briefly on the shoulder.

On the way back to school, the students sensed something was wrong and stopped joking and fooling around. Their small furnace no longer looked so marvellous. It was removed without explanation. The school now built two very big furnaces, each two storeys high and the Party Secretary invited two master steelmakers to come and teach selected senior students how to refine iron. In this new attempt they used not only iron ore but also broken iron pots, buckets and beds—anything they could find. This met with success. A new song did the rounds:

> Work, work, work!
> We have exceeded the quota by one half!
> While we all cry 'Make the Great Leap Forward!'
> Our targets will be even more ambitious
> Like rockets soaring up to Heaven!

Li Yao does not know how much steel was made by his school. Jining city boasted that it had made 8 tons, a good contribution to the national output of 10.7 million tons. But as everyone knew years later, the cost had been enormous. Much of this steel was of poor quality and the total production was only 2 million tons more than it had been in 1957. Great Leaping had resulted in great waste.

The Great Leap Forward led to a frenzy of uncoordinated activity, misdirected production and enormous problems of distribution.

Useless piles of iron lay everywhere. Doctrinaire new policies were applied uniformly across divergent regions. Agricultural production suffered. From 1959 until 1961 there was a national shortage of food. Famine stalked the land. Farmers all over the country did not have enough to eat and city dwellers were short of basic provisions. Millions of Chinese died of malnutrition. The size of the 1958 harvest was grossly exaggerated, obscuring the problem and delaying an effective response to food shortages. China continued to ship grain to the Soviet Union in return for loans and technical assistance. Tension between the two countries grew.

Li Menglian was in Hohhot studying, leaving the Li family in Jining with three growing teenagers to feed. Initially, they had a little more food than many others. The two middle school children each received 34 *jin* (17 kilos) of grain each month, while each parent, as teachers, received 29 *jin*. Ordinary people only got 27 *jin*. But gradually, supplies of meat, oil and vegetables ran low. Before long all the family grew malnourished. The situation in the countryside was terrible. Li Yao's fourth uncle became so hungry that he came to the Li family in Jining begging for help. He stayed with them for two weeks while Li Tiren and Li Yueheng, hoping to save his life, brought out their best food: porridge, steamed bread and pickles. When he left, they gave him half a bag of millet, hoping this would help his family survive.

Li Yao's parents always tried to save some steamed bread or a bowl of rice from their meals for him. Meat was rare even though Jining had a meat processing cooperative. On one notable occasion, the family was able to buy a sheep's head and hoof through a friend to make a memorable feast. There was a pharmaceutical factory at the meat-processing cooperative which made traditional medicines from liver. The Li family discovered that liver left over after making medicine was just horrible but they forced it down because they were so hungry. Yet Inner Mongolia was better off than many other parts of China, especially the inland provinces. Once again, people fled north to escape famine in Shandong and Hebei.

Growing up, David never suffered from a lack of good food. But when the family moved to the Adelaide suburb of Broadview

Gardens when he was thirteen, the milkman, the butcher and the greengrocer no longer made their rounds. The vegetable garden declined. Glasson had discovered the supermarket, so much more convenient. Processed foods were just starting to arrive.

At Lushan in 1959, an expanded meeting of the Politburo took place. After a disagreement with Mao, Peng Dehuai was abruptly removed from all his positions. Ordinary people were astounded. Li Yao had read the popular novel *Guarding Yan'an*, which had portrayed General Peng as a great commander. It was hard for Li Yao to believe that Peng was now in such disgrace. He was China's Minister of Defence, an important CCP leader, a veteran of the Long March and a real revolutionary hero! The political atmosphere changed. Li Yao's parents stopped talking to others and Li Yao no longer heard them laugh. At his middle school, the teachers seemed a lot more cautious. Then the Anti-Right-Leaning Movement began, to identify any Rightists who had infiltrated the CCP, the government or the military.

A new slogan appeared warning people not to fly the 'white flag of the bourgeoisie'. At this, Li Yao became very anxious about his family background and his nickname, 'Little Literary Giant'. At his school, members of the Youth League had already begun 'pulling out the white flag'. He started to have nightmares, crying out in his sleep. His parents were very worried not knowing what was wrong. The Secretary of the Youth League soon identified two White Flags in their class. Li Yao, although relieved not to be targeted, was puzzled. Why those particular boys? Only three or four years older than himself, they had always treated him like a little brother. Li Yao thought of the saying 'Illness comes in by the mouth, disaster stems from careless talk'. Those two boys liked to talk and make jokes. Perhaps they had said too much.

Now every afternoon, at meetings after class, the two White Flags were criticised by their classmates. Li Yao remained silent until the class monitor confronted him saying, 'You should speak up and criticise them.' When Li Yao replied, 'I don't know how,' the monitor mocked him: 'You are a Little Literary Giant. Why can't you criticise them? They have been writing nonsense. You are still young, don't copy them.' Li Yao got the message. He had to criticise these two or face the music himself.

At this time, the work of the futurist Russian poet Vladimir Mayakovsky, who wrote in the language of the streets, was very popular in China. People called him a brave Bolshevik whose poems were his spear and dagger. Li Yao had an idea. He would write a poem against the two White Flags in his class using the declamatory style of Mayakovsky. He quickly set to work, writing a poem that ended:

> The red flag of the proletariat is flying high
> The white flag of the bourgeoisie has been torn down!
> Fire! Fire to Zhang Jun!
> Make our world a better place!

As Li Yao read out his poem, his classmates sniggered. The class monitor looked sullen. Li Yao froze, wondering, 'What on earth will happen now?' But the next day, things changed dramatically. The teacher in charge of the school magazine asked if he could publish Li Yao's poem. He found it beautiful, just like one by Mayakovsky, a real spear and dagger. Li Yao was happy but wondered about the wisdom of naming one of the boys. Could the third line just read, 'Fire! Fire! Fire!' When the teacher agreed, Li Yao thought, 'I really am lucky.'

The two White Flags in Li Yao's class were not disciplined further but their self-esteem had been badly dented. Neither would be admitted to university. Other White Flags were kicked out of school. Sessions for 'Planting Red Flags' began. Li Yao's teachers explained that this slogan stood for becoming 'Red and Expert', that is, both socialist-minded and professionally competent. Not that it was entirely safe to excel. Being a Little Literary Giant was no longer such a great idea. Nevertheless, Li Yao continued to dream of becoming a writer. Perhaps he could be a proletarian writer like Mayakovsky or Gorky. They clearly held high the great red flag of Marxist-Leninism. Li Yao admired Gorky's novels and enjoyed reciting passages from Gorky's poem 'Sea Swallow'. He had read Nikolai Ostrovsky's socialist realist novel *How the Steel Was Tempered*, and was inspired by his stirring phrases:

> Man's dearest possession is life, and it is given to him to live but once. He must live so . . . that dying, he might say: all my life, all my strength were given to the finest cause.

Li Yao's parents were continually afraid he would be drawn into some anti-Rightist confrontation. They urged their son to become 'Red and Expert' and join the Communist Youth League. Li Yao and his sister grew more actively involved in school study groups reading *Mao Zedong Thought*. But practical applications were also important. Lin Biao, vice chairman of the CCP Central Committee, advised:

> To grasp and apply truly, we must combine study with reality. Only by linking it with reality can we understand it, fix it in our minds and apply it.

To overcome his family history Li Yao resolved to do exceptionally well by relating Mao's work to some important problem. He read Mao's essay 'Report on an Investigation of the Peasant Movement of Hunan'. When it was written in 1927, the CCP was still largely concerned with the problems of urban workers, as was the Communist Party in Soviet Russia. But after visiting the countryside near his home in Hunan, Mao revised his thinking and now argued that revolution in China should be based on the violent struggle of poor peasants against the landlord class. By January 1927, peasants in Hunan were ruthlessly attacking their landlords. Landowners were given tall paper hats and led about on ropes, pursued by crowds shouting abuse. Some were imprisoned and even killed. Mao explained how this was a very good thing:

> Revolution is not a dinner party. It is not painting, embroidering, or writing. Not so dainty, nor so modest. Revolution is an insurrection, a violent act by which one class overthrows another. The rural revolution is a revolution in which the peasant class overthrows the power of the feudal landlord class.

Li Yao thought Mao must be right. Feudal landlords should be brought down. When peasants were so downtrodden, violent revolution was inevitable. It was lucky that his grandfather had still been a poor farmer in 1927. It was even better that because he had died in 1946, no-one had been able to make him wear a tall hat or lead him around on a rope. Li Yao carefully studied two important essays by Mao that had been recommended to him by his teacher. In 'On Contradiction', Mao argues that capitalism is internally contradictory because different social classes have conflicting goals, which leads to class conflict, economic crisis and then revolution. In his second essay 'On Practice', Mao stressed that knowledge must be tested by experience to determine its truth. Yet although Li Yao and Li Mengqi studied Mao's writing diligently, when they graduated from middle school in 1962 they were not asked to join the Communist Youth League. Their poor family background barred the way. It was very disappointing, especially for Li Mengqi who was such a good student. Only their elder sister Li Menglian was accepted. With her positive outlook she had performed well in every political campaign. Li Yao's parents always urged him to learn from her.

In 1963 David, no doubt on his parents' advice, chose to stay at school for a fifth, 'Leaving Honours' year. This suited his parents who planned to be away that year on their first overseas trip. Their youngest son would stay with his sister Beverley and brother-in-law Dick, whose home was inconveniently located on the other side of Adelaide, two long bus trips from Enfield High. Having learned to drive at sixteen, David decided that his best option was to drive the family car to school each day. His one difficulty was how to pay for the petrol. He had no income. Officers from the South Australian Education Department visited Enfield High seeking teacher training recruits. When David learned that there would be a small stipend, he signed on the dotted line. Petrol problem solved. When his parents returned from their trip, they were most surprised to learn their son intended to become a primary school teacher.

CHAPTER 9

The wind in the tower

Gil and Glasson moved from one country town to another every couple of years. As an incoming headmaster, Gil tried to make a good impression among country people, who tended to be suspicious of outsiders. The Walker children were told to be on their best behaviour, which really meant remaining quiet while adults did the talking. Gil wanted to be seen as a respectable gentleman, one who did not smoke, drink or swear. He quietly placed his diplomas on his office wall but never proclaimed he was a university graduate. In the 1950s, graduates were still a rare and rather suspect breed. Where Glasson was a city person, never at ease in the socially exposed goldfish bowl of a small town, Gil was a quiet country boy who liked to keep himself to himself. He had inherited the conservative politics of small business people whose interests were best served by political stability and a strong economy. He never paraded his views or tried to convert others. Nor did he ever belong to a political party, attend political rallies or go to meetings agitating for change. His politics, like his income, was a strictly private matter.

In small communities, it was hard to keep religion private. Arriving in a new town, one of the first questions concerned which church the Walker family would attend. In South Australia there was always a Methodist church nearby. While it was necessary to turn up, it was no good to be too religious. If you were, you ran the risk of being labelled a 'bible basher'. Gil and Glasson steered a careful middle course. They went to the local Methodist church about once a month and sent their children regularly to Sunday school. But once inside the family home, religion was largely forgotten. Their children were not asked to say prayers before bed or a simple grace before meals. Religion seemed a necessary public display, not a sustaining system of belief.

The country pub was another important Australian institution. Down to 1970, women were not allowed into the public bar of a hotel. Their place was among the potted palms of the 'ladies lounge'. Not that this worried Glasson. As a non-drinker, she would never have entered a bar of any sort and nor would her husband. Gil's mother, May, had drummed the importance of good behaviour into him. Drinking alcohol and any association with saucy women were particularly bad. Gil never knew the byplay, rough jokes, storytelling and rowdy mateship to be found in the boisterous world of the pub.

By the end of the 1950s, having set up a reliable gerrymander, Tom Playford had completed his first twenty years as premier of South Australia. Although a wily politician, he was personally incorruptible. High office never changed his simple lifestyle. Meanwhile in Canberra, Robert Menzies was on track to become Australia's longest serving prime minister. His long rule became known to wits as the 'Ming dynasty'. Gil and Glasson admired Menzies. With his eloquence and commanding presence, they felt he was a statesman rather than a mere politician fretting over votes. Menzies was a figure able to connect Australia to the larger, more consequential English-speaking world. He embodied the British spirit, the history and rich pageantry of the monarchy, the proven record of British democracy, freedom and fair play. Menzies celebrated the rousing cadences of the English language and emphasised that Australians were a valued branch of the adventurous British race, on whom the future of the civilised world was said to depend.

Gil and Glasson were not wealthy people. Nevertheless, they considered themselves far removed from the unions, slogans and rallies of the working class. To them, the Labor leader Arthur Calwell was everything Menzies was not: a union man, an Irish Catholic and certainly no statesman. They were embarrassed to think he might ever become their prime minister. Imagine this craggy man with his rasping

Australian accent taking tea at Buckingham Palace! Many years later David learned that Arthur Calwell would be giving a seminar in the History Department at the Australian National University (ANU). He decided to go off to hear him, still expecting to encounter the rather crude fellow conjured up in childhood by his parents. To his surprise, the small seminar room was packed as Calwell spoke about his life in politics. David saw before him, as expected, the battered face and harsh voice, but Calwell's talk was thoughtful, self-deprecating and perfectly suited to his audience. Ingrained stereotypes collided with reality.

Through the Cold War, Menzies regularly out-manoeuvred the Australian Labor Party (ALP), suggesting their patriotism was always suspect. He rarely wasted an opportunity to emphasise how international communism was bent on world conquest. 'Red China' was the immediate danger. As a teenager David largely agreed, happy to echo the *Advertiser* in warning that the Chinese were about to invade defenceless Australia. His beliefs on these big geopolitical questions had not yet been challenged by any reading of Chinese history.

Li Yao as a student at IMNU in 1966

In 1962, at the age of sixteen, Li Yao was admitted to IMNU. A dream had come true and his mother had not lost face. Even so, no-one was getting carried away with excitement because in reality, Li Yao did not want to be a teacher. The Li family already had too many teachers. From kindergarten to university they covered nearly all subjects: Chinese, English, physics, chemistry, biology, mathematics, physical education. All too often, teachers were dismissed as 'poor knowledge tellers' becoming a target for every political movement. The Li family always tried to stay well clear of politics. At IMNU, Li Yao, as an aspiring writer, had wanted to study Chinese. Yet, due to the current political situation, he found himself enrolled in the Division of English in the Department of Foreign Languages.

In September 1962, the Eighth Central Committee of the CCP adopted a new 'Basic Line' stating that true socialism would take a long time to implement. Class contradictions and class struggle would continue as long as different social classes remained. Because the bumpy road to socialism coexisted with the road to capitalism, there was also an ever-present danger that capitalism might win out. The Chinese people had to remain vigilant and steel themselves for a long fight. There could be no letting up on class struggle.

Li Yao, his three sisters and younger brother filled out many long forms as they applied for admission to university. Their parents insisted they provide as much detail as possible, saying that the officials would appreciate honesty and be more inclined to admit them. Their children struggled to list every detail of the cattle and land their family had owned before Liberation. But after confessing that their third uncle had escaped during the Suppress the Counter-Revolutionaries Movement, they could not say where he had gone. They just wrote 'fled to escape punishment'. There was no way of refuting the rumours he had escaped to Taiwan.

Li Tiren insisted that his children reveal his past service with a Guomindang army unit. He seemed to regard this as something honourable and in no sense a crime. But it gave his children another big label: they were now children of a Guomindang lieutenant *aide-de-camp*. When they explained that their father held this position for a mere forty-eight hours, they were told: 'one hour even one minute is enough, your father used to be a Guomindang lieutenant *Aide-de-Camp*'. But, they would argue, 'he was fighting against the Japanese'. Back came the reply, 'Why didn't he join a band of Communist guerrillas? Only guerrillas led by the Communist Party fought the Japanese. The Guomindang didn't fight the Japanese.' Li Tiren's children had no answer, they did not know why their father had not joined the Communist guerrillas. But now they had to deal with the reality of their dangerous new label. The children's university files were stamped 'politically unreliable'.

Students with files bearing this stamp would never be admitted to a leading university. Peking University would not take them. Tsinghua University would not take them. But students categorised as 'politically unreliable' never knew this stamp was on their file, it was a secret not revealed until the Cultural Revolution when Red Guards took student files from university archives. Although Li Yao's elder sister Li Menglian was an excellent student, she was excluded from university in 1959 and was only saved by a sudden stroke of luck. The President of Inner Mongolia University thought it was wrong to prevent so many youngsters with very high scores in the entrance examination from having a university education. He went ahead and enrolled some students who had been labelled 'politically unreliable'. Li Menglian was among them, admitted to the Department of Biology.

By 1962, the class struggle had intensified. Li Yao's parents became very worried that Li Yao and his second sister, Li Mengqi, would not get into university. Her geometry, algebra, physics and chemistry were much better than Li Yao's and he was sure she would be admitted. But unaccountably, Li Yao found that he was accepted as a student at IMNU while his sister was not. They both had a politically suspect background. Why was he so lucky? He thought of his mother's story about the magpie singing so cheerfully on the roof when he was born. Had the magpie known he would become a university student? The truth was more prosaic. IMNU, just like Inner Mongolia University, decided to admit a small number of 'politically unreliable' students. He was just lucky to be among them, a lucky Rooster born at *La-Ba*. Three years later, when his younger brother, Li Xin, applied for a place, he was rejected. He missed out on a university education.

At the end of August 1962, Li Yao left Jining to attend IMNU in Hohhot, the first time he had been away from home. The Three Difficult Years were coming to an end but many people still did not have enough to eat. Li Yao's mother worried about him. She gave him a bag of fried oatmeal (a Mongolian staple food that would store well) and a bag of steamed buns. His parents must have saved hard to buy this food. Li Yao's one comfort was that his sister Li Menglian would be studying nearby at Inner Mongolia University where he could visit her every Saturday, his only entertainment. She always saved some steamed bread or a piece of cake for him and sometimes took him to movies at the university auditorium. They saw *Dream of Red Mansions* there.

Through Li Yao's middle school years, the relationship with the Soviet Union, the 'Big Brother', had been very friendly. Studying Russian was all the rage. Li Yao had enjoyed Russian literature and by the time he left school he could write simple articles in Russian. But friendship turned to enmity in the 1960s. The gloves came off when the Soviet leader, Nikita Khrushchev, not only denounced Stalin but called Mao a 'geopolitical adventurist' and an 'ideological deviationist'. The friendship was over. The Union of Soviet Socialist Republics (USSR) withdrew 1400 technicians from China. Then in 1962, Khrushchev refused to go to war with the United States during the Cuban Missile Crisis. In China, studying Russian was now out and learning English was in.

Before Liberation, Inner Mongolia had no universities. IMNU was the first, founded in 1952. In 1962, the university enrolled only forty English majors, one of whom was Li Yao. He soon fell in love with English literature and was no longer disappointed at not studying Chinese. He set himself a new goal: to gain admission to graduate school where he could pursue further study and avoid becoming an oppressed middle school teacher. Although he knew his grand plan might fail due to his poor political background, he remained hopeful.

Like English majors all over China, Li Yao began to study the basic text, *College English* by Xu Guozhang. Inner Mongolia was a remote place where English was a new major, but Li Yao found, to his surprise, that he had excellent teachers. The first, Liu Qingrong, was a new graduate from Beijing Foreign Studies University (BFSU). Despite his fine academic record he had been sent to Inner Mongolia, a frontier ethnic minority area because he came from a landlord family. Other English teachers at IMNU were Rightists or people with a problematic history. Their students knew little about their past. They only saw teachers who were hard working and knowledgeable, though not particularly approachable.

While Rightists were being weeded out in China, communists were under attack in Australia. That said, there were significant limits to government power, as the newly elected Prime Minister Menzies discovered when he tried unsuccessfully to ban the Australian Communist Party in 1950. However, well into the 1960s, individuals on the left were kept under regular surveillance by Australia's spy agency, the Australian Security Intelligence Organisation (ASIO). The ANU academic C.P. Fitzgerald had a very large ASIO file. As a recognised sinologist and author of *The Birth of Communist China*, Fitzgerald was regarded as a potential traitor by those on the right of Australian politics. Nevertheless, he retained his ANU position, spoke out freely on the case for recognising China and was later promoted to a full professorship. When the teacher and writer Helen Palmer returned from her visit to China in 1952 she was not so fortunate; the NSW Department of Education refused to re-employ her for eighteen months.

Conditions for learning English at IMNU were far from ideal. Li Yao heard no native speakers, no recorded voices. The state-of-the-art language laboratories now found at IMNU were as yet undreamt-of luxuries. During his four-year course, Li Yao never met a foreigner. Most students spoke English poorly with a strong local accent. Even today, Li Yao is a diffident English speaker. He jokes about being the great translator who cannot speak English. He was a reader, not a talker. He worked hard. At the end of his first year, he was reading *Robinson Crusoe*, *Pride and Prejudice*, *Gulliver's Travels*, *Tales from Shakespeare* and *Alice in Wonderland*. He was in the top three in his class. Not all his classmates were impressed. One told him, 'You can't always have your head in a book, you need to be more down-to-earth.' But Li Yao liked reading. It had got him where he was and he was not about to stop.

Jin Xigu, a tall man of about forty-five, took the intensive reading class. It was rumoured that Teacher Jin had worked for the Chinese Academy of Social Sciences in Beijing before being sent to IMNU in 1960. Li Yao was sure he was a White Flag hurled into the remote grasslands. He adored this learned teacher, who was as proficient in English as in Russian and the first translator Li Yao had ever met. Jin's translations of Władysław Reymont and Eliza Orzeszkowa were published by the prestigious People's Literature Publishing House in 1959. Reymont was a Polish writer who had won the Nobel Prize for Literature in 1924, while Orzeszkowa, another Polish writer, had been a finalist for the Nobel Prize in 1905. To have translated a Nobel Prize winner was a great accomplishment. To have this great translator as a teacher at IMNU in far off Hohhot was nothing short of miraculous. Li Yao always looked forward to his classes with Teacher Jin even though this watchful man seldom smiled and never dropped his guard.

With this fine teacher, Li Yao was inspired to try his own hand at translation. For his first effort he chose an English version of 'The Lighthouse', a short story by the Ukrainian-born Russian writer Vladimir Korolenko. Li Yao was all nerves as he handed his translation to Teacher Jin. He hardly slept that night. But the following day his teacher smiled and invited him home to discuss his work. Jin's dormitory room was austere, a single bed, a small bookshelf, a desk, a chair. Li Yao noticed a photograph on the desk. 'My son and daughter in Beijing,' Teacher Jin explained with a warm smile. He liked Li Yao's translation and praised his choice of Chinese phrases. To this point, Li Yao knew little of translation theory. Jin told him: 'Good literary translation depends on faithfulness, expressiveness and elegance. You should practice listening, speaking, reading and writing until you can reach this goal,' adding, 'this takes cultural understanding.'

The difficulties and importance of 'faithfulness', 'expressiveness' and 'elegance' for translation were first discussed by the renowned nineteenth-century scholar Yan Fu. After studying in London, he had brought Western ideas to China by translating classics such as Adam Smith's *The Wealth of Nations*, John Stuart Mill's *On Liberty* and Thomas Huxley's *Evolution and Ethics*. Li Yao had heard of Yan Fu, and his three much-debated keys to translation, but this was the first time he had heard a teacher discuss these questions using examples drawn from his own translation work. The meeting changed him. He left the dormitory believing that translation was a great calling that opened the world to curious readers. He wanted to be a translator. But it was not that simple. His university did not train translators. On behalf of the Chinese people, it trained teachers to be 'Red and Expert'.

On 5 March 1963, the *People's Daily* published a new instruction from Mao: 'Learn from Comrade Lei Feng'. Best take notice. Lei Feng was a simple fellow, an orphan born in 1940 who became a loyal PLA soldier. After his death in an accident in 1962, the Shenyang Military Command told its soldiers they must learn from the example of this model citizen. Soon Chinese news media were writing about him. He was admired for his diary entry: 'Everybody is painting his own life picture. Some paint it white, some grey, some pink and some brilliant red. I will always keep my picture brilliant red.' Mao's call to emulate Lei Feng ignited a nationwide campaign. With a past to overcome, Li Yao could see the advantage of learning from Lei Feng. When the Secretary of the Youth League in his class suggested that they should pay attention to the little things, Li Yao wracked his brain. What little things had Lei Feng done? He thought of Lei Feng's simple life and how his socks had been full of darns. He could learn from those socks. Li Yao took out his clothes. None were great, but the clear winner was an old coat so patched and worn that it barely held together. He put it on. When the Secretary of the Youth League spotted him wearing this garment, he gave Li Yao a thumbs-up sign, the first time in years that Li Yao had been given a thumbs up. He felt a bit Redder than before.

The learning did not stop there. Li Yao went off with his classmates to wash clothes for PLA soldiers. He helped farmers growing vegetables. He could feel himself becoming Redder and Redder. But still he failed to be accepted into the Communist Youth League. He grew despondent and frustrated. His parents wrote encouraging him to listen to Chairman Mao, 'Learn from Comrade Lei Feng', and be 'Red and Expert'. Li Menglian told him to be strict with himself, but Li Yao really did not know how to be strict with himself. He gradually gave up any idea of joining the Youth League and turned back to what he did best: studying. During this time he read Romain Rolland's *Jean Christophe*; Tolstoy's great works, *War and Peace, Anna Karenina* and *Resurrection*; and Dostoevsky's *Crime and Punishment, The House of the Dead* and *The Idiot*. He particularly liked the French writer Rolland who had received the Nobel Prize in 1915 for his 'lofty idealism'. Li Yao still remembers his words: 'Human beings need brightness. Sunshine alone is not enough. The brightness of heart is necessary.'

Li Yao lived on very little. He shared a dormitory with fourteen others in bunk beds. University tuition was free, the state paid for his accommodation and food at IMNU and he got 5 yuan from his parents every month. Li Yao was frugal, only buying necessities like soap and toothpaste. With all the money he saved, he bought books from second-hand bookshops. His biggest purchase, costing 8 yuan, was for *Jean Christophe*, a novel about a young musician, a Beethoven transposed to the modern world. The original *roman-fleuve*, it flowed like a river, emotions dictating its events. These volumes remain on Li Yao's bookshelf today.

Li Yao decided to follow Rolland's words: 'Every successful person has to make a start. Start bravely and find a successful way. The worst enemy is to have no strong belief.' He was determined to read as much as possible but soon found that the more he read, the less Red he became. Had he forgotten the old saying: 'The tree craves calm but the wind will not die down'?

Late in 1963, Sino-Soviet relations declined further. After years of Cold War, Khrushchev was now committed to an improved relationship with the United States. Mao, believing this was a sign that the USSR was lapsing into capitalism, attacked Khrushchev for revisionism. Mao launched the Four Clean-ups Campaign saying: 'From our highest organisations down to the grass-roots we must everywhere give constant attention to the training and upbringing of successors to the revolutionary cause . . . They must be genuine Marxist-Leninists and not revisionists like Khrushchev.'

During the second half of 1964, university students from all over China, except those studying in Foreign Language Departments, were told that their classes were suspended for three months while they were sent to the countryside. By autumn many thousands of students from Beijing and Shanghai plus 1000 researchers from the Academy of Sciences shared food, housing and work with the peasants. As students of foreign languages, Li Yao and his English class remained at the IMNU. Under the direction of the University CCP Committee, they took classes in Socialist Education where altruism, courage, perseverance and confidence in the building of socialism were highlighted. This program began with 'Ego Education'. Students were asked to confess any repressed bourgeois ideology. One classmate owned up to listening to Soviet Radio, which by then was considered dangerous enemy propaganda. This confession kept Li Yao awake at night since he too had once listened to forbidden radio stations.

When Li Yao was at middle school, his family did not have enough money to buy a radio. So Li Yao learned from a classmate how to make a crystal receiver. It was much easier to make than a valve radio, needing only a wire coil, a capacitor, a piece of crystal, earphones and wire for antennae. As it was a passive system based on the power of the received signal, it had a very limited range. Through his headset, Li Yao could hear the *Wulanchabu People's Radio.*

This was enough. Every day, after class, Li Yao listened to radio serials, music and stories. Then one evening, around midnight, he heard a loud statement issuing from his headset: 'This is the *Voice of America.*' After a few short sentences, there was signal noise interrupted by a great burst of static. Although he had heard nothing of importance, it made him very afraid. It was against the law to listen to enemy radio. *Voice of America* clearly came from the enemy. Li Yao felt his heart thump furiously and he broke out in a cold sweat, though it was midnight and he was at home, lying on the *kang* with his sleeping parents and siblings beside him.

The next morning, Li Yao did not dare tell his parents what he had heard. In fact, he did not dare speak of it for many years. But he was curious. How was it possible that his little crystal receiver could hear *Voice of America*? America was so far away, on the other side of the earth. The next night, even though he was very sleepy, he stayed up until midnight. Putting on his earphones, once again he heard: 'This is the *Voice of America*', a phrase which made him both excited and scared. Once again, he heard just a few sentences, signal noise then a great burst of static. Once again, he had really heard nothing. As a youngster with a poor grasp of physics, he failed to understand that because *Voice of America* sent out such extremely strong signals, his little crystal receiver would at times be able to pick up its broadcasts. As his Chinese station interfered with the signal, only a few sentences came through. Li Yao continued listening to his radio. One night he heard another voice: 'This is *Japanese International Radio NHK*.' Again, his heart began beating violently. He took off his headset and stared at it in the dark. Was his little radio set some kind of monster tempting him to break the law? He stopped listening to the radio in the middle of the night.

The Communist Youth League continued to ask students to demonstrate party loyalty by revealing their hidden secrets. The Political Instructor praised the classmate who had confessed that he had listened to an enemy radio station. Everyone should learn from him. Li Yao wanted to show loyalty but didn't know what to do. After some agonising, he decided not to say anything about listening to the radio. It was long ago and he had heard nothing of substance. But the Political Instructor still wanted self-criticism. So Li Yao wrote an article accusing himself of wanting to be a famous writer, for reading too much Western literature and being influenced by it. When his article appeared in the school journal *Leap Forward*, the Instructor praised him for his solid analysis of bourgeois ideology. Once again, Li Yao thought, his pen had saved him just as it had four years earlier with his proletarian poem.

A Chinese proverb states: 'the wind sweeping through the tower heralds a rising storm in the mountains'. In 1964, a very popular drama called *Youth* was performed at IMNU. Two of Li Yao's activist classmates took part. The drama called upon young students to remember the need for class struggle and to break away from bourgeois ideology. The wind was sweeping through the tower. Three reactionary students were expelled from the Russian course. Li Yao's classmate Qin was criticised but not severely punished, saved by his poor peasant background. The one hit by the storm was Li Yao himself, and this time his pen could not save him.

Li Mengqi had finally managed to come to Hohhot to attend university. Li Yao got into trouble after he introduced her to the Branch Secretary of the Communist Youth League in his class. His fellow students started to criticise him: he came from a landlord family, he was a political underachiever, he was Expert but not Red, professionally competent but not at all socialist-minded. They accused him of trying to corrupt the Branch Secretary in order to find himself a backer. Li Yao felt wronged. It had never occurred to him to try to find a backer and he knew nothing about corrupting anyone. Li Yao had just thought the Branch Secretary was an honest young man whom his sister might like. As it happened, his sister and the young man were not at all interested in each other. But this was not how his class saw things. They met several times and criticised Li Yao harshly.

It was the first time Li Yao had ever been criticised. He was just eighteen years old and didn't know how to deal with it, let alone how to tell his parents. He later discovered the real reasons behind the campaign. His class was like a small society where many were already masters of the art of class struggle. Someone in their number wanted to get rid of the Branch Secretary. He was accused of many things, of which the crime of being corrupted by Li Yao, filial grandson of the landlord class, was only one. As a result of these intrigues, this Branch Secretary was ousted from office, replaced by the main actor who had manoeuvred against him. Li Yao could see that he had been just a gun in their hands. Li Yao was pardoned, but after these events he lost any desire to join the Communist Youth League.

David began the summer of 1963 with a holiday trip to Waikerie with his good friend Ian Anderson, setting up a tent in the local caravan park on the River Murray. They had a plan. They would earn some money during the vacation by fruit-picking. Their first job was to remove stubborn bushes from a paddock for a rather nasty farmer. Miserable work for little pay. After a sweltering morning in the sun, they downed tools and returned to the caravan park where they spent the rest of the afternoon swimming and fishing, then wandered into town. They found that the grocery shop carried a few paperback books. The cover that caught David's eye was *Advertisements for Myself*, by an American author called Norman Mailer. Sitting on the riverbank, the elder Rooster became totally engrossed in this mixture of essays, fragments and reflections on contemporary America. It was unlike anything he had read before. Mailer was brash, funny, opinionated and self-important. He set a bad example, just the type of book his parents and teachers would not have recommended. From now on David became fascinated by contemporary American writing. If this was what modern writing was about, there might be something in it. He began to read. For his generation, America had replaced Britain as the cultural powerhouse of the modern world.

Returning to Adelaide at the end of 1963, Gil and Glasson gave their youngest son a wonderful present—a smart Japanese transistor radio. He began taking an interest in what was happening in the world. Waking early on the morning of 23 November, he caught the 6 a.m. news bulletin to hear that President John F. Kennedy had been assassinated in Dallas, Texas. The events of 1963 gave David a lot to think about.

CHAPTER 10

Ghosts and monsters

A colleague from Peking University tells David that when he was a schoolboy during the Cultural Revolution, his teacher always emphasised his devotion to Chairman Mao, urging his pupils to follow his lead. One morning storming into the classroom, he waved a newspaper above his head. On the front page was a photograph of an African-American sailor with a Mao badge pinned to his bare chest. Pain and blood meant nothing to him! The class was impressed although some thought quietly, 'If our teacher wants to demonstrate devotion, why doesn't he pin a badge to his chest?' Even so, it was not easy to demonstrate that you were keeping to the right path. Authorities were skilled at finding error. The smallest detail could prove telling. Who would have suspected that a small gourd in an amateur painting was a satirical assault on the CCP?

In China, the trigger for the real disaster, the Cultural Revolution, occurred in November 1965. It took the form of a review of a new historical drama, *Hai Rui Dismissed from Office*. Some may have thought this play no more than an entertaining tale in which an official is sacked for criticising a corrupt Ming emperor. Mao knew better. It was a cleverly disguised attack on his dismissal of the senior CCP figure Peng Dehuai. Time to act. Mao ordered Yao Wenyuan, the Shanghai critic, to write a savage review. A fierce debate ensued. After the disastrous Great Leap Forward and the years of widespread famine, there was growing opposition in the CCP to some of Mao's ideas. These cadres remained committed socialists but thought there were better ways of building China's future. Mao disagreed. His critics were 'leading the country back to capitalism'. He dismissed one CCP Central Committee member after another. The Cultural Revolution was underway, a concerted effort to use China's young people to purge capitalist and traditional elements from Chinese society.

The critic Yao Wenyuan went on to denounce two newspaper columns that had gently questioned policy failures during the Great Leap Forward. Soon the whole country began to criticise the three cultivated authors of these 'poisonous arrows'. Deng Tuo was a poet and journalist, a collector of painting and calligraphy. Wu Han, who had written the play about Hai Rui, was a professor of history at Tsinghua University and deputy mayor of Beijing. Liao Mosha was a witty and accomplished writer. At IMNU, students soon began writing critical articles denouncing these rogues. There was no end to the fiery meetings. Although Li Yao was off on an education internship, he and his class were expected to participate.

On 25 May 1966, teachers at Peking University put up a big-character poster denouncing their CCP Committee for trying to suppress the growing student movement. When the content of the poster was acclaimed by Mao, an unprecedented storm of activity was unleashed across university campuses all over China. In Inner Mongolia, the Cultural Revolution quickly gained momentum and intensity, exacerbated by the growing tensions between China and the USSR. On 3 June 1966, Gao Shuhua, a young teacher in the Department of Foreign Languages at IMNU raised a big-character poster accusing the university president, Ji Zhi, of 'stubbornly following the path of revisionism and opposing the Mao Zedong line'. Gao had been political instructor for Li Yao's class. Li Yao remembers him as a good young man from a working-class background, an active CCP member. By the end of August, Gao and his supporters had formed a Red Guard unit called 'The East is Red Fighters' General Brigade'. Most students joined. Opposing them were around 300 academically distinguished but more conservative students who supported the university president, calling themselves the 'Anti-Japanese Military and Political University Division'. Before long, the two camps were plastering posters all over campus. Students no longer went to class but stayed up all night arguing. Li Yao was keenly aware of the threat this campaign posed for his family but he could say nothing. While nominally with 'The East is Red Fighters', he tried to stay under the radar. Things were getting far too risky far too fast. He stopped reading novels.

A couple of days before Gao's first poster went up, an editorial in the *People's Daily* had called on the masses to 'sweep all "ghosts and monsters" from the earth'. Cadres, intellectuals, workers and peasants were told to use Mao's Thoughts to break free of the 'mental shackles' imposed for so long by experts, scholars and bourgeois authorities. The CCP Committee at IMNU could no longer sit idly by. They went hunting for ghosts.

The first ghost and monster identified in the Division of English was Teacher Jin Xigu, the renowned translator. Students and staff gathered in the amphitheatre where CCP Branch secretary Wang Lvan announced: 'Jin Xigu is a wicked ghost and monster, standing against the Communist Party and Chairman Mao. His thoughts are anti-communist.' The room fell silent. His heart pounding, Li Yao glanced across at Teacher Jin. His head was hanging down and his face was white. Wang Lvan roared: 'Down with Jin Xigu! Down with Jin Xigu! Down with ghost and monster Jin Xigu!' Deathly pale, Jin lifted his head and fixed his eyes on Wang. He raised a tightly clenched fist but said nothing. Li Yao was shaken. Jin was his respected teacher, someone he wanted to emulate. Li Yao thought of his own father. When would he be exposed as a ghost and monster? The clamour continued. Wang urged everyone to write posters criticising their teachers for anything they felt was revisionist. Their Great Leader, Mao, would back them.

Before long, new ghosts and monsters had been identified among the teachers: those who had returned from abroad, those who had studied at Cambridge or Oxford, those who had published books or were well regarded. It was summer, and even in a northern city like Hohhot, the days could be hot. The ghosts were forced to run around the campus or work in the sun. Some collapsed. Most were old. They wore tall paper hats and carried large signs stating their name and crimes. The situation was serious and frightening. All over the nation, in the cities and in the countryside, ghosts and monsters were paraded while students recited Mao's inflammatory words: 'Revolution is not a dinner party.' Then they chanted 'insurrection is justified, insurrection is justified!'

Jin remained in the eye of the storm. Students and teachers continually put up posters criticising him. It was noticed that Li Yao had not joined in. He was warned: 'You are Jin's favourite student. If you do not expose him, you will be criticised. Draw a sharp line between yourself and this ghost and monster.' Li Yao grew afraid. He wrote a poster denouncing Jin's bourgeois ideology and reluctantly put it up in the hallway, hoping that it would soon be covered up. He did not want Jin to see it. But only ten minutes later, Jin appeared. He read Li Yao's poster from beginning to end, his face expressionless. Li Yao fled the building, ashamed.

People like Jin were described as 'dead tigers'. They were locked up and made to write long confessions. Meanwhile, the net spread wider. Wang Lvan himself did not escape. Exposed as a 'capitalist roader', a man with power in the Party who opposed Chairman Mao, he was subjected to a very brutal struggle. Li Yao saw him in a tall paper hat but did not feel very sympathetic. He could never forget how Wang had set Jin Xigu on the road to perdition.

One day, Li Yao's elder sister came to see him. As a new graduate, she had been sent to a Grassland Research Institute in remote Xilingole. Returning from a short course in Nanjing she had gone to see their parents in Jining. Her news was not good. She told Li Yao how their father was being criticised every day. Then, to Li Yao's surprise, she added: 'What worries our parents even more is something about you.' Apparently, Li Tiren had once boasted: 'My son learns English and can understand English broadcasts.' He meant the English version of *China Radio International* but some of his colleagues insisted that only Britain and America had English broadcasts. His son must have been listening to enemy radio! His parents wanted Li Yao to stop writing to them, it was not safe. As his sister left she warned: 'Don't speak casually. Don't write anything. Don't get caught on the wrong side.'

The first students to call themselves Red Guards came from Tsinghua University in Beijing. For a time they met secretly in the ruins of the nearby Yuanmingyuan or Old Summer Palace. But their meetings did not remain secret for long. Mao soon ordered their stirring manifesto to be broadcast. Similar groups then appeared all over China. On 18 August 1966, Mao, wearing an olive-green military uniform met Red Guards in Tiananmen Square and gave them his strong support. It suited Mao to be at the head of their mass campaigns. They could help him suppress the increasing power of the communist bureaucracy. Mao now pitted peasants and workers against experts and officials, bypassing the CCP. Old rivals were fair game. There were enemies on all sides. Growing elitism had to be crushed.

That August, a crowd of around 800 000 gathered in Tiananmen Square to see the Great Leader. The young people had responded to Mao's call. The following day, they took to the streets of Beijing, to attack the 'Four Olds': old thoughts, old culture, old habits and old customs. Soon they were fomenting chaos throughout the country, destabilising the Party and government instrumentalities at all levels. Streets were given new revolutionary names and were plastered with posters and the sayings of Mao. This devastating campaign brought untold destruction to traditional Chinese culture.

The new campaign in China did not go unnoticed in Australia. News about it came in continually from Australian Associated Press, Reuters and international sources like the *New York Times* who had 'China watchers' in Hong Kong. Diplomats would also report on what they saw in the streets of Beijing: men being beaten with ropes, Red Guards vandalising houses and throwing the contents out the window, people forming a 'circle of shame' around their victims as they were marched down the street, buses being stopped so that Red Guards could harangue the passengers. Even the traffic lights were wrong. Red should not mean 'stop'. It had to mean 'advance'.

All across China, rampaging Red Guards destroyed or damaged anything old they could lay their hands on. To have something labelled 'feudal', including Beijing's impressive old city walls, was an invitation to have them destroyed. Sometimes it took an act of defiance from a brave individual to save a cultural treasure. As David travelled across China, he heard many stories of what had been lost and rather fewer of what had been saved. On one occasion he went with Karen to see the Fahai Buddhist Temple just out of Moushikou near Beijing. Dating from 1439 it is made up of several temple buildings with curved tiled roofs. Visitors are given torches in order to see what is really special, the frescoes around the inner walls. They are in remarkable condition, fresh and vibrant. The whole Buddhist pantheon is there, joined by earthly emperors and their gorgeously robed consorts. There is a wonderful assortment of lively animals: elephants, lions, tigers and monkeys. The whole lot was about to be destroyed. But when Red Guards stormed the temple entrance, they encountered a very determined old man who risked his life, blocking their way until they backed off. A rare victory.

Painting of a lion at Fahai Temple at Moushikou

At IMNU, the students began to burn books. Art students smashed their plaster models, music students smashed valuable records. Red Guards in Li Yao's class ordered him to burn his collection of English books. He quickly hid his favourites, *Jean Christophe* and *Pride and Prejudice*. He picked up *How the Steel Was Tempered* and other 'proletarian' novels and took them to the Red Guards, arguing that English books of this kind should be kept, not burned. After some time, they agreed. His relief was short lived. They instructed him to burn his pillow embroidered with the six characters: *Happy Together*. Li Yao was horrified. His mother had given it to him. She had made it when she got married. But the Red Guards said, *Happy Together* represents old thoughts and old culture. It must be destroyed! Borrowing a pair of scissors, Li Yao cut out the six characters. That night, lying there with his head on the damaged pillow, he could not get to sleep for a long time, thinking of his mother, his family and what lay in store for them all.

Li Yao was unaware that in coming days, a great many people would die. During what became known as the Red Storm, 114 000 households in Beijing were searched and their property confiscated. Across the country, 10 million households were affected. People were like little boats, tossed in rough waters, waiting for that huge wave to dash them on the rocky shore. Li Yao did not know if his family was being searched, if their books were burned, if the little they owned was gone, if his parents had been sent to the countryside. One nightmare followed another.

The last photograph taken of the Li family together in 1966

Australians found the chaos in China and the actions of 'the hooligans known as Red Guards' very hard to understand. China appeared an insular, almost friendless society. Even Australian communists did not approve of what was happening. Laurie Aarons, general secretary of the Communist Party of Australia, thought the ideological and theoretical justifications given for the Great Proletarian Cultural Revolution were 'ludicrously opposed to the enlightened ideas of Marxism'. To further questioning, he added: the 'adulation of Mao is already far more extreme—and absurd—than that ever lavished upon Stalin'. Aarons thought China had lost a lot of goodwill among the communist bloc by refusing to come out in support of Vietnam. Sitting in the student cafeteria at the University of Adelaide, David heard students refer to the Cultural Revolution as a bright new dawn. To him, everything happening in China seemed remote and hard to follow. It was never discussed by Gil and Glasson around the kitchen table.

A few days after serving the Revolution by cutting up his pillow, Li Yao bumped into a fellow student from Jining who whispered: 'Two days ago I saw your father paraded in a tall hat. Your house has been confiscated. Be careful the Red Guards don't criticise you.' Li Yao couldn't hold back his tears. His father was an honest but vulnerable person. How could he survive such cruel and public humiliation? Li Yao had no-one to confide in. There would be no more *Happy Together*, no family reunion. His mother's hopes would be shattered. Li Yao had a family photograph, taken at Spring Festival in 1966 when they were all back in Jining. No-one had known then that this would be the last picture of the Li family together.

A week later, at the university post office, Li Yao happened upon a distant relative from Li village named Liu who was not from a landlord family. He asked Li Yao, with a sort of schadenfreude: 'Did you know that your parents are back in Li village?' He glanced back at Li Yao triumphantly as he walked away. Li Yao thought, disaster follows disaster. His parents had been sent to the countryside! Li Yao did not know how to deal with the news. He was only twenty years old. He knew that many people sent to the countryside were committing suicide. Li Yao could only pray that his parents would find a way to hold on. Red Guards were already active in the rural villages of Inner Mongolia, most of them just teenagers, although their leaders were slightly older. Some blackened their faces before conducting their raids on homes and families. They were harder to recognise that way and much more frightening.

As bad as things were for Li Yao, they were harder for his younger brother. Li Xin was sixteen and at middle school in Jining. Jining was a small city where everyone knew everyone else. The news soon got around that his parents were being criticised and that Li Tiren had been mocked and derided in his paper hat. The Red Guards in Li Xin's class were very pleased. They pounced on the news. Li Xin became their target. Red Guards covered his bed and quilt with posters. They kept him awake, trying to force him to confess his parents' crimes. He was filled with anger and fear. His parents had been forced back to Li village, their home in Jining was taken and their few possessions confiscated. Their books were burned. Li Xin was left homeless. He went to a distant relative, asking if he could stay the night. They sent him away, too afraid to help. Li Xin had to live on the street.

Li Yao with his brother Li Xin in Jining, 2018

Red Guards in Li village had prepared a homecoming for the returning Li parents. When Li Tiren and Li Yueheng stepped off the train, they were immediately surrounded by youths chanting: 'Down with landlords Li Tiren and Li Yueheng!' They were pushed, shoved and beaten up. Red Guards who had been her students grabbed Li Yueheng and roughly chopped off her hair. The couple were sent to live in a dark, abandoned cave. It was damp and cold. They had brought nothing with them from Jining. A few days later, Li Yao's uncle arrived, dismissed from his position as chemistry teacher in Hohhot First Middle School and now labelled a disgraced counter-revolutionary. This uncle had served in the Nationalist army but had managed to rebuild his life after Liberation. It was a different story now. He could not escape his past.

In 2021, Li Xin found self-criticisms made by his parents in 1966, written on the back of an old calendar. Li Tiren wrote:

> Through my experience of labour, I understand the endless wisdom of working people. Labour skills are not easy even if they appear simple. I now appreciate the integrity and selflessness of working people. I must learn from them and reform myself through labour. This is the direction the Party has pointed out to me. I will listen to the Party and follow the Party.

Li Yueheng wrote:

> When I was young I went to boarding school. Since graduating, I have been a teacher for over 30 years. After Liberation the Party trained me to work as a teacher for the people. Now after 16 years I feel more honoured than ever to have been given this role. With my heart and soul, I have always tried to struggle for the cause of education. The new society provides me with the warmth of a big family. I love being an educator, working with innocent children, and would like to work for them for the rest of my life. Recently, I often think back to the times when I would guide children studying the works of Chairman Mao. Now I feel very sad to leave them.

Li Yao thinks about the reasons why the peasants of Li village had acted so harshly to his parents, people they knew well. First, the peasants wanted to change the name of Li village. They started calling it Fanshen village and later Happy village. They had taken Li land, cattle and property. But perhaps things had not really 'turned over' (*Fanshen*) because they too had suffered in the last ten years. It may have seemed to them that the Li family were doing better: they lived in cities, the adults were teachers and their children studied in universities. The Li family were still above them, still doing well. But now the Cultural Revolution had arrived, this elite family could finally be knocked to the ground. The peasants were filled with a righteous hatred and an excitement they had never felt before.

Standing behind them, urging them on was the giant, godlike figure of Chairman Mao.

When he found himself homeless, Li Xin made his way to see Li Yao in Hohhot. He was only able to stay a few days. They had no money so Li Yao went to the school cafeteria to get some food. He found fresh lychees, fruit rarely seen in Inner Mongolia. Li Xin ate them for the first time. He still associates the sweet taste of lychees with the bitter taste of the Cultural Revolution and the actions of the Red Guards. The brothers sat together and talked, all the time worrying about their parents. When Li Xin was leaving, Li Yao looked around for something he could send to his father. Li Tiren had been driven away in such a hurry that he only had the clothes he was wearing. He would need stout clothing for working in the countryside. Li Yao picked up an old coat and a pair of gloves and asked Li Xin to take them to him.

With nowhere else to go, Li Xin went to stay with his maternal grandparents in Fengzhen. They had heard the worrying news that their daughter and son-in-law had been sent back to Li village. But there was nothing they could do. The grandfather was now over eighty and suffering dementia. In Fengzhen, Li Xin met up with old classmates. One day they heard that Mao was asking students and Red Guards to travel through China for a Mass Exchange of Revolutionary Experiences. They would be given train tickets and food. Needing both, Li Xin set off to Lanzhou, Xian and Beijing with his classmates. On 25 November 1966, Chairman Mao met the Red Guards in Tiananmen Square for the eighth and last time. Around 2.5 million Red Guards and young students gathered to see him. Despite mixed feelings, Li Xin was caught up in the excitement and drama. His family history was problematic but he too was being inspected by Chairman Mao.

In July 1968, Li Xin and his classmates at middle school were told that as 'educated youth' they now had to spend time in the countryside. Some students were sent to farms run by discharged and retired PLA men, others, especially those like Li Xin with a poor family background, were sent to the grasslands. It was a very long trip. With a group of fifty students, Li Xin took the slow and overworked steam train from Jining to Baotou via Hohhot. A bus took them on to Bailingmiao. Another stop. The final 40 kilometre journey on to the grasslands was made on horseback. Eventually, they reached the White Mountain People's Commune (Chagan'aobao). Over the horizon lay the People's Republic of Mongolia. On arrival the students split up. Li Xin and a group of thirty stayed together in a long dormitory building. They were now the Yellow Cliff Production Brigade.

Li Xin was just eighteen and he stayed there for three long years. Where Li Yao has a scholarly demeanour, Li Xin has the rougher aspect of a man who has endured hard times. He had started smoking on the grasslands and speaks with the throaty voice of a veteran smoker. He has a good sense of humour but his loud laugh often ends with a coughing fit. He is kindly disposed towards the odd Australian couple travelling around China with his brother. He tells them in his gravelly voice that he was lucky to have been sent to the grasslands rather than to a village to work as a farm labourer. On the grasslands they had milk and mutton to eat, and then, with a gesture to the horizon, more freedom in being in such a remote place.

The hours were long but the work was not too heavy. The really hard work was hauling up water in the morning for the cows, which took two hours. Li Xin shows David his tough, calloused hands. Li Xin remembers how an old woman wearing a high headdress would milk the cows, singing songs in Mongolian as she worked. Some songs she had made up herself. By this time, pastoral life for Mongolians had been radically reorganised. The old way of life was disappearing. It was less common to see traditional dress. After the cows had been given water, Li Xin and a Mongolian herdsman would take the sheep out to graze and then bring them back at night. Sometimes they were joined by a lama who had turned to herding following the destruction of the local Tui Lama Miao temple by Red Guards. Li Xin has a rare photograph of the temple just before it was destroyed.

There is a primal beauty in the grasslands. In summer the grass is long and green and thick with flowers, yellow poppies, little carnations, blue daisies and pea flowers. At every step there are insects. The air is clear, the sky is blue and the sun has a gentle, nurturing warmth. The harsh sun of an Australian summer is not welcome here. In winter, the temperature sinks to minus 40°C, a world of snow and sky which reduces humans to specks in the landscape. Li Xin was lucky to have warm sheepskin clothing, thick boots and a sheepskin hat. He needed them. Occasionally, in winter he was able to tuck a sheep's carcass under his coat and get it home to his family.

David and Karen go back to Chagan'aobao with Li Xin and a group of his old classmates. The travellers are barely out of Baotou when the beautiful sight of watermelons piled high on roadside stalls stops them in their tracks. Out they hop. The watermelons are tapped, tested and closely interrogated. After some jocular bargaining, three large watermelons join the expedition. These roadside stalls remind David of his childhood in Cadell. The party arrives at a hotel in Bailingmiao. Half the town seems to have turned up for a welcome banquet with lots of smoking, speeches and *baijiu* toasts. The men said, 'This is our second home town. We old comrades have come together again after fifty years. We welcome warmly the visitors from Australia.' David pushes back his chair, stands as steadily as he can and thanks them all and Li Yao translates. 'It was a privilege to be here sharing their stories.' The Chinese hotel room is comfortable, with its clean white cotton quilts covering hard wooden beds and its little table with cups for tea. A notice in the shower offers sound advice: 'Please watch your steps in order to be dangerous.'

Outside the old dormitory building
at Chagan'aobao

The next morning the party drives to Chagan'aobao. The river running through Bailingmiao is almost dry. The grass looks in need of rain and seems overgrazed. Large patches of yellow soil are exposed. No flowers to be seen. Inner Mongolia is in drought. The two cars draw up in front of a couple of farmhouses with enclosed courtyards. Some inquisitive children peek out but no-one else is around. Small white goats sleeping in the sun on the windowsills show no interest in the foreign visitors. Not far off is a long, low building made from bricks, packed dirt and straw. Much of the roof has fallen in. There is a dirt floor. This had been home to the middle school students during the Cultural Revolution. Li Xin points through the broken window at his old *kang*, now just a dusty platform piled with a few bundles of straw. He inspects it all closely, searching for memories. After the obligatory photos the party gets back into their cars for the short drive to Tui Lama Miao. Standing at the site, it is hard to imagine that this desolate pile of rubble had once been a thriving centre for Tibetan Buddhism. Yet in the surrounding vastness are whisperings that speak to the human spirit. David imagines lines of red-robed monks chanting and clearing away mental obstructions as they meditate on the image of a Buddhist figure:

> . . . on his forehead there is a white syllable *Om*, a black syllable *Eh* on the heart, and a green syllable *Ah* on the crown, a yellow syllable *Le* in the navel, a red syllable *Re* on the throat, and a blue syllable *Am* in the secret place to protect the body, speech and mind.

There is a famous saying, 'Buddha dharma resides in the mundane world'. Dharma teachings are living and never leave us alone. The only problem is we do not use them.

Some adjoining buildings still remain within the old temple complex. These were the monks' quarters. Made of mud brick they are now in a state of photogenic decay. Traces of a delicate floral pattern run across the central roof beam. During the Cultural Revolution it was prisoners not monks who were confined here. One of the visiting group recalls how he had to guard them, often letting them out to get some sun in the courtyard. But they all had to be securely locked away whenever the Red Guards came by. A woman approaches and is recognised. One of their middle-school group who decided to marry and stay here. It looks as if her life has not been easy. She shows the foreigners a few surviving photos. There she is as a teenager, robust and vital, her two long plaits swinging behind her back, just like a girl from a propaganda poster of the 1950s. Here she is with her husband, newlywed, and in another with short hair, she is a young mother with a toddler.

Not far away on a low hillside was a tourist establishment, a large cluster of concrete *ger*. Many seem deserted but in some you could have a Mongolian meal. The party goes in and the food comes out, corn porridge, yoghurt, hard white squares of Mongolian cheese, plates of salad vegetables with a dipping sauce, juicy black and white sausages, a large plate of dumplings, a bowl of oat noodles, some cabbage dishes and a great platter of baked lamb falling off the bone. The party drink milk tea with roasted barley and chat about life on the grasslands. A sturdy man in blue satin comes in to sing. He spends a long time getting his microphone and sound system set up, but he should have left it at home, all the beautiful and now familiar Mongolian folk tunes emerge distorted and far too loud. A modern innovation.

One of Li Xin's old classmates was the son of a doctor so he had been given the responsibility of looking after the other students. He said that they had been a pretty healthy lot. Their main problem was 'stomach complaints' because the diet was so heavy in meat. In winter, no vegetables were available. To treat these stomach problems, he had collected eagle droppings, mixing them with wild herbs to make a folk medicine. He rationalised his approach in this way: the eagle eats only meat yet its stomach is very strong, so its droppings are sure to contain something that will benefit people.

Students returning home after years in remote rural areas faced many problems. Jobs were few, it was hard to find a place to live and their disrupted education had left them with few skills and poor marriage prospects. Li Xin returned to Jining in July 1971 where he went to live with Li Yueheng. He got a job in Jining Hardware Factory as an ordinary worker.

CHAPTER 11

White pigeons

As Australians returned to civilian life at the end of the war, their attention turned to work, marriage and family. From 1946, births rose dramatically creating the 'baby boomer' generation. Although he was born at the end of 1945, David always considered himself a 'boomer'. With numbers came power. Baby boomer needs and preferences had economic, political and cultural consequences that continue to this day. Across the Western world the boomers shook things up, pushing the oldies aside. Women, workers and youths became more assertive. The music got louder and the cry went up, 'make love not war'.

Towards the end of 1963, the Walkers moved to the leafy surrounds of Hazelwood Park in the prosperous eastern suburbs of Adelaide. Their new home, built of Basket Range sandstone was set in a quiet cul-de-sac. For Glasson the sandstone clinched the sale, its streaks of orange, gold and yellow were so contemporary. This was a superior building material and after years of Education Department houses, Glasson was more than ready for a superior home. From her kitchen window she saw large gum trees in the park where, morning and evening, senior kookaburras taught their young the ancient art of loud laughter.

The move suited David. Wattle Park Teachers' College where he began his training as a primary school teacher was just a twenty-minute walk away. His parents remained unenthusiastic about his proposed career but, as Glasson was rather too fond of saying, teaching was something to 'fall back on'. There would always be a need for teachers, classrooms and chalk. From the onset, David planned to also complete a Bachelor of Arts, enrolling in English and History at the University of Adelaide. He soon realised that his university subjects were much more thought-provoking than the rather lame Wattle Park curriculum: principles and practice of teaching, educational psychology, art, music and physical education—subjects no student could fail. He passed music without ever drawing a tuneful note from his recorder. He worked much harder at the university, doing sufficiently well in his first year to be invited into the History Honours program. His parents greeted this news with a mixture of teacherly pride and poorly concealed disbelief. Gil never saw the point of history. Why waste time raking over the past? Besides, university was a place for superior brains. How would his son ever fit in?

The campus of the University of Adelaide was not far from the city centre, on a gentle slope leading from North Terrace down to the River Torrens. Along North Terrace stands a proud collection of public buildings erected by Adelaide's progressive colonists, civic leaders who valued knowledge and learning—the State Library, the Museum and the Art Gallery. The university was right at home in these cultivated surroundings. During his first year, even as a part-timer, David grew very attached to university life, a revelation to a boy from a quiet suburban home. The university was a place where everything seemed discussable. Opening the student newspaper, *On Dit*, gave him plenty of food for thought. Attending tutorials in the offices of university staff, he was surprised by how many books they had. Working in a room full of books seemed a very attractive proposition.

One day, in the university's Barr Smith Library, David met an old friend from Enfield High School, Cathy Passmore. She was fair-haired, blue-eyed and attractive, the thoughtful daughter of English immigrants who had ended up in one of the barren housing estates in the far northern suburbs near the satellite city of Elizabeth, named in doubtful tribute to the new Queen. David had his eye on Cathy, a popular girl with a little trail of suitors. Although she found him quite amusing, she felt she could do better. Talking together, they strayed into politics. At that time, David was still inclined to follow the Walker line which was reflexively conservative, never taking ideas coming from the ALP seriously. After rolling out his views self-importantly, he was astonished to find Cathy was quite unconvinced. She insisted that Menzies was deceptive, he really looked after the rich and took no real interest in ordinary people. Only Labor believed in social justice. Perhaps for the first time, David heard an intelligent person make the case that there were at least two sides to the political debate.

On Dit was another eye-opener. It had plenty to say about racial prejudice and often poked fun at the sacred cow of the long-standing 'White Australia' policy, introduced when the first Federal Parliament passed the Immigration Restriction Act in 1901. David had not met any Asian students at Enfield High School or Wattle Park Teachers' College. At the university, few took Arts subjects, although in these days of the Colombo Plan, which offered scholarships for Asian students to study in Australia, Asian students were much in evidence on campus, especially around the library. One day David, assuming his role as comic impersonator, subjected his friend Ray to an impromptu impression of Chinese English. Ray was unimpressed, quietly indicating that Chinese students were standing nearby. What would have been a winning performance at Enfield High fell flat on the steps of the Barr Smith Library.

As Ray was studying philosophy, he felt obliged to question everything. He and David were often seen outside the Arts building, holding forth on topics of the day: apartheid in South Africa, immigration reform, the downward thrust of communism and the presence or absence of God. It took quite some time before it dawned on David that Ray may have been homosexual. At the time this was a crime. The Adelaide Vice Squad, a special police unit formed to prevent crimes like illegal gambling, prostitution and drug- dealing, was in the habit of hurling anyone they thought was homosexual into the River Torrens. In one notorious case this had led to the death by drowning of an Adelaide University academic, Dr George Duncan. Homosexuality was one subject Ray could never speak about.

On Dit regularly carried articles about sexuality accompanied by obligatory pictures of buxom young women. With the introduction of the oral contraceptive pill, the 1960s had become the decade of sexual revolution. Censorship and the nature of obscenity were hot topics. In the letters column, David noticed contributions from some of his lecturers condemning the obscenity trial of the satirical magazine *OZ* which was then taking place in Sydney. Even so, censorship remained the ruling doctrine at Hazelwood Park. No copies of the inflammatory *On Dit* could ever be left lying around.

In state politics, the ALP remained where it had been for decades, on the opposition benches. But studying Premier Playford closely was the young Labor politician and rising star Don Dunstan, first elected to parliament when he was only twenty-six. Glasson was suspicious of Dunstan. She thought he spoke far too fluently, went to the theatre, had fancy foreign ideas about food and sometimes wore bright modern clothes, quite unsuitable for parliament. Even worse, despite being educated at one of Adelaide's best private schools, he was on the political left. David grew curious: anyone Glasson found so politically objectionable must surely have some redeeming features. In time it became clear that Dunstan, perhaps more than any other Australian politician of the 1960s, understood the baby boomers' appetite for change.

During the 1960s, fear of Asia remained widespread in Australia. The journalist Donald Horne detected a fatalistic acceptance of the idea that sooner or later Australia would be overwhelmed by China. Adelaide's *Sunday Mail* published maps with arrows showing how the 'red menace' would make its way through South-East Asia down to Adelaide. The call went out for more migrants to populate the country. British ones like Cathy's family, the blue-eyed, blond-headed Passmores if possible. Failing that, European ones would do.

David was too young to notice the Korean War and knew little about the Malayan Emergency. Vietnam was another matter. Menzies had sent Australian advisors there in 1962, arguing that if the Vietnamese 'domino' was allowed to fall, the rest of South-East Asia would surely follow. Like most of his compatriots, David had never met anyone from Vietnam and knew nothing about the country. Yet in April 1965, Menzies announced he would send an infantry battalion to the Republic of Vietnam, insisting that it was imperative for Australia to support America. The only way the army could increase its recruitment numbers was by conscription. How would conscripts be selected? By lottery, with birth dates drawn at random from a barrel to determine who would be called up.

In March 1966, when David was twenty, his 'marble came up'—he was a lucky winner in the conscription lottery. He was summoned to an army medical examination. Apart from extreme short-sightedness, he was not in bad shape, but perhaps not army material? Surely they would take only the very fittest and strongest? After struggling with the eye chart and being prodded and poked, they dismissed him, 'You're not up to much are you, son?' But two weeks later, the new conscript was told he had passed the medical and must report for military service on completion of his university studies.

Towards the end of September 1966, Li Yao lined up with his classmates to walk to the railway station in Hohhot. Everyone was in very high spirits because they were off to Beijing to be inspected by Chairman Mao, the Great Helmsman. As they were leaving, Red Guards pulled Li Yao and two others aside: 'We have orders. You can't go to Beijing. Your parents have been sent to the countryside.' The pariahs watched as the others marched off, waving the red flag and singing:

> Sailing the seas depends on the helmsman
> Making anything grow depends on the sun
> Raindrops nourish the rice and the rice grows strong
> To make revolution we need Mao Zedong Thought.

The rejects returned to their dormitories where they were set demeaning tasks, scrubbing floors, cleaning toilets and emptying rubbish bins. Family background determined everything. 'A hero's son is a real man. A reactionary's son is a rotten egg.' They were called 'dog's whelps'. But in Wonderland, as Alice knew so very well, up was down and down was up. What was this? Li Yao was standing there with his mop when Han Tong, head of the Red Guard unit in their class, suddenly appeared. Quite unexpectedly, he handed over train tickets to Beijing. The three pariahs hurried to the station. Arriving in Beijing the next morning, it was frightening to see Red Guards everywhere. Li Yao had heard how they beat up people from the landlord class. But they soon were able to join their astonished classmates. When Li Yao explained, 'Han Tong gave us train tickets', they were reluctantly allowed to stay.

The night before the review, Li Yao was too excited to sleep. As dawn broke, each student was issued with two steamed buns and some pears and they all began walking towards Tiananmen Square. On arrival, the atmosphere was incredible, deafening noise and singing and a sea of waving red banners in all directions. Israel Epstein, one of the very few Western journalists in Beijing watching these rallies recalled 'the enthusiasm was real'. He saw from close by how Mao, Zhou Enlai and other leaders 'sat down on the flagstones in the square surrounded by rejoicing youngsters'. When he glimpsed the distant portrait of Chairman Mao high above the rostrum, Li Yao forgot his fears, thinking, 'Chairman Mao, at last I am at your side!' It was 1 October 1966, National Day, the seventeenth anniversary of the founding of the People's Republic of China. Around 1.5 million people, mainly students, were there in the square. One of them was the dog's whelp, Li Yao.

On their second day in Beijing, Li Yao and his classmates made their way to BFSU out in Haidian. English majors were gathering to criticise the authors of their English textbooks, Xu Guozhang and Wang Zuoliang. As Red Guards marched these professors towards the stage, Li Yao pushed his way forward. He saw that neither of these teachers he admired seemed intimidated. Professor Wang outlined his academic career at Southwest United and Tsinghua universities. Shouting loudly, the Red Guards accused him of working for the American army. Wang smiled: 'Yes, I was interpreter for Brigadier General Waters during the war against Japan.' Immediately the heckling began: 'Down with Wang Zuoliang! If he does not surrender, let him perish!' while Wang stood there in silence.

No landmark in Australia's settler history approaches the historical power of Tiananmen Square. The world changed there in 1949. Driving down the beautifully lit Chang'an Avenue past the square at night is to feel the weight and gravity of China's rise. Throughout the day there are always crowds of people there, taking photographs in front of the Monument to the People's Heroes or posing for selfies with the curved roofs of the Tiananmen building in the background. Tiananmen Square is flanked by two gigantic Soviet-style buildings. One is the National Museum, the other the Great Hall of the People. Traditional details have been added to the Stalinist architecture of the Great Hall: its twelve massive pillars sit on lotus petals, a Buddhist symbol of purity. In 2016, David and Karen, as 'foreign experts' at Peking University, were invited to a National Day event in the Great Hall. No bags, mobile phones or cameras were allowed.

It was a grey, very cold evening. In such weather, red warms the spirit. An enormous red carpet led up the steps and into the hall. There were 2000 guests but Karen and David found themselves seated on table number five, right near the front. They spotted their Australian colleague Colin Mackerras who had been visiting China since 1964, over on the far side of the room, at table one or two. At their own table, solicitous officials looked after a very old Chinese woman, a veteran of the Long March. The line of dignitaries on the stage made short speeches while beautifully groomed waiting staff whisked away the plates as courses came and went with military precision. In front of each guest was a perfect peach. There was no chance for David to taste it because suddenly the event was over and the guests filed from the hall. In the throng on the stairs they met Colin, who had managed to pocket his peach. That evening, Li Yao sees his two Australian friends on CCTV (China Central Television). Taking a photograph with his phone, he sends it to them by WeChat.

After their momentous days in Beijing when they saw Chairman Mao, Li Yao and his classmates had returned to Hohhot. At this time, many students changed their name to demonstrate their revolutionary spirit. As this seemed a good tactical move for someone from a 'bad background', Li Yao became Hong Tao ('Red Wave' or 'Revolutionary Wave'). But the change lasted only a few days. No-one could believe that this bookworm had really become Red and revolutionary. But in that autumn of 1966, Li Yao soon saw another chance to show his Red credentials. Red Guards and students had been instructed to travel across China promoting rebellion. They were told to visit important sites like Yan'an, the endpoint for the Long March;

Jinggang Shan, where the Red Army was born; or Ruijin, which had sheltered the Communists in the 1920s. At IMNU, one team after another raised the red flag, sang revolutionary songs, held high a portrait of Chairman Mao, and set off for the train station. At last only Li Yao and seven classmates remained. No-one wanted to be seen with them. The discards set off for Ningxia Autonomous Region which lies between Shaanxi, Gansu and Inner Mongolia.

Before he left, Li Yao went to see Teacher Jin Xigu who had sent a message to say he wanted to return Li Yao's copy of *Ordeal*, an account of how the Russian intelligentsia had painfully adapted to post-revolutionary society. Li Yao had not seen Jin since the dreadful poster incident. He still felt ashamed as he rang the doorbell. Jin seemed much thinner. Li Yao could only tell him as he took back his book that he was going off to Ningxia. 'Take care,' Jin Xigu replied kindly. It was the last time Li Yao would see him.

The great revolutionary journey turned out to be its own kind of ordeal. As train travel for students was free, everyone was in on the act. Li Yao and his group had to stand for most of the thirty-six-hour trip. On arrival, they collapsed onto beds at the reception station. They all loved Ningxia rice, but found little to do and wandered aimlessly about town reading posters. The following week they continued to Lanzhou, capital of Gansu province. They found the platform full of students, pushing, shoving and shouting, the train doors already closed. One smart aleck half-opened the window in his carriage to mock those stranded below him. When his glasses fell off, Li Yao's classmate pounced. Negotiations commenced. Smarty would get his glasses back if he wound down his window and let them in. Done. They squeezed into a carriage packed with Red Guards. Twenty-four hours later they reached Lanzhou where they saw big character posters everywhere. They failed to find any famous Lanzhou melon and missed out on the town's equally famous stretched noodles. The reception station only provided steamed buns and rice.

Next stop Sichuan. An even more crowded train: people sat in the aisles, luggage racks, under seats, in the toilets. Stopping and starting, it took three days to reach Chengdu. Li Yao's legs were covered in bruises. At Chengdu Institute of Geology, the little group flopped down onto makeshift beds on the floor. No-one had the energy for revolution, they just tucked into free sweet potatoes from the reception station, food they rarely saw in Inner Mongolia.

What should they do next? Chengdu was the home of Tang poets Li Bai and Du Fu and of the great philosopher Zhuge Liang from the Three Kingdoms period. But Du Fu's cottage and Zhuge Liang's Memorial Hall were closed, so they set out for Dayi, 48 kilometres from Chengdu, to see the manor house of Liu Wencai. Liu was a notorious reactionary landlord whose manor had shot to fame in 1965 for its *Rent Collection Courtyard,* a series of ceramic sculptures created by students and staff of the Sichuan Art Academy. With no transport available, the students decided to walk to Dayi. These dog's whelps would toughen themselves on their own Long March. They set off like PLA soldiers, with a quilt in their backpack and heads held high. Local farmers smiled and greeted them warmly. It took them two days to get there.

At Dayi, they stayed at the beautiful middle school, established by Liu Wencai before Liberation. Remembering his parents, Li Yao thought, Liu did not just take rent from farmers, he also opened a school. Visiting the famous courtyard, they learned that Liu had owned nearly 700 shops and many banks, pawnshops and houses. The courtyard contained 114 life-sized ceramic characters: eighty-two men, thirty-two women and one dog. The realism of these sculptures shocked the students. When farmers fell behind in their rent, Liu would lock them in a cell where the water was waist deep. An old woman told them how she had once been locked in such a water dungeon. She showed them a cell with iron bars where you could still see the imprints of bloody hands on the walls. Returning there in the 1980s, Li Yao found this cell greatly changed. The water had drained away, the iron cage had been removed, and a wooden sign saying 'opium den' now hung on the door.

Returning to Chengdu, they learned that everyone had been ordered back to school. Li Yao heard from Li Xin that their indomitable mother had persuaded the Jining Revolutionary Committee to allow her to return to Jining. Very excited at this news, Li Yao decided to try to see her on his way back to Hohhot. Under cover of darkness, he slipped inside the house of a distant relative. There was his mother standing in the dim interior. Astonished, she exclaimed, 'You are really taking a big risk!' She was thinner now and her hair remained ragged where the Red Guards had hacked at it. It was upsetting to see her like this. His mother tried her best to console him: 'People are suffering all over the country, Liu Shaoqi and so many old revolutionaries have been arrested. Compared to them, we are nothing!' She continued: 'Everything will be all right. I am negotiating. Your father will be allowed back soon.' She added, 'Your father is fine, he's working for the production team.' Li Yao was dismayed. His father was sixty-one years old. What use would he be to a production team?

That night, lying on the warm *kang* beside his mother, he experienced a surge of happiness. His family was still alive. To live is to win. At daybreak his mother told him he had to leave. He must not be seen. Li Yao could hardly bear to go. He tried to give his mother some money, but she would accept very little. 'Don't worry,' she said, 'the government will pay us wages.' Despite her frailty, Li Yueheng remained a tower of strength, as resolute and dependable as ever.

When Li Yao returned to Hohhot, there were no staff at the university, only Red Guards and students. There was no possibility of any academic work. The students divided into two camps: the radicals and the conservatives who went for each other hammer and tongs. Li Yao's class was soon sent off to the Hohhot First Woollen Mill to experience the 'Three Togethers' with the workers, 'eat together, live together, labour together'. Li Yao preferred life at the mill to the strife-torn university.

At this time of turmoil it was no easy thing to keep city bureaucracies functioning. In Shanghai, during the January Revolution of 1967, a mass meeting of a million workers called for their city officials to be replaced by workers from the Shanghai Commune. This change did not work well. Mao disapproved and soon put in place his own more controllable Revolutionary Committee. In Beijing there were high-level meetings and sharp struggles between radicals and conservatives on major issues of principle. Students, egged on by Mao's wife Jiang Qing and her supporters in the Central Cultural Revolution Group, called for radical change: 'We shall turn the old world upside down . . . create chaos and make a tremendous mess, the bigger mess the better!' Meanwhile, the *People's Daily* called on everyone to 'learn from Shanghai'. Law and order broke down across China. As Israel Epstein observed, 'Each side claimed to be totally right, actively denouncing the others who were totally wrong . . . Those professing error had to be knocked down!'

In the Inner Mongolian Autonomous Region, constant clashes continued between competing groups. A number of academics were arrested. Li Yao grew dispirited by these ceaseless power plays. He had had enough. He took off to Baotou, a large industrial city near Hohhot. His quiet escape did not last long. While out walking in Baotou, he came upon a poster announcing that Han Tong, a Red Guard, had been shot by an army officer. He could not believe it. Remembering Han Tong's kindness in giving him the train ticket to Beijing, he rushed back to Hohhot to find out what had happened.

Back at IMNU, Li Yao was told by his shocked classmates how 'The East is Red Fighter's Brigade' had organised a sit-in at the Military Command Headquarters where they had called on the Deputy Commander to meet their representatives. He refused to see them. For three days the students continued to protest. Wrapped in blankets, they took turns at blocking the main gate. Shortly after noon on 5 February, Han Tong had stood on a stool shouting slogans into a microphone: 'Defend Chairman Mao with your blood and your life!' An officer bellowed: 'Shut up! Or I'll kill you!' Han Tong shouted back: 'I am a revolutionary, I am not afraid of death!' At which the officer shot him in the chest. Murmuring, 'take me to hospital', Han Tong died, the first student shot by the PLA during the Cultural Revolution.

This incident alarmed Beijing. Premier Zhou Enlai ordered representatives from the Inner Mongolia Communist Party Committee, the PLA Military Command, and representatives of Red Guards to Beijing. In the Great Hall of the People, he chaired tough negotiations between these parties, talks that continued for two months. Meanwhile, the struggle between warring factions in Hohhot grew more intense. A huge memorial event was organised for Han Tong. When it was discovered that the military planned to steal Han Tong's body to destroy any incriminating evidence, Li Yao's class hid the body at the top of a water tower at the university until it could be safely handed over for a formal autopsy. Then the evidence was clear. Han Tong had been killed with a military pistol by Military Training Director Liu Qing.

Li Yao's class made a red flag with big golden characters reading 'Han Tong Combat Team'. Facing the flag, they swore to:

> Learn from Han Tong.
> Defend Chairman Mao with our blood and life!
> Seek revenge for Han Tong, our comrade-in-arms!

In 2015 while walking across the campus of IMNU, Li Yao stops near the Teaching Building, pointing to the second floor. During the Cultural Revolution he had been holed up here with almost 500 other students, Red Guards and workers for almost a week. Opposing factions of conservative students had blocked all the entrances and exits. Luckily, the cooks supported the besieged students. Li Yao had helped to haul food up to the second floor in buckets. There was much shouting, flag waving and defiance. Eventually, a PLA general was sent in to end the siege at the Teaching Building but armed clashes continued all over Hohhot.

Not long after these events, a student Li Yao knew named Ouyang Ruchen was caught by militant Red Guards. He and a Mongolian friend, Mo Rigen, were subjected to ferocious questioning. Asked about his family background, Ouyang answered honestly, 'Landlord'. The Red Guards jumped on him like 'tigers and wolves', beating him to death and throwing his body out the window. When Mo Rigen said he came from a poor peasant family, he was also badly beaten but he survived. Ouyang's brutal killing hit Li Yao hard. Where was the Cultural Revolution leading? He felt like a person trapped in a nightmare. It was always 'struggle', never a moment of peace. His classmates held high the Han Tong flag and fought against rival factions. They went off to Han Tong's home county to support rebels there. That ended with three classmates landing in jail. Li Yao thought of them as good people, but what was the point of this constant fighting?

One day a note arrived asking Li Yao to hurry to the apartment where his eldest sister and her new husband were living. Li Yao was astounded to find his father there. Sobbing, he cried, 'Dear Dad! Is this really you?' A worried Li Menglian told him to quieten down, they must not be overheard. Li Tiren explained that he and Li Yueheng were now back at work in Jining. Things were a little better, they were still being criticised but it was good to be back in their old town. Together again, the children celebrated their father's arrival quietly with food from the school cafeteria. But their time together was too short. Li Yao had to be on his way before dark. Two days later, Li Tiren stole away to Jining.

On 13 April 1967, the CCP Central Committee released a 'Decision . . . on the Issue of Inner Mongolia', drafted by Zhou Enlai and approved by Mao. 'Eight Red Articles' rationalised the rebel protest as an understandable 'revolutionary act' while gently rebuking the PLA for 'making a mistake in picking direction'. Everyone was to be rehabilitated. Li Yao's class were moved by this outcome. Han Tong was named a revolutionary martyr. Released from jail, their three classmates were welcomed back as heroes. While it seemed a great victory, establishing peace was not so easy. Some of the military objected strongly to the 'Eight Red Articles' and armed conflict with more deaths continued in Hohhot. Remote villages and grassland areas were slow to recognise the new policy even though the CCP Central Committee dropped leaflets explaining it from planes. 'Struggle' continued.

In January 1967, readers of the *Advertiser* learned from a London journalist who had just returned from China about the 'fantastic convulsions' paralysing the country. He had seen 'millions on the march' and reported the prevailing mood as 'hysterical and apprehensive'. Red Guards were everywhere. In April, Nationalist Chinese leaders in Formosa (now Taiwan) told the Australian prime minister Harold Holt that 'Communist rule in China is beginning a slow process of disintegration', a poorly informed prediction that has failed to eventuate.

A monument for Han Tong was put up in his village. In large characters it stated: 'Revolutionary Martyr Han Tong is immortal!'

Seeing this, Li Yao thought of Han Tong handing over the train tickets. He pictured Han Tong shouting: 'Defend Chairman Mao with your blood and life!' He saw a plane flying across the sky, leaflets dropping like snow, then changing into flocks of white pigeons. But he never saw the pigeons land and he did not know when his country would be at peace.

CHAPTER 12

Snowstorm on the grasslands

Late in 1967, Li Yao had graduated and was waiting to be assigned a job. The plum jobs in the big cities would almost certainly go to activists or students from worker or poor peasant families. Dog's whelps knew they would be sent to remote areas. Li Yao hoped he would not end up back in Jining because he could not bear to see how his parents were being treated. Posters were plastered all around their house: 'Down with landlord Li Tiren! Down with landlord Li Yueheng!' If Li Yao turned up there, another poster was sure to appear: 'Down with dog's whelp Li Yao!' He begged the Red Guard leader in his class not to send him back home. Big mistake. He was ordered back to Jining.

On a bitterly cold day early in February 1968, Li Yao left IMNU. He had lived there for five years and eight months, arriving as a boy of sixteen and leaving as a young man of twenty-two. His goal had been to gain a Master's degree and become a writer. No chance of that now. It seemed unlikely that China would ever again want independent scholars, writers, translators or artists. He was torn by conflicting emotions. He loved his university for giving him knowledge and ideals. He hated it because his new knowledge and ideals had been trampled on.

Li Yao's parents were overjoyed to see him. As a new graduate, it seemed likely that he would get a job, even if it was a teaching position somewhere remote. He was feeling sorry for himself until his mother reminded him that the whole country was suffering, not just the Li family. Chastened by her words, he went down to the Jining office which assigned jobs to new graduates to discover his fate. There he was greeted by a smiling middle-aged man, the deputy editor-in-chief of the *Wulanchabu Daily.* When Li Yao heard that this man wanted him to work for his paper, he could not believe his ears. The deputy editor explained that the paper had chosen 'Yu Deshui and yourself from about one hundred graduates'. Li Yao was bowled over. He knew Yu Deshui, a real Red Expert, CCP member and a recent graduate from the Department of Chinese Literature at Inner Mongolia University. Li Yao thought, 'How can I measure up to him?' He was a star.

The deputy editor must have guessed what Li Yao was thinking. Picking up a newspaper from the table he asked, 'Did you write this?' It was Li Yao's article in the *Inner Mongolia Daily,* 'Han Tong—Your Comrades-in-Arms miss you!' The deputy editor smiled: 'We have looked into the matter. We know you were a member of Han Tong's Combat Team. We know you have been a proletarian rebel. We are rebels too! We want you to fight alongside us.' Li Yao wanted to tell him that he was not really a proletarian rebel. He was a dog's whelp whose parents . . . But he said nothing.

Introducing himself as Zhang Jizhong, the deputy editor explained that the newspaper was aware of Li Yao's background. 'Your parents are being criticised. But we also know that they are very honest people. More importantly, we know that you always came first in the school composition contest and you were the editor of the *Blackboard Newspaper.*' Li Yao never dreamed that anyone from Jining would ever speak so well of him. The deputy editor quickly got down to tin tacks. 'You know that power struggles throughout Jining are still very intense. We hold power today but may be out on our ear tomorrow. So, go through the formalities straight away, then get out of the way until your appointment has been finalised. We will pack you and Yu Deshui off to Guyang County where you can interview the locals. By the time you return, the paperwork will be done. Even if someone objects, it will be too late.'

Li Yao stood there nodding repeatedly. Once again his pen had miraculously changed his fate. He rushed home to tell his parents the good news. They were delighted. They had been so worried that their landlord background and his father's suspect history would harm their son's job prospects and they had expected he would be sent to the countryside. But now it was clear he was going to be a newspaper reporter. For the first time in ages, there was laughter in the Li family.

The following day Li Yao and Yu Deshui took off for Guyang County. Getting there was slow work, nine hours by train to Baotou, an overnight stay in a small hotel, then a reluctant old bus eventually deposited them in Guyang. It was bitterly cold, not the best time to travel. But Li Yao did not give two hoots about the foul weather. He was on his way to becoming a journalist even though he was well aware that he would not be able to write whatever he wanted.

Yu Deshui was five years older than Li Yao and treated him like a younger brother. In Guyang County they interviewed lots of people, hearing harrowing accounts of poverty and hardship, stories that weighed heavily on Li Yao. His mother was right. There had been too much suffering. Ten days later, the two men returned to the newspaper office having successfully avoided anyone who might have opposed their appointment. The day after Li Yao's return, deputy editor Zhang told him that a big storm had just swept across the Damao grassland. An old herdswoman called Eerdunqiqige and her daughter Wu Guiying had suffered severe frostbite while trying to protect their commune's sheep. Li Yao was being sent out to interview the herders and write a report: his first assignment as a working journalist.

In 1953, the CCP had called for Producers' Cooperatives to be established on the grasslands. Each consisted of about fifty households, taking group ownership of animals, assigning work to the herders and paying them a subsistence allowance. By 1958, almost all herder households had joined a cooperative. They were then merged into larger People's Communes, each of about 650 households. Policies towards the Mongolian herders became more assimilationist with the CCP taking the 'modern view' that settled life was more 'advanced' than traditional 'nomadic' life. Pastoral households were allowed a few of their own animals, some cows, horses, sheep and goats. Some family members still moved across the seasonal pastures with their animals while most of their family remained at a fixed base where the children could go to school and the adults could attend nightly CCP meetings. One old Mongolian herder summed up his new situation: 'It was alright to be poor, but not to be rich. It was alright to work, but not to rest. It was alright to be hungry, but not to be full.'

Long Mei and Yu Rong, the Heroic Little Sisters of the Grasslands, 1964

Eerdunqiqige and her daughter came from the New Baolige Commune. It was already well known for two sisters, Long Mei and Yu Rong who had grown up there. In February 1964, aged just eleven and eight, these little girls were in charge of 384 sheep when a severe snowstorm occurred. After running about trying to keep the animals together, the girls collapsed in the snow only to suffer severe frostbite requiring amputations. Duly honoured as 'heroic little sisters of the grassland' they were celebrated by the *Xinhua News Agency* and the *People's Daily.* Long Mei and Yu Rong became famous and their touching stories were made into a book for children, a play, a film, and a Peking opera.

Li Yao was now getting the chance to write his own heroic story. Impatient to get started, he quickly hit upon a promising title: 'Heroic Mother and Daughter of the Grassland'. But getting to Damao was very difficult. He had to take a train to Baotou, then another train to the grim steel town of Baiyun Obo, and then go on by bus to Bailingmiao, the administrative centre for Damao. At Bailingmiao, Li Yao looked forward to seeing the famous Guangfu temple built in 1703. He was depressed to discover it had been severely damaged by Red Guards, who had taken away all the lamps and the silver religious objects and defaced the sacred images. The monks had been sent packing.

The Revolutionary Committee of Damao Banner sent a Mongolian propaganda officer to Bailingmiao to take Li Yao to the New Baolige Commune. They rode together into the depths of the grassland. It was the first time that Li Yao had ever been on horseback and the first time he had been out into the grassland. The sky arching above him was intensely blue, and the grassland, white in this winter season, was vast, rolling peacefully to the distant horizon. Li Yao felt as free as a bird. Way out here in this tranquil place, he could forget all the years of trouble and pain.

Li Yao was made welcome by the production team. He was told that Eerdunqiqige was recovering from surgery at the army hospital in Hohhot. But Wu Guiying, who had recovered more quickly, was there and she told Li Yao her story.

She had gone out one fine morning to herd sheep. In the afternoon a storm had rolled across the grassland, driven by a fierce north wind. She had never seen such snow. The temperature dropped precipitously. The noise of the wind was unrelenting. The world turned white and Wu Guiying knew she was lost. Back in the commune, watching the gathering storm, her mother grew increasingly anxious. When her daughter failed to return, her mother rushed out to find her. For hours, Eerdunqiqige struggled through the snow, falling, getting up again and falling once more. Quite suddenly she saw her daughter. Deafened by the roaring storm, they guided the sheep towards a small depression offering some shelter. Eerdunqiqige held Wu Guiying in her arms and tried to warm her daughter's frozen body. The snow kept falling. Mother and daughter clung together until morning when worried members of the production team, fearing the worst, finally found them alive. Eerdunqiqige had suffered severe frostbite. Li Yao marvelled at this strong maternal love, expressed in the ice and snow. He was sure he would be able to write a moving story.

Li Yao visited Eerdunqiqige in Hohhot, where she was lying in a hospital bed after having one leg amputated. She was a woman

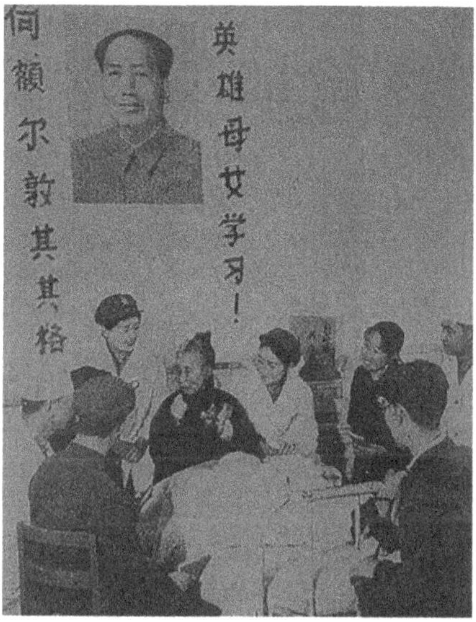

Eerdunqiqige in her hospital bed in Hohhot.
Li Yao is at the foot of the bed.

of about sixty, with an open, unsophisticated manner, whose dark Mongolian face was deeply lined by the elements. As she only spoke Mongolian Li Yao had to interview her through an interpreter. On being told that he was a journalist who wanted to know her story, Eerdunqiqige shook her head. What had happened to her was not something to be impressed by. Things like this happened every winter on the grassland. On the very same day, more than a dozen people in her production team had suffered frostbite. Li Yao should go off and write about them. She had just been trying to save her daughter, something any mother would do.

Li Yao met several herders who had also been out in that terrible storm. He has never forgotten Qimude Haorilao an eighteen-year-old lad. With one foot amputated he was getting around on crutches. In recompense, the commune had given him the *Selected Works of Mao Zedong* and some copies of *Quotations from Chairman Mao*. Li Yao felt bad that he had not been able to write anything about Haorilao. He had to stick to his assigned task, 'Heroic Mother and Daughter of the Grassland'.

All fired up after his interviews, Li Yao quickly finished his article for the *Wulanchabu Daily*. He thought he had done well. Then the *Inner Mongolia Daily* asked if they could republish his report but when they read it more carefully, they were not satisfied. Their editor-in-chief said, 'You told a moving story, and you write elegantly, but you don't tell the readers where Eerdunqiqige got her strength from. How did she manage to survive the storm?' Li Yao hesitated: 'Perhaps it came from her great motherly love?' The editor-in-chief stepped closer, patted him on the shoulder and replied: 'You are a naive young man. Remember, you are now a journalist, writing for the Party newspaper, you are not fooling about writing pretty pieces at school.'

On further reflection, the editor's eyes suddenly lit up. 'Great motherly love. Yes, that is a very good angle. But first we have to ask, who is our mother and what is great motherly love?' A puzzled Li Yao wondered where all this was going. 'Do you know this song?' asked the editor humming the well-known tune 'Father and Mother are not as close as Chairman Mao'. 'Yes,' Li Yao nodded, 'I know it.' Then, 'Who is our mother?' asked the editor. 'Our mother is the Party and Chairman Mao! The strength shown by that woman comes from our Great Party and from Chairman Mao. You must write it like that. I'll send an experienced journalist to the grassland with you and you can do a repeat interview. You must write an article that will make a big splash!'

The 'experienced journalist' turned out to be editor Ji Zhiheng. Together they re-interviewed Eerdunqiqige and Wu Guiying. Ji's questions were designed to elicit just the right kind of answers. 'Did you remember Chairman Mao's teachings when you struggled in the snowstorm?' he asked. Eerdunqiqige was an illiterate woman who only spoke Mongolian. Her daughter knew some Mandarin but her vocabulary was limited. Li Yao could not believe that they would remember Mao's teachings during a snowstorm that threatened their lives. But Wu Guiying was young and twigged to what was going on. When Ji asked, 'Did you think of Chairman Mao's saying "Firstly, do not fear hardship and secondly, do not fear death"?' 'Yes,' she nodded while her mother looked on uncomprehendingly. The revised article, now called, 'Red Hearts Dedicated to Chairman Mao', read:

> The north wind howled as the heroic mother and daughter of the grassland struggled through snow and ice to protect important state property, the flock of the People's Commune. Remembering Chairman Mao's teachings 'Firstly, do not fear hardship and secondly, do not fear death', they shouted loudly, 'Be resolute, fear no sacrifice and surmount every difficulty to win victory!' As they fought the storm, the grassland seemed to be singing to them, 'Father and mother are not as close as Chairman Mao'. Greatly encouraged by Chairman Mao's deep maternal love, they conquered adversity.

The editor-in-chief was pleased. He told Li Yao: 'You are very clever, I believe you will be a good journalist.' Li Yao did not know what to say.

The article appeared on the front page of the *Inner Mongolia Daily* on 5 May 1968. It caused a stir. The Party Committee of the Inner Mongolia Autonomous Region called on people everywhere to learn from this 'Heroic Mother and Daughter of the Grassland'. Eerdunqiqige became an activist, promoting the works of Chairman Mao, and attended all kinds of events to talk about her experience. Wu Guiying became deputy director of the Revolutionary Committee of Damao Banner. This was a miraculous change in their circumstances. They were as famous as Long Mei and Yu Rong. As a young journalist who had only been working for three months, Li Yao was pleased to be valued by his newspaper. He had made a splash. But deep down, he remained uneasy. He could feel eyes upon him; the kind simple eyes of Eerdunqiqige; the clear bright eyes of Qimude Haorilao; and other eyes too, full of scorn and derision.

Both the English and Russian editions of *China Reconstructs* reprinted Li Yao's article. David and Karen, visiting Canberra in February 2020, decide to go to the National Library to find the article. No chance of Li Yao doing that in Beijing. He was bunkered down in his apartment as the coronavirus began to spread. Canberra had not yet reported any cases. Walking up the steps of the National Library on the shores of Lake Burley Griffin, David had a sense of homecoming. He loved the place. Since its opening in 1968 he had spent a lot of time here looking at manuscripts and newspapers. The library had a full set of *China Reconstructs* in pristine condition. In the heavy volume for 1968, Karen found a small article on Inner Mongolia. It celebrated all the good things that were happening. 'Life has become brighter and more attractive and prosperity is evident everywhere,' it claimed. Evidently there was no *ger* in the vast grasslands that did not have 'hanging on its walls a portrait of Chairman Mao'. The herders were kept busy with nightly discussions and political broadcasts. The article noted how no-one rode out to graze sheep or cattle without *Quotations from Chairman Mao Tse-Tung* in their pocket. Whenever a visitor arrives 'the first thing he says is "How is your study of Chairman Mao's works getting along?" Then he takes out his copy of the *Quotations* and reads a few passages with his host.'

In the September 1968 issue of *China Reconstructs* Karen locates Li Yao's article now bearing the title, 'A mother and daughter save the Commune's sheep'. No author or translator is acknowledged. A small photograph shows Eerdunqiqige (here called Erdonchichig) smiling cheerfully beneath a large portrait of Chairman Mao. The article opened with quite a flourish: 'One early spring morning before sunrise, as rose-tinted clouds threw a reddish glow over the snow-covered Ulantsab grasslands, a young herdswoman set out to graze a flock of 276 sheep . . . In her pocket she was carrying *Quotations from Chairman Mao Tse-tung*.' In this version, the mother goes to look for her daughter, but after finding her gets lost herself while trying to locate all the sheep. It gets dark as the daughter, frantic with worry, tries to find her mother. At last, in the 'hazy moonlight', she sees some 'vague forms of moving sheep' and there is her mother crawling along in the snow. She has lost her gloves and one shoe. The mother urges her daughter to go off to get help saying, 'Chairman Mao teaches us: so long as a single man remains, he will fight on. As long as I am alive the sheep will be safe.' Two hours later her daughter arrived to rescue her with two commune members and a camel.

In summer, Li Yao returned to Eerdunqiqige's commune. The grassland was now green, an ocean of waist-high grass. Eerdunqiqige now had a new prosthetic leg but she could not get used to it. She was still working but crawling about everywhere. She and her family were very happy to see Li Yao. To her unsophisticated mind, it was his article that had changed her life. Taking him by the hand she told him, 'You are closer to me than my son!' Li Yao knew she meant it. She instructed her son to kill a sheep, took out some rice she had stored which was hard to get on the grassland, and set her daughter-in-law to make a fine meal. It was like a festival. Li Yao was very touched.

There were no hotels anywhere about, so Li Yao stayed at Eerdunqiqige's hut. He lay next to her on the *kang*, like a son. The night was very quiet. As he lay there Li Yao was disturbed by a sudden commotion outside the window. He sat up, listening intently. The sheep had all woken up as if from a nightmare and were thundering down the hill. Hundreds of sheep rushed past. Eerdunqiqige's son, sleeping in the next room, jumped up and grabbed his shotgun, shouting that a wolf was coming. Eerdunqiqige knelt by the window and putting her hands together prayed: 'Long live Chairman Mao, long live Chairman Mao, long live Chairman Mao'. Li Yao could see her dark silhouette and the streak of white in her hair. He had the disconcerting feeling that she regarded Chairman Mao as some sort of god, a god who had miraculously changed her life. Did she regard Li Yao as a guardian angel, one who, waving his pen like a wand, had turned her and her daughter into heroes? Only gods and angels had such power. Outside, the sheep gradually quietened down. Her son must have chased the wolf away. Eerdunqiqige lay down and fell asleep. But Li Yao lay there, eyes wide open, feeling a sense of guilt, as if he owed a debt to this simple old woman. Li Yao knew he and his journalist colleagues had used her for their own advantage.

When he entered the university in 1964, David soon found that students were expected to read and the reading lists were long. The weekly one-hour tutorials in English and History rarely had more than six students, leaving those who had not done their reading seriously exposed. The tutorial was not a therapy session, designed to make students feel comfortable. The failure rate in the big first year subjects was high, up to 50 per cent. There was nothing for it but to knuckle down and prepare for classes. The tutorials were not only academically demanding but also quite formal. Although the decade was later to become famous for its youthful upheaval and rebellion, in tutorials, students were seldom addressed by their first name either by the tutor or by other students. David became Mr Walker, which he found awkward as this title had always been reserved for his father, Gilbert J. Walker, Headmaster.

While David has no memory of any library at the Teachers' College, the Barr Smith Library at the university was a shrine built in honour of the book. Its spacious main reading room was furnished with handsome desks fitted with elegant reading lamps. He would make a beeline for his favourite spot at the back and pile it high with books. For a change of scene, he went off to the State Library with his fellow student Trevor Horton. This was an even bigger and more ornate building. Built in the 1880s, it stood as a proud affirmation of the central role assigned to knowledge and learning in advancing the new colony. The ground floor reading room had a high glass ceiling. Books on the upper floors were reached up flights of echoing stairs. Each floor had secluded reading bays or alcoves, several of which housed the History Section. Sitting there, surrounded by books, Mr Walker and Mr Horton felt that they had the place to themselves. But the books that surrounded them were mostly by authors from overseas.

The University of Adelaide focused on British and European history, although some Asian history was taught, mainly that of India and China. The first course in Australian history was not introduced until 1965. As with history, so with literature. Courses in Australian literature were rare. During the 1960s, the English Department had one eccentric academic, Brian Elliott, delivering one of the first Australian literature courses in the country. Elliott seemed a rather grumpy fellow, trading in the base coin of Australian literature while the really big professors discoursed on the greats: Chaucer, Shakespeare, Swift, Austen and Coleridge. Struggling to complete university subjects on top of a full teachers' college workload, David was attracted by Australian Literature and Australian History as subjects which might be less demanding. Like most of his classmates, he doubted that Australia had either a history or a literature worth studying. That had to mean shorter reading lists.

Taking a break from his studies, David started doing the rounds of Adelaide's bookshops. Across the road from the university was the Argonaut bookshop, a reminder of his undistinguished career as the fitful rower, Sestus-26. Opposite the State Library, a Red Cross charity shop had a big selection of second-hand books. The best bookshop of them all was Mary Martin's, a local institution owned by Adelaide's very own Max Harris, poet, daring modernist and enemy of polite society. David caught occasional glimpses of him, an alert, slightly pudgy fellow who wore his dark hair rather longer than was considered acceptable. Harris seemed every inch the writer, a figure far too important to speak to or approach.

As he began to read more widely, David experimented with writing. With no experience of the theatre, he embarked on a five act play. Not long after completing this masterpiece he made the mistake of reading it. That occasioned a short trip to the bottom of the back yard. Behind a stone structure that Gil and Glasson called their 'feature wall' was a large 44-gallon drum serving as an incinerator. In went the pages. The little fire danced and crackled. No memory survives of what the play was about. What made him write it? He had enrolled in a class on Elizabethan and Jacobean drama taught by Dr Allan Brissenden. Unlike most of the English Department, Brissenden was still in his thirties, approachable and Australian-born. David loved Brissenden's classes and the language of this English drama. Before long, after a drink or two at a student party, he would thrill his audience with a small serving from Thomas Kyd's gory revenge play, *The Spanish Tragedy*:

> Oh eyes! No eyes but fountains fraught with tears;
> Oh life! No life but lively form of death;
> Oh world! No world but mass of public wrongs,
> Confus'd and fill'd with murder and misdeeds . . .

John Webster's rousing melodrama *The Duchess of Malfi* also formed part of David's repertoire but he believed that for sheer emotional power, dramatic gestures and sonorous phrasing, nothing surpassed his rendition of Othello's death speech: 'Soft you, a word or two before you go.'

Although David had burned it, he did not regret writing his play. It had taught him something. Now he turned to poetry. He did this with some qualms. He understood that it was not considered a very manly pursuit. His Enfield High friends thought poetry was better left to girls. But David's mop of 'girlish' curly hair had already left him wondering if manliness would ever really be his thing. His woodwork teacher had once singled him out in front of the class as the 'most feminine boy' he knew. Getting his own back, the elder Rooster had tossed his curls and adopted some alluring, come hither poses for his appreciative classmates. Never a well-controlled class, their raucous laughter could be heard several suburbs away.

David had been introduced to poetry as a child. At primary school everyone had to learn Dorothea McKellar's 'My Country' and bits of Banjo Paterson, the poet who introduced the nation to Clancy, the shearer who turned his back on the crowded city for a carefree life as a drover in the bush. By high school, nineteenth-century English poetry had come into its own, led by William Wordsworth. Gil was quite a fan of Coleridge's, 'The Rime of the Ancient Mariner':

It is an ancient Mariner,
And he stoppeth one of three,
'By thy long grey beard and glittering eye,
Now wherefore stopp'st thou me?'

Gil struggled to go further than that but felt that he hardly needed to. What a great opening that was! That was real poetry. Tennyson, so sonorous and high-sounding, was another high school staple. When Enfield High wanted a rousing motto for the school magazine, it found 'To strive, to seek, to find, and not to yield', the last line of Tennyson's poem 'Ulysses'.

By late adolescence, the figure of the poet offered David an escape from the confines of an undemonstrative suburban household. The most appealing exemplar was that wild man of Welsh letters, Dylan Thomas. Often drunk and always disorderly, Dylan Thomas was everything a poet should be. What seems surprising now is that David even managed to get a couple of his own poems published in the Jacaranda Press anthology *Under Twenty-Five*. A year later, he was too busy writing his Honours thesis in History to think of poetry. His career as a poet was over.

David's Honours thesis 'Mates and Diggers' focused on a group of popular Australian novelists who had written about war, nationhood, manliness and the bush legend in the late 1940s and 1950s. David was motoring along now, working hard, sprouting opinions left, right and centre, convinced he was onto something. He ended 1967 on a high with a Tinline Scholarship, no money but a proven ticket to postgraduate study. Previous Tinliners had taken off overseas, to Oxford or Cambridge. While the elder Rooster wanted to go to the University of Chicago, as a conscript he was not allowed to leave the country.

CHAPTER 13

Facing contagions

Without asking, our dreams borrow from scenes in our waking lives, twisting them into troubling phantasmagoria where nothing is ever as it should be. Childhood memories often inhabit these strange lands. David has an insistent memory of a certain house in Freeling, standing at a fork in the road not far from the small town centre. One day, when he was about seven years old, walking down that road, he looked up at the house straight ahead of him. It had a wide veranda affording a good view of the road below. Sitting there most days was a young boy, studying the cars and the passers-by. As David approached, the boy began waving at him very enthusiastically, arms flying everywhere. Embarrassed, David had quickly run home to ask his parents about the strange waving boy. Gil explained, 'This poor lad is a "mongol" who suffers from a terrible disease that has affected his brain.' As David grew older, 'mongol' joined a list of cruel names flung around the school yard. Boys were always yelling out, 'you mongol', 'you idiot', 'you imbecile' or 'you cretin'.

The medical terms 'mongol', 'mongoloid' and 'mongolian idiocy' date from the 1860s. For over a century, these invidious names linked China with a dreadful disorder, language that was not changed until the 1960s when 'mongolism' became 'Down syndrome' or 'Trisomy 21', although the older terminology still lingers on. Taking a break from his university studies on a wintry afternoon, David was scanning the shelves in the Red Cross bookshop—friends knew to look for him there—when he came upon a curious book that took him straight back to the waving boy in Freeling. He paid threepence for a little red volume called *The Mongol in our Midst* by Dr F. G. Crookshank. Published in the 1920s, it contained carefully classified photographs: 'high-grade' and 'low-grade racial Mongols', 'Occidental Mongols' (Turks, Finns, Lapps and Russians), 'sporadic Mongoloids' and 'Mongolian imbeciles'. Drawing on such features as the epicanthal eye fold, the Buddha-like disposition of lower limbs into 'horizontal planes' when seated, and the presence of a 'transverse line' on the palm, Crookshank advanced his argument that mongols had evolved from orangutan apes.

While much reprinted through the 1920s, Crookshank's book failed to engage the elder Rooster who felt his threepence had been wasted. But returns on investment can take time. Crookshank now sits on his bookshelf along with a line of other 'yellow peril' offerings from an odd collection of racial theorists. For many years David has pondered the ways in which settler Australia thought about race and their country's location in the Asia Pacific. It is a jigsaw puzzle, with many scattered pieces, but no agreed final picture. How could there be? Even so, David argues that anxiety about 'rising Asia' has had a profound impact on Australia's development and has influenced how the country has approached questions of defence, security, population and the importance of being white. It was easy, too easy perhaps, for settlers to picture their continent as a temptingly empty prize, unhappily located on the edge of crowded, desperately poor Asia.

Politicians soon found this was an image they could use. A young nation seemingly under threat provided a great rallying cry for flag-waving patriots. Nothing focuses the mind like the battle for survival in a dangerous world. Writers also warmed to the theme. The prospect of a threatened nation had the makings of a gripping yarn replete with a full cast of valiant heroes and cunning oriental villains. On 1 January 1901, the Commonwealth of Australia became the first new nation of the twentieth century. What were the odds of this infant's survival? Australia kept a wary eye on rising Asia, particularly China and Japan.

From the 1880s, invasion stories warned that one day, an Asian enemy would take over white Australia. Some began connecting the dots. Invasion stories warned that yellow would replace white, just as white had replaced black. These 'yellow peril' anxieties are lodged deep in the European imagination where, like a deadly virus, they quietly mutate and adapt. There was, of course, a gracious, elegant and civilised China, the China of gorgeous *chinoiserie* and willow pattern plates, but settlers all too often saw only the dark side, imagining a cruel oriental race bent on conquest, a conquering race that was also the bearer of horrible disease. From the late nineteenth century, Australians linked Chinese people (without good cause) to loathsome and disfiguring maladies such as smallpox, leprosy and 'mongolism'. Sharp distinctions were drawn between the clean, 'white' continent of Australia and the contaminating dirt and contagion of China.

Australians were not only frightened of Chinese disease but also of the machinations of Chinese masterminds, brilliant minds serving evil ends. The greatest mastermind of them all is Dr Fu Manchu who began his long fictional career in 1913. In a series of popular novels, this amoral doctor displays an astonishing command of languages and a mighty brain. Despite a vast medical knowledge, he never heals the sick. He is a bioterrorist, creating new and fearsome diseases to use against anyone standing between him and world domination.

David now has a growing collection of cheap Fu Manchu paperbacks. Harder to come by were the posters. He was in Beijing in 2010 with his daughter Veronica when they noticed a large private collection of film posters for sale. There were wonderful finds. Two striking posters now hang in his study, advertising 'Le Masque de Fu Manchu' (1965) and 'The Castle of Fu Manchu' (1969).

The prototype for such sinister figures can be traced back to the Mongol invasions of the thirteenth century. The achievements of Genghis Khan in establishing a trading empire stretching from Siberia to India, Vietnam to Hungary, Korea to the Balkans has been forgotten by many, overtaken by the spectre of the barbarous conqueror bent on destruction. Crookshank attributed the 'Occidental Mongol', 'the mongol in our midst' to the mass rape of European women by Genghis Khan's armies. It is a short step from having nightmares of a fearsome racial enemy to believing that these people are busy plotting your destruction. Most of Australia's invasion writing feeds upon conspiracies which flourish when societies confront unknown dangers, not unlike the troubling responses to the coronavirus pandemic that weighs on us today.

In Australia in the late 1950s, the Catholic intellectual Bob Santamaria claimed to have seen documents revealing how China planned to take over the world, cleaning up Australia along the way. Santamaria was a tireless Cold War warrior, broadcaster and newspaper columnist. In his radio broadcasts, he sounded obsessive, with a rapid-fire, high-pitched delivery. On the other hand, this urgent little man always seemed to know what he was talking about, especially when it came to the menace of Communist China.

Santamaria explained Chinese intentions. He believed they had a twenty-year timeline and a three-stage plan to conquer the West. Australia was clearly doomed. It would fall under China's control by the mid-1970s. Using trade as a weapon, Australia would be inexorably drawn into the Chinese 'co-prosperity sphere'. According to Santamaria, Japan's failed 'co-prosperity plan' of the 1940s provided the blueprint. China would complete what Japan had started. Santamaria was struck by Lenin's prophecy of 1918 that the communist road to Paris and world domination lay through Beijing. There it was. Lenin had a plan and half a century later it was being seamlessly implemented by the infinitely patient Chinese. In the early 1960s, bookshops in Adelaide prominently displayed Denis Warner's *Hurricane from China*. Its front cover shouted, 'What you MUST know about Mao Tse-Tung's plan for world conquest'.

According to *On Dit*, most of the students at Adelaide University during the 1960s were quite conservative in their political and social views, especially the men. Seventy-five per cent of them supported Australia's involvement in the Vietnam War and at least two-thirds supported conscription. On social matters, almost one-third were regular church-goers and over half agreed that homosexuality was a crime. Arts students were more inclined to question conservative opinion. A Bruce Petty cartoon summed up how things were going in Vietnam. An aide advises President Johnson: 'We've still got 1/3rd of the pacified 3/5ths of the southern ½ of Vietnam on our side.' That Petty was a funny man, but *On Dit*'s photographs of the war were disturbing—bodies of soldiers, wounded children and the destructive aftermath of US bombing raids. An editorial warned that Australians had to be 'clear in our own minds as to why we are in Vietnam'. Glasson Walker was certainly clear in her mind that the army was keeping the Chinese communists out of Hazelwood Park by stopping them in Vietnam. Her son was not so sure.

Throughout 1967, *On Dit* continued to carry articles on the war. In the wider society, particularly around Anzac Day, contrasts were drawn between the valiant patriots who had served in earlier wars and self-indulgent modern youth who seemed less inclined to serve their country. While the *Advertiser* was convinced that stopping China in Vietnam was the right policy, *On Dit* published letters highly critical of Australia's submissive response to American policies. A detailed report came in from a summer school held in Canberra by the Australian Institute of Political Science. Speakers reiterated that Australia did not need to exist in such a 'miasma of fear, hatred and suspicion' over the threat of China. *On Dit* reprinted an article from the *New Statesman*, explaining that the Allies could never 'win' the war in Vietnam without invading the north and committing troops to hold down the entire peninsula in perpetuity. Was Australia prepared for such an enormous expenditure of men and money?

In the pages of *On Dit*, communism itself was looking much more complicated than it did in the mainstream media. V.C. Funnell, lecturer in politics at nearby Flinders University, reminded *On Dit*'s readers that 1967 marked the fiftieth anniversary of the Russian Revolution. In his opinion, events in China were unlikely to turn out exactly as Mao planned. In the future, Funnell believed, 'communism as a political creed may be unrecognisable'.

On Dit interviewed Malcolm Salmon, an Australian journalist who had lived for several years in North Vietnam. While Salmon, as a communist, opposed the 'unjust' and 'hopeless' war, he was reassuring on the China threat. 'Chinese influence in Hanoi' he said, was at an 'all-time low'. The North Vietnamese were far from impressed with Mao's Cultural Revolution, regarding it 'as anathema and not at all helpful to their own cause'. He thought Chinese intervention in North Vietnam was very unlikely. Based on their historical experience, it was an axiom of 'good North Vietnamese politics' never to let 'Chinese troops on your soil'. David did not consider *On Dit* the sole repository of truth, but it made him aware of dissenting opinions on the war, many of which were reinforced by his growing interest in the battle raging in American politics.

Through the year, dissent on campus increased. The Campaign for Peace in Vietnam established a group at the university. At a Special General Meeting of the ALP Club, a resolution was passed stating that 'the Australian government should withdraw their troops immediately from Vietnam'. A motion was also circulated signed by Adelaide University staff urging 'de-escalation of all military operations by all parties in South Vietnam'. This, David noted, was signed by nine members of the History Department and by eight Department of English staff. He suspected these academics might well know more about the political situation than he did.

At the time of writing, the great coronavirus pandemic continues to spread outside China. David and Karen are locked down in Melbourne. Talk of the vulnerable 'elderly' has never been more common. Whatever these two imagined themselves to be in 2019, they are 'old' people now. An email arrives from the equally 'elderly' Li Yao to say that Beijing is coming back to life. Nevertheless, he is staying indoors where he is pressing on with his translation of Mary Gaunt's *A Woman in China*. He spends an hour each day walking in his small apartment, a few paces up and a few back, up and back, up and back. On television, David hears President Trump repeatedly refer to COVID-19 as the 'China virus'. The indefatigable mongol is in our midst again, spreading disease. Rumours circulate. An email attachment arrives in Melbourne, sent by an even older relative in Queensland. It proves to be a fresh remake of an old story: 'China's plan to conquer the world'.

Standing in their way, thank goodness, are courageous Queenslanders who have twigged to what the Chinese are up to and are bravely alerting the world to the dangers ahead. The email outlines the ten steps of this process from:

1. Creating a virus and the antidote.
2. Spreading the virus.

All the way down to . . .

10. Getting back to full production while the rest of the world has been brought to a standstill.

Each step is supported by revealing so-called facts. Wasn't it very suspicious that Beijing and Shanghai had largely escaped the virus? Was there more to this pandemic than Australians were being told?

Retired Australian Liberal Party Senator Bronwyn Bishop, speaking on *Sky News*, advanced her own theory. The Chinese, she claimed, had created the coronavirus to 'get rid of non-productive Chinese' because then 'they don't have to be fed'. That done, they would 'export the virus' to the United States to determine 'whether or not it is possible for this sort of action to send the rest of the world into recession'. She insists that this deadly virus has provided an opportunity for China to fatally weaken the West and grab the spoils. While few of Bishop's parliamentary colleagues would support this nonsense, suspicion runs deep and seems to be getting deeper. In June 2021, a survey undertaken by the Australia Institute revealed that over four in every ten Australians feared China might invade their continent. As an historian, David is exasperated that in seeking to explain these 'astounding' results, researchers look only to contemporary political explanations and appear wholly unaware of Australia's long and constantly reinforced history of anxiety about rising Asia.

Late in 2019, a senior Australian journalist, Peter Hartcher, warned Australians about a secret CCP document outlining the Chinese government's plans to dominate the world stage by 2049, a year that marks the centenary of the founding of the People's Republic of China. There is a proven appeal to any conspiracy, particularly a Chinese conspiracy, involving a secret document, a precise timeline and uncanny levels of detailed planning. But one can question the need for this appearing in a serious foreign affairs essay—there is so much else of importance to discuss in the Australia–China relationship, material that Hartcher is more than competent to tackle. Since Hartcher's essay appeared, the global pandemic has occurred. Evangelical Christians invoke the First Horseman of the Apocalypse on his white horse, his bow swinging back to release poisoned arrows that spread pestilence abroad. How many other unforeseen global shocks will disrupt Chinese planning before 2049? Nevertheless, it is likely that as its power grows, China will become the focus of new conspiracy theories. For its part, China has generated its own conspiratorial views pushed by 'Wolf Warriors' on the Internet who argue that the virus originated in America and was released to harm China. There are choppy waters ahead.

When David was a conscripted university student contemplating his possible role in stopping China's advance through South-East Asia, Li Yao was coming to the end of his quiet journalistic life. A Cleansing the Class Ranks Movement had started up. On 25 May 1968 the CCP Central Committee released comments by Chairman Mao on *The Experience of the Beijing Xinhua Printing Factory Military Control Commission in Mobilising the Masses to Struggle against the Enemy*. Mao had dispatched army propaganda teams to selected universities and factories to conduct struggle, criticism and reform experiments. New instructions were about to be rolled out.

In Inner Mongolia, Li Yao's parents were locked up again. Back to the future. They were compelled to answer dozens of questions they had answered countless times before. For his part, Li Yao was told he needed more working class education. Plucked out of his newspaper office, he was sent off, along with several of his unsound contemporaries, to the Jining Meat Processing Plant. He readily conceded he knew little about canning meat. As things turned out, the meatworks was not such a bad place to be. He could buy very cheap meat left over from making canned beef. As for the workers, they were a pretty friendly bunch who consumed their politics with a large grain of salt, unconcerned about the finer points of revolutionary practice. Most were young people, around Li Yao's age. Some of the bolder spirits cooked up large chunks of beef very slowly in a big pot of peanut oil. As soon as the head of the workshop had disappeared, they scooped the meat out and concealed it until it could be safely eaten. The workers invited Li Yao to join them which, in the name of re-education, he was always pleased to do. For Li Yao, beef cooked in peanut oil brings back happy memories. Whenever the workers put the illicit beef in front of him, he thought, 'Just the sort of re-education I need!'

Eating alongside the workers, it seemed to Li Yao that a flash of lightning had lit up the dark sky, a fleeting moment, but a glimpse of light. Human warmth and good humour were very rare in those days. Li Yao would have liked to stay in that factory forever, not just for the beef but for the healing friendships he had formed there. He was happier but it bothered him that his parents were still locked up being criticised every day. They could not go home. Before his mother was locked away, she had told him, no matter what happens, he mustn't visit them. She was afraid that he might be kicked out of the newspaper office. All Li Yao could do was buy some canned beef and ask his youngest sister to send it to his parents. Then he heard that his mother had developed ovarian fibroids and needed surgery, but the hospital refused to admit her after they learned she was being criticised at her school.

Li Yao was shocked and angry. He sought out the person in charge at the hospital and fired off question after question: 'Chairman Mao taught us to practice revolutionary humanitarianism. What is revolutionary humanitarianism? My mother has been a teacher all her life. Why isn't she allowed to see a doctor?' They replied, 'Because the Leader of the Workers' Propaganda Team at the school has told us that your father was a historical counter-revolutionary and landlord. Your mother is being criticised and cannot come to the hospital.' Li Yao argued and argued, to no avail. Finally, he found an old classmate of his eldest sister who was working at this hospital as a doctor and asked her for help. His mother was finally admitted in order to undergo a total hysterectomy. This major operation normally required two weeks' recovery in a hospital ward, but his mother was abruptly discharged after only one week. When Li Yao asked the hospital to let her remain there a few more days, they refused. The Leader of the Workers' Propaganda Team at their mother's school had requested that she be sent back to accept criticism. Li Yueheng was willing to face any hardship. She got up from her bed, saying nothing, and left the hospital. That might seem about as bad as it could get. Not quite. A huge storm was about to sweep across the grasslands engulfing millions of Mongolian and Han people.

On 13 October 1925, the first Congress of the Inner Mongolia People's Revolutionary Party (IMPRP) had been held in Zhangjiakou, attended by representatives of the Communist International, the CCP, the Guomindang, the Feng Yuxiang National Army and the Mongolian People's Revolutionary Party. Two years later, the IMPRP met again in Ulaanbaatar. This city was now the capital of the Mongolian People's Republic, formed in Outer Mongolia with assistance from the USSR. In following years, while Mongolian nationalists consolidated their hold on Outer Mongolia, the IMPRP failed to develop an effective base in Inner Mongolia and by 1927 the party ceased to exist. Although scattered supporters made attempts to re-establish the IMPRP after the anti-Japanese War, the party was formally dissolved in April 1946 and many of its members joined the CCP.

On 6 February 1963, a letter addressed to the Russian-backed Mongolian People's Republic was discovered at the post office in Jining. The letter claimed that a recent meeting of the defunct IMPRP was calling for the unification of Inner and Outer Mongolia. Adding fuel to the flames, it also strongly condemned Chinese colonisation of the grasslands. Three years later in May 1966, Ulaanhu, Chairman of the Inner Mongolia Autonomous Region, lost his freedom and political power. More in sorrow than in anger, the CCP claimed that they had trusted Ulaanhu. Yet he had betrayed their trust by heading a secret Mongolian separatist organisation. This snake in the grass had colluded with the USSR and the government of the Mongolian People's Republic. He was seeking to destroy 'the integrity of the Motherland' by attempting to set up an independent state. All the old fears of Mongolian subversion were now updated, fuelling a massive paranoia directed at Mongolians which reached its peak during the Cultural Revolution.

In April 1967, the Cultural Revolution Group of the CCP Central Committee sent General Teng Haiqing to head a 'newly born red regime' in Inner Mongolia. Ulaanhu remained under house arrest in Beijing. Teng soon began a campaign to 'dig out' the poison of Ulaanhu. It was now a top priority to 'uproot Ulaanhu's sinister black line and eliminate his pernicious influence'. From February 1968, events took an even darker turn, as persistent attempts were made to uncover and purge members of the IMPRP, an organisation that no longer existed. A concerted campaign of Counter-Revolutionary Scooping Up and Elimination began.

One Mongolian herder remembered how his 70-year-old grandmother, still wearing traditional Mongolian dress, was forced to do physical labour followed by a 'struggle' session at the headquarters of the production brigade. To the sound of loud roars from the 'heavily armed people's militia' she was called a 'monster and freak' and draped in posters denouncing her as a member of the IMPRP. At night, revolutionary crowds burned grass outside her cell window and she was made to stand in the heavy smoke in a 'jet plane posture', her arms behind her back. This campaign to purge Mongolian separatists inevitably spread to their possible Han associates. The net grew wider and wider as the campaign rolled out across Inner Mongolia. Panic was in the air.

In Jining, Li Yueheng knew nothing about the IMPRP, but Li Yao knew a little. He had read about them in *Red Road,* a novel by the Mongolian author Zaragahu. *Red Road* described a struggle in 1946 in north-east Inner Mongolia between some members of the IMPRP and the CCP. Based on his reading, Li Yao thought the Counter-Revolutionary Scooping Up and Elimination Movement would target Mongolians and have nothing to do with him and his family. They were Han people. But over time, more and more people, both Mongolian and Han, were branded as counter-revolutionaries. Suddenly the net fell. Li Tiren was locked up first and then Li Yueheng, even though she had just been released from hospital. The Workers' Propaganda Team and the PLA Propaganda Team who were running the school insisted that Li Yueheng was a member of the IMPRP even though she had never heard of this organisation.

Li Yueheng had always been a very committed teacher. Before the Cultural Revolution, she was considered an Advanced Education

Worker and was elected as a deputy to the Second and Third People's Congress of Jining City. When the Scooping Up and Elimination Movement began, most of the deputies of this People's Congress were branded as IMPRP even though most were Han Chinese. So Li Yueheng was locked up. It was winter and Jining was bitterly cold. Li Yueheng was pushed into a room with no bed and no heating. When she asked where she could sleep, the guard pointed to the cement floor. A shocked fellow teacher, ashamed at what was happening, gave her some old posters to lie on.

When Chinese guards wanted to find out if someone was a member of the IMPRP, they would interrogate them using 'wheel tactics' or sleep deprivation. As people broke under the pressure, they would be forced to name their associates. Li Yueheng knew that if just one person in a family was identified, it was immediately assumed that the whole family was implicated. She was very afraid of incriminating her children, especially Li Yao, working in Jining. She flatly denied that she was a member of the IMPRP and refused to testify against anyone. That was unacceptable. For seven days and

Li Yueheng and Li Tiren in later life

nights her accusers refused to let her sleep. They hung an iron bucket filled with sand around her neck and sometimes beat her. But, as Li Yao explains, as a mother, she was as brave as Eerdunqiqige. She protected her children with her life. She would rather die than bring disaster upon them.

In the winter of 1968, thousands of people like Li Yueheng were persecuted in Inner Mongolia, especially ethnic Mongolian people. Years later, the Special Prosecutor's Office reported that 340 000 people had been imprisoned and cruelly punished. Over 16 000 people were killed. A report sent to General Teng in Hohhot stated that entire villages ran away in terror whenever a team arrived hunting for members of the IMPRP. Premier Zhou Enlai's niece, Zhou Bingjian, had been sent to the Xilingole grassland as an 'educated youth'. When she saw at first-hand the catastrophe occurring on the steppes, she wrote to her uncle. Realising the situation was very serious, Zhou Enlai instructed the central government to rehabilitate the persecuted cadres of Inner Mongolia urgently. In May 1969, an order went out for the situation to be corrected. On this document were characters written in Mao's hand: 'do so'.

After months of brutal torture, Li Yueheng's health had deteriorated sharply. In accordance with the new policy, the Workers' Propaganda Team decided to rehabilitate her. But when they released her, she refused to budge. She said, 'First you must give me a proper explanation. Why did you torture me? What made you think I was a member of an organisation I knew nothing about? Go on, explain yourselves.' The Workers' Propaganda Team were at a loss. They begged Li Tiren simply to persuade her to go home. He was very shocked when he saw his wife. She had become so much thinner and had difficulty walking. Borrowing a wheelbarrow, Li Tiren took her home to look after her. An old ballad runs:

> This crescent moon, it shines over our land,
> In our land do we know how many families are content?
> And how many families suffer too much torment?
> How many husbands and wives sleep in one bed?
> While how many are adrift so far away from Home?

CHAPTER 14

The study class

By the end of the 1960s, relations between China and Russia had deteriorated sharply. Inner Mongolia's long border with the USSR and the Russian-backed People's Republic of Mongolia put it right at the centre of any potential conflict. The Chinese considered Inner Mongolia a first tier province, first to be attacked if there was a war. It sent 70 000 troops to guard its northern borders. The Soviets stationed a similar number of their troops in the People's Republic of Mongolia, ready to cross into China. By 1969, after months of tension, a conflict erupted over the control of an island in the Ussuri River which flows through Heilongjiang province. The CIA concluded that China now saw the USSR as its foremost enemy.

Jining was a strategically important city. Amid rising tensions, the government organised the people of Jining to begin digging hundreds of miles of anti-tank trenches on the northern outskirts of the city. The land was very rocky and the work was hard but it was believed to be vital for the defence of the Motherland. Li Tiren, who was still being criticised as a historical counter-revolutionary, looked a lot older than his sixty-four years. Despite his age, he was sent out like everyone else to haul stones and dig trenches. Each day he set out early and returned late, so tired that all he could do was lie groaning on the *kang*. Li Yueheng would prop him up, trying to get him to eat something. But as the days passed Li Tiren grew thinner and more and more exhausted.

By November 1969, Li Yao was back in Jining working as a journalist. When he was sent off to conduct an interview in the little town of Salaqi, his father accompanied him to the railway station. He was proud of his journalist son. It was very cold. Li Tiren stood there on the platform as the icy wind ruffled the fur on his hat. The train started to move away. Li Yao looked back at his father waving to him and felt an inexplicable melancholy as he disappeared from sight.

Li Yao had to stay overnight in Hohhot. On the way back to his hotel, after calling in on his sister, he experienced a sudden nosebleed. He was surprised. This was unusual. His colleague Tian Wenzhong jumped up to help as Li Yao entered their room with blood all over his face. Once he was cleaned up, Tian told him that the *Wulanchabu Daily* had called to say that his father was taken ill. Li Yao must return home as soon as possible. He needn't worry about the interview, Tian could do that. Li Yao was very worried. His father had seemed tired and thin but not ill when he said goodbye at the station. What had happened? He could not call the family as they had no telephone. He had to wait for daylight to catch the next train back to Jining.

That night, the electricity went off as it often did during the Cultural Revolution. A single candle, flickering nervously, lit the hotel room. Li Yao could not sleep, he lay there worrying. He thought about his father, such a kind, unassuming man. He had never harmed anyone and yet had gone through so much. The next morning, Li Yao returned to Jining with his elder sister and brother-in-law. Entering the narrow alleyway leading to the family home, they saw the characters 'Down with the landlord Li Tiren' scrawled on the wall. A string of white paper hung from the courtyard door, signifying that someone had died. This shocked Li Yao but he did not connect it with his father. Then he saw it, the coffin lying in front of their window.

Crying out, Li Yao rushed inside. There was his mother. She was very controlled. 'It's no use crying,' she said. 'Your father has gone, his suffering has ended. Now we must live. No-one will help us. We have no relatives or friends to fall back on. The head of your father's school doesn't care. People will avoid us. All we can do is save ourselves. We are the only ones who can send your father to heaven.'

Li Yao and his sister were dazed and confused. They could not understand what had happened. Why had their father died so suddenly? To their surprise, their mother told them that Li Tiren had not been ill. On the morning of 26 November he had gone off to the school to work. Winter had set in and the classrooms needed to be kept warm. Li Tiren found a stove in one of the rooms was not working. The air vent was blocked. Moving a desk onto the teacher's platform, he had climbed up to fix it. He was old and unsteady. Standing there, he must have felt dizzy and lost his balance. He fell, striking the edge of the concrete platform, breaking his neck. Li Tiren died on the teacher's platform where he had stood for most of his life, without a word, a stream of blood flowing from his left nostril.

Hearing this Li Yao turned pale, remembering the blood flowing from his own left nostril the previous day in Hohhot. Who knows what governs our destiny? Li Yao believes he and his father must surely be connected by fate. Was Li Tiren searching for his son as he left this world? Looking at the coffin, Li Yao wanted to tell him: 'Your blood is not frozen, it still flows in my body!' But there would be no answer. Li Tiren was gone. Two simple wreaths were placed by the coffin. Only his wife and children stood near it. None of Li Tiren's former colleagues, friends or relatives paid their respects. Did they think this historical counter-revolutionary had got what he deserved? The body was taken back by horse and cart to Li village for burial in the family cemetery. No headstone could be placed on the grave. There were campaigns against cemeteries, they wasted land. Two years later, the Li family cemetery was destroyed by poor peasants and Red Guards. Li Tiren's burial place would not be marked until 1996.

Visiting Li village, we walk up the hillside to Li Tiren's grave in the partially restored Li family cemetery. The two Australians pay their respects, not yet knowing the painful circumstances in which many in the family had died. The village itself is no more than a small collection of walled houses surrounded by well-tilled fields. Dogs bark but nobody is around. Coming to a well, lined with well-formed stones, Li Yao tells his friends to look at it closely. There are carvings. These were the stones that his grandfather, Li Hai, had prepared for his own hillside grave. When the cemetery was destroyed, the frugal villagers had reused the damaged stones to line their well. Li Yao says other stones were used as doorsteps. When misfortune befell one family, they had removed their gravestone doorstep, thinking it had brought them bad luck.

In December 1969, Jining became an Inner Mongolia Front Command Post under PLA control. Military notices plastered the walls. Walking past a poster one day, Li Yao noticed that ten counter-revolutionaries had just been punished. Snowflakes were drifting to the ground. He slipped and almost fell on the icy road. Pushing his way through the small crowd, Li Yao saw that one of these men had come from IMNU. Then he saw the name, Jin Xigu, aged fifty-one, born in Hunan to a landlord family. Li Yao felt ill. Beside Jin Xigu's name was a small red cross. It indicated that the English teacher and gifted translator Li Yao had so admired had been shot.

Li Yao wanted to know more. At length he heard that Jin Xigu had been arrested on the charge of malicious abuse of Chairman Mao and the CCP. His wife and children had done the patriotic thing and testified against him. They had heard him scolding Chairman Mao and asked the Workers' Propaganda Team and the PLA Propaganda Team of the university to come and hear it for themselves. After listening from behind his door the evidence seemed clear. He was reported to the Public Security Bureau and arrested at once.

Exactly how Teacher Jin was tortured in prison Li Yao does not know. But a classmate saw Jin Xigu being driven to the execution ground dressed in tattered black trousers and a worn jacket. He had a rope around his neck to stop him from shouting reactionary slogans. He knelt on the ground. The police fired two shots and he fell over, his legs twitching as he died. At the execution, a Red Guard activist, one of Jin's former students who was known to Li Yao, had run about flaunting his power, posing as a proletarian revolutionary soldier. Returning to the university after this terrible scene, Li Yao's classmate had come across Jin's son casually playing basketball. Li Yao thought back to his final visit to Jin Xigu's dormitory to collect his copy of *Ordeal.*

One day Li Yao proposes a trip to the small city of Yanggao. We arrange to meet at Beijing's main railway station. There is no better place to see China on the move than among the crowds drawn here day and night. Li Yao gives careful instructions about where to wait. The masses flow past, travellers with the smartest suitcases you could ever hope to see, alongside country people with their belongings in hessian bags and large cardboard boxes. The chimes of the great station clock, although getting on a bit now, boom out 'The East is Red'. Briskly, Li Yao gets his friends through the outer gates to the common waiting area where a vast monitor board displays exotic destinations, trains were leaving for Ulaanbaatar and Moscow. Guards are making sure that everyone stays in well-ordered lines. Li Yao pushes forward. Can these old people go down to the platform early? The guard, a smartly dressed young woman, waves the party through and no-one seems to object.

It is an eight hour trip to Yanggao. Li Yao and his Australian friends are the only people to disembark. Most tourists get off at the next stop, Datong, home to some of the finest Buddhist statues in the world. The travellers head towards a small group of taxi drivers sitting in the sun, chatting. Li Yao asks them how much it will cost to get to the hotel. One driver produces a figure which makes them all laugh. 'No, no,' says Li Yao, 'we are locals. Give us the local price.' More laughter as another driver, looking the party up and down replies, 'You sure don't look like locals to me.' Finally, when Li Yao gets a fare he can accept, the travellers, waving, slowly move off in their battered taxi. The taxi drivers wave back, all smiles.

This is Li Yao's first trip back to Yanggao in almost fifty years. He seemed preoccupied, a bit on edge. At the end of 1969, just a few days after Jin Xigu's execution, Chairman Mao had issued new instructions. Tens of thousands of Inner Mongolian cadres were to be sent to Hebei and Shanxi provinces to attend classes in Mao Zedong Thought under PLA supervision. Mao wanted to 'drive actors, poets, dramatists and writers out of the cities and pack them off into the countryside'. Li Yao and thirty journalists from the *Wulanchabu Daily* learned that they were being sent to Yanggao County in Shanxi province, along with a thousand others from Jining and surrounding districts.

When they reached Yanggao railway station around midnight, PLA soldiers marched them to their barracks, about 2 kilometres away. They found themselves in a very big camp surrounded by high walls. It had been built in the 1950s along Soviet army lines. PLA men stood guard 24 hours a day. Each of the camp dormitory buildings was divided into four compartments around a central walkway, each compartment holding four double bunks. So there were thirty-two people per building and around 2000 people in total in the camp. Staff from the *Wulanchabu Daily* remained together in one of these barracks.

That evening, the little party is waited on at their hotel restaurant by a team of cheerful waitresses. After a beautiful meal—and no doubt under instructions from Li Yao—the head waitress brings in a king-sized bowl of watermelon. The outer green skin is elaborately carved, a still life by an old master, the mottled green, white and red of the fruit set against the imperial yellow of the large bowl.

The next morning the taxi driver from the railway station, an old friend by now, drives the party to the camp. It stood on one side of a long and narrow road lined with poplar trees. Its high brick walls are still there, keeping in the ghosts. No-one appears to be standing guard. The grounds are overgrown with weeds, windows are broken. The site is abandoned. Li Yao soon finds his old barracks. Through the dirt on the window, one can still see the bunks, some old chairs and a scattering of rubbish. Li Yao leads the way to the grey amenities block where the meals had once been served. There are mountains in the distance. Between camp and mountain the railway line curved north to family and freedom.

Li Yao standing outside his old barracks in Yanggao in 2014

The camp was run on army lines. Li Yao and his colleagues found themselves in the Second Platoon, Second Company, Third Division,

Fourth Battalion under two young soldiers: Guo Erdan, a nineteen-year-old man from Hebei province, and Chen Yongshen, a young Shanghainese. To them, young and old, all were fair game, even senior newspapermen like Li Yao's editor-in-chief. The *Wulanchabu* group had been told to take food stamps with them to last thirty days, but it soon became clear that their stay was indeterminate. Discipline was strict. There were five prohibitions: no letters home, no phone calls, no leaving the camp, no forming groups, no gathering in pairs. A few zealots tried to fit in by resorting to slogans: 'Strongly support the Party Central Committee's decision. Resolutely enforce discipline!' But it was clear to all that from that day they had lost their freedom.

According to the analects of Li Yao, some places in the barracks were better than others. An upper-level bunk had advantages. Granted, there was more climbing and the space between the roof and the bed was particularly narrow but sleeping there made it harder for others to see what you were doing. To be even more secure, it was a good plan to have a trusted friend sleeping in the bunk opposite. With some effort, Li Yao got himself an upper bunk. His good friend Tian Wenzhong, whose father was a Rightist, lay opposite. By now Li Yao trusted few people, but he was sure Tian would not betray him.

Officially, the camp was for re-education, a place to study the works of Chairman Mao. Lin Biao, designated as Mao's successor, had ordered all workplaces to conduct a daily study of the Chairman's works. For lack of space, the group from the *Wulanchabu Daily* sat on their beds to conduct this compulsory reading. The superiority of the upper bunk became clear. Hoping not to lose his language skills, Li Yao had smuggled three English books into the barracks: *Pride and Prejudice, Alice in Wonderland* and *Path of Thunder* by Peter Abrahams. When he was sure that no-one could see him, Li Yao would take out his English books. Tian provided cover. If a PLA snoop appeared, Li Yao would be warned in time to whip out his *Selection of Mao Zedong*. Thanks to Tian and the upper bunk, Li Yao never got caught.

Despite his solid communist credentials, the journalist Israel Epstein was arrested and placed in solitary confinement during the Cultural Revolution. He too found that one of the most difficult things to endure was not being able to read. For days, he could only look at patterns made by spots of damp on the wall. His only printed material was his package of toothpowder which he propped up as his sole piece of literature and art. Encounters with his jailers were Kafkaesque. 'What am I charged with?' he would ask. His interrogator snapped back, 'Don't try and worm anything out of us. You know perfectly what you have done, or you wouldn't be in this place. Make up your mind to spill the beans. To pretend you are here wrongly is to insult the Proletarian Headquarters, adding to your crimes.' Like Li Yao, he thought about Alice's upside-down *Wonderland* world:

> I'll be judge, I'll be jury,
> Said the cunning old Fury
> I'll try the whole case and condemn you to death!

There were a lot of people for the PLA to re-educate, especially all the categories of 'black elements': landlords, rich peasants, counter-revolutionaries, Rightists, capitalist roaders, reactionary academic authorities and bad elements. When education sessions took place in the camp, those from a 'bad' family background had no choice but to sit there, heads lowered, not knowing what to say as their critics abused them. It was an absolutely one-sided process with no right of reply.

One of the group, Wang from Henan province, told an emotional story about his family. Before Liberation they had been very poor. One day, as he went with his mother to beg, the landlord's dog had bitten his leg. Wang rolled up his trousers to show them his scars. As he told this story, he suddenly fell to the ground, crying. It seemed very odd. Wang was nearly forty. The incident had happened years ago. No-one dared say anything. They had to look sympathetic and show how critical they were of the landlord class. Wang was taken away for acupuncture. After this incident, he became an activist, trusted by the PLA and reporting everything to them. To ingratiate himself, he fetched water for his platoon, swept the yard and did good deeds until the PLA called him a 'living Lei Feng'. His colleagues avoided him.

At one class education session, people were asked to relive the past by eating the meals of very poor people. Serving bad meals came easily to the camp kitchen. One of their educational offerings was made of bran and frozen cabbage mixed with a little flour, a meal not good enough for pigs. Nevertheless, everyone ate it voraciously. It was important for people with a 'bad' background to eat 'eagerly' in order to show how revolutionary they had become. Finishing this meal, Li Yao and Tian glanced at each other but said nothing. Wang loudly declared that this was much better than any of the meals he used to have. With meals like this, his mother would not have needed to beg and he would never have been bitten by the landlord's dog.

Class education included revolutionary criticism. The 'students' were required to criticise Liu Shaoqi, past president, and Deng Xiaoping, secretary general of the CCP, both now repudiated by Mao. They then had to criticise Ulaanhu, the deposed chairman of the Inner Mongolia Autonomous Region. After three years of criticism from 1966, everyone was quite aware of their crimes. Going after them yet again was ugly and depressing. They struggled to look interested.

As the inmates were confined to their barracks, those with handyman skills looked for ways to kill time. They fashioned branches into clothes hangers, they turned tree roots into pipes. They made brooms. Wang reported these activities to the PLA who called a general meeting. The head of the study class screamed at them all, 'This is the fast current under the ice'. He was tall and dark and had excellent lungs: 'It is a concrete manifestation of the class struggle and it must be firmly dealt with.' Thunderous applause. Comrade Wang joined in, shouting, 'Keep the class struggle in mind! Down with Liu Shaoqi, down with Ulaanhu! Down with all reactionaries!' After three days criticising handyman work, no-one dared do it again.

After three months, camp life continued in its tedious way with no sign of ending. The Five Prohibitions were strictly implemented and no-one could write or call home. One day Zhang Yingqing, a newspaper colleague, told Li Yao that he had just seen a girl he knew from Jining through a gap in the camp wall. She was in Yanggao visiting her grandmother. Recognising Zhang Yingqing, she agreed to post some letters for him. 'I will come back in three days,' she said. 'Have them ready.' Zhang, Li Yao and a few close mates busily wrote letters home. Li Yao tucked his inside his copy of *Marx's Youth*. Pretending to be swapping books, he collected seven other letters and quietly passed them to Zhang. Zhang gave them to the girl at the wall. Everyone was jubilant at this great success.

That afternoon, the entire camp was hastily called together. Over 2000 people stood there nervously, wondering what had happened. Liu Hanying, in charge of the Third Division, stepped up to the podium to announce that certain people in the camp had attempted to defy Chairman Mao. 'This morning, Zhang Yingqing from the *Wulanchabu Daily* tried to send letters home. They were intercepted.' Li Yao and his friends were aghast. Liu continued: 'We must firmly fight against those who want to destroy Chairman Mao's revolutionary line.' Wang bellowed: 'Resolutely defending Chairman Mao's revolutionary line! Down with Liu Shaoqi and all reactionaries!' Everyone had to join in. Liu Hanying shouted into the microphone, 'Comrades! This is a textbook example of class struggle. We must raise our class consciousness, draw a clear distinction between ourselves and the enemy. From today, we will carry out in-depth Great Revolutionary Criticism. Zhang Yingqing, you must be honest about your problems and accept scrutiny of your politics!'

Action against Zhang Yingqing started immediately. He was moved to another room and his colleagues were ordered not to speak to him. They stared at him or pointed and said nothing. Zhang was unafraid. He just could not understand how the PLA had got hold of those letters. He had watched the girl walking away with them in her hand. He later learned that a PLA soldier had noticed the handover and followed the girl. After seeing her put the letters in the mailbox, he had reported it. The leader of the study class had called the post office and retrieved them.

As Zhang was moving out of his room, he brushed past Li Yao saying, 'Don't admit anything. I'll take it all on myself.' Unfortunately, a woman called Qiu had seen Li Yao pass his copy of *Marx's Youth* to his friend who lived in her dormitory. When this friend returned the book very quickly, she guessed that it might contain a letter and reported the incident to the PLA. Li Yao was brought to the Company Commander's office. His Platoon Leader asked, 'Do you know why I asked you to come here?' 'No,' Li Yao replied. The Platoon Leader stood up, slapping the table. 'Don't play funny games!

We know what you've been doing!' Li Yao stared back, thinking of the old saying 'A scholar can't engage rationally with a soldier'. Li Yao, a dog's whelp and an intellectual (a stinking number nine), knew it was best to stay silent. His Company Commander shouted: 'You must be honest and explain why you broke the discipline of our study class.' Although he already knew the answer, the Platoon Leader asked, 'How many letters did you collect?' When Li Yao still didn't reply, he yelled, 'Don't forget you are a landlord puppy! How many letters did you collect? Tell the truth!' Li Yao said; 'Seven.' Passing him a few sheets of paper, the Platoon Leader snapped, 'Explain how you did it! Don't miss a single detail!' and Li Yao was left alone with a young guard to make his report. The guard, seeing Li Yao looking so angry and perplexed, tried to help. 'Just put down a few lines. It'll be OK. They don't have time to take much notice of you now. They've gone off to a meeting. It will be a big day tomorrow!' So Li Yao wrote his brief report. When he finally returned to his bunk, Zhang's bed was empty.

The next day, the Study Class was asked to examine a letter the inmate Li Daning had sent to her husband in Jining. Li Daning just said she didn't know when she was coming home and complained about the rigidity of camp life. 'We get up every day as soon as the bugle call sounds from the barracks, then we have to do exercises and military training,' she wrote. 'Our quilts have to be folded like pieces of tofu. We have to sing revolutionary songs and read quotations from Chairman Mao before dinner.' She said nothing against the CCP or Chairman Mao. Regardless, 2000 people had to criticise Li Daning and her letter for an entire week.

Following this episode, the PLA and informants like Wang watched Li Yao and his friends very carefully. The beat of revolutionary criticism grew louder. Everyone was tense, on edge, watchful. Discipline, punishment and humiliation ruled. A man named Yang hanged himself in a grove near the barracks. After this, discipline was tightened. Guards kept the lights on through the night. Two people kept watch, alternating in pairs every two hours. Lying in bed, thinking of his father and his widowed mother, Li Yao found it very hard to fall asleep. Dreams plagued him.

There was his father holding a book. He asks his son to read with him adding, 'You should be a writer.' A sudden gust of wind sweeps the book away. His father disappears. Li Yao cries out in his sleep until his colleague shakes him awake.

Li Yao began to think about writing a novel. He remembered a young Mongolian girl he knew called Hamutu. She had been assigned to the Wulanchabu Song and Dance Troupe during the Cultural Revolution. Her father, Galasen, had been a very famous 'Living Buddha', an exponent of Tibetan Buddhism which had been important in Inner Mongolia from the late sixteenth century. Li Yao had heard of various Tibetan Buddhist precepts but understood that it was forbidden for a Living Buddha to marry. How had Galasen married and had children? Hamutu told him that she had one little sister and two younger brothers, living with their mother in a small compound in Hohhot. As a 'secret population', no-one but the Public Security Department knew their true identity. When her father died, Hamutu had to attend his memorial service as his niece, not his daughter. The Cultural Revolution brought the family's peaceful life to an end, they became ghosts and monsters. Red Guards wrecked their house and confiscated their property. Her mother, a very beautiful woman with four young children to protect, was distraught.

Moved by Hamutu's story, Li Yao had visited her pariah family in Hohhot. Her Mongolian mother was indeed very striking, though worn down by poverty and grief. Li Yao gave jackets to Hamutu's younger brothers who were dressed in rags. He gave shoes to Hamutu's beautiful little sister. Now he lay in bed thinking about Hamutu and her ostracised family. He could picture her mother's beautiful but glassy eyes. The outlines of a novel came to him: a Living Buddha falls in love with a beautiful shepherd girl but pays a huge price for his devotion.

Li Yao began to write. Every morning, while he sat in his upper bunk pretending to read Chairman Mao, he wrote his novel. Even Tian did not know what he was doing. Through the day, during political meetings, Li Yao mapped out his story in his head. At night, in the dim light of the barracks, he pressed on. Six months later, he had a complete first draft. What a foolish enterprise. This was no time for literary creation. It was a time for struggle and self-criticism. There could never be enough self-criticism. Chairman Mao had spoken out against the novel: 'using the novel to oppose the Party is a great invention'. Li Yao had done something very dangerous. There were over thirty people in his barracks and absolutely no privacy. He became very afraid he would be discovered and reported.

Lying in bed, Li Yao could feel his manuscript hidden in the mattress. Things became especially dangerous whenever the guards called an emergency muster in the middle of the night. Then everyone had to roll up their quilts and go marching into the mountains until dawn while the PLA scoured the barracks. Li Yao was sure his hidden 'time bomb' would blow him to bits. At last he decided it had to be destroyed. But how to do this among thirty people with eyes everywhere? It was winter, so he could burn it in the stove, though he felt sure he'd be noticed. As Wang had discovered, snooping on others was a sure way to get ahead. So Li Yao sneaked just a few pages into the stove every other day or so when he hoped no-one was looking. It took him six months to write the novel and a month to burn it.

After about a year, Premier Zhou Enlai decreed that internees would be allowed to write home. Everyone knew the PLA would read their letters, but it was better than nothing. Li Yao wrote to his mother. Her reply saddened him. She was still being criticised. While that had not changed, Li Yao learned that his maternal grandfather had died and his frail grandmother was now living in Hohhot with his elder sister. Li Yao thought of his dear mother. Her husband was dead, and now her father. Her mother was very old and frail. She had no relatives to help her and Li Yao could do nothing.

After a little over eighteen months Li Yao's detention finally ended in July 1971. The camp had been an education. He left Yanggao knowing much more about moral ugliness, treachery and wilful cruelty. In 2014, as Li Yao and his Australian friends leave the abandoned camp they see that a uniformed guard is now standing at the gate. Rather than explain he had once been an inmate, Li Yao tells him that he had been a guard there himself many years earlier and was just having a look around.

CHAPTER 15

Meeting places

One morning in March 1968, a red and white EH Holden stood in the driveway of 513 Glynburn Road, Hazelwood Park. A young man of twenty-two could be seen loading a small suitcase and a box of books into the boot of the car. David was about to head off for his new life as a PhD student at the ANU. The drive from Adelaide to Canberra, over a thousand kilometres, was the longest he had ever undertaken. For some years Glasson had said it was time for him to strike out on his own but he always replied that his home was far too comfortable. Their little battle of wits developed into a game. 'Still here?' She would ask, as he returned from university. 'Still here,' he would say, 'these leafy eastern suburbs are hard to leave.' But he was finally on his way. Glasson was a little tearful, not like her at all, while Gil seemed anxious about the long trip ahead. But it was high time David left the nest.

When his Honours results came out, several interstate universities had invited him to join their doctoral programs. As conscription had closed the door to an overseas scholarship, he was advised to go to the ANU which had a large postgraduate program. The ANU had no colleges to match the great halls of Oxford and Cambridge, but it did have University House, a residence for postgraduate students and visiting academics. It had a fine dining room, a bar, a music room, a library and a long tinkling pond. As soon as David learned that he had been accepted as a PhD student in the History Department at the ANU Research School of Social Sciences, he booked a room at University House.

On his way to Canberra, David stopped overnight in the small town of Yackandandah in Victoria's high country. The next day he drove down the Hume Highway past the Dog on the Tucker Box 'five miles from Gundagai'. This was a road he remembered from holiday trips as a child. At Yass he turned onto the Barton highway towards Canberra, cooler country over 500 metres above sea level. Along the road the poplar trees were showing autumnal colour, preparing themselves for winter. He drove through silent, gently undulating grazing country, a line of blue hills in the distance. Scattered outcrops of beautiful granite rock marked this ancient landscape. Over a ridge, there was Canberra, set among trees. It was all very quiet until flocks of sulphur-crested cockatoos began their meetings high in the scribbly gums, squabbling and screeching, setting a bad example. He found out later that the name 'Canberra' derives from a Ngunnawal word meaning 'meeting place'.

China was not on David's mind as he entered the city but it had been for the city's designers Walter and Marion Burley Griffin. They had drawn up plans for their 'ideal city' on *feng shui* principles: water to the south, a tall mountain to the north, low hills to the east and west ensuring harmony, peace and prosperity. Accordingly, Canberra is built on a north–south land axis intersected by an east–west water axis. But what David was more aware of was some scattered university buildings set back from the lake. He knew his uncle Alan and his family lived somewhere in the suburbs. He would catch up with them down the track, now it was getting dark and he had to locate University House.

At University House, David was directed to his room in Block A. It was quite large, with a mellow, crafted quality to the furnishings, nothing dark or heavy, well-suited to the scholarly life. His bathroom even had a heated floor for the very cold winter months. There was a balcony overlooking the main carpark and the cheaper rooms of the eastern annex. That evening, the new scholar ventured down for his first meal. In the high-ceilinged dining hall, over a hundred people were sitting at long polished wooden tables. Entering that great hall, it seemed to him that he alone was out of place.

Queen Elizabeth II opened University House in 1954, not long after ANU itself was founded. Douglas Copland, who had been Australia's

Minister to Nationalist China in the late 1940s, was its first vice-chancellor. Although inclining to the conservative side of politics, he supported recognition of the People's Republic, arguing that 'whether we like it or not Australia does belong to the Eastern Hemisphere'. He was among those who believed Australia had to know Asia better. In appointing him vice-chancellor, it was hoped that the ANU would help prepare Australia for its Asia-Pacific future. That said, at the time of the royal tour, faith in British practices and precedents still ran very deep. University House drew upon the rituals and ceremonies of the great British universities. Each evening the Master, a world authority on classical Greek pottery, would gather with a select company of scholars for sherry and conversation before proceeding, fully gowned, to dinner. Only when this distinguished party had taken their place on the elevated platform in the dining hall were the residents allowed to enter. This was the nightly ritual of High Table.

David grew quite fond of the ceremonial trappings of University House, especially the practice of retiring after the evening meal for conversation over a glass of port. There was no shortage of jocularity, banter and nonsense. On Friday nights it was off to the bar, where beer was served in silver tankards. Little did they know that the academic world they would enter was soon to become much more cut-throat as student numbers expanded, funding grew tighter, and the pressure to publish intensified. These were the best years of that University House world.

As he got to know other residents, David came to appreciate that he had fallen in with a quite unusual collection of people. In its first twenty years, the ANU had built an international reputation for research. It already had associations with two Nobel Laureates, Lord Howard Florey and Sir John Eccles. There would be more to come. By world standards, postgraduate scholarships at the ANU were generous. For overseas students, three years in the mysterious land down under was very appealing. The ANU drew people from around the world. While David would not have used the term, he had entered a 'community of scholars', a multicultural community established well before multiculturalism was adopted as government policy. But were the 'fine minds' so beloved by academe found only in men? There were many more males than females at University House. David was still largely unaware of how being male had made his entry into this community so much easier.

He was a pampered fellow. They all were at University House. A team of maids, mainly older European women, looked after the rooms. Maria was in charge of Block A. She often knocked ever so softly on the door and, receiving no response, would enter only to find the great thinker still asleep. 'Oh!' she would cry, 'you are sleeeeping', and she would then come back later to clean his untidy room.

While David had moved among Arts students at the University of Adelaide, he found every discipline and field of inquiry gathered at University House. Most of his friends now came from the sciences—mathematics, physics, chemistry, neurophysiology, microbiology. It was an unusual mixing and mingling of backgrounds and disciplines. It was only in University House that he could get to know a fellow like George, a neighbour in Block A whose PhD in Physics was on a topic that David had no chance of understanding. George moved through University House like a galleon in full sail, impeccably dressed and often wearing a smart bow tie, more cultural attaché than student. This tall, imposing figure had a mysterious white Russian background and a huge collection of classical records, dominated by Wagner.

Early in 1969, there was a new sighting, Karen Wilson, a Zoology graduate from Victoria University, Wellington, bringing the total number of female postgraduate students at University House to eight. David was impressed to learn she was doing her PhD at the star-studded John Curtin School of Medical Research. He was not at all sure what her work on the graft-versus-host reaction was about but it was clear that she knew much more than he did about the immune system. This new scholar was very attractive with large, expressive eyes and a lively manner. She wasted no time in getting involved in University House theatrical and artistic activities. David found she could even draw tunes from her recorder. As an avid reader, she was happy to be introduced to Australian writing. One afternoon, the two of them sat together on the shores of Lake Burley Griffin talking about Martin

Boyd's novels, what a strange place Canberra was and how fascinating it would be to travel to China. They were married in January 1971.

David and Karen with friends in 1970

It was not until 1971 that Li Yao was released from Yanggao camp. He waited to be told what the authorities had in store for him. He noticed how PLA informers were well looked after. The snoop Wang was elevated to the Propaganda Department of the CCP Committee for the Wulanchabu League. Less glorious assignments awaited Li Yao and his colleagues. Zhang Yingqing was not allowed to resume work as a journalist but was sent off to become an agricultural labourer. Li Yao found his own destination would be the May 7th Cadre School.

Those who had fallen foul of the camp authorities had a nastier fate. Hu Yixi from Baotou Railway Administration had slipped out of the barracks one day to farewell his girlfriend who was heading off to southern China. When he was discovered, the PLA organised a 'Great

Revolutionary Criticism'. There was a flurry of nasty posters. Then Hu was led through the barracks, while the 'students' hopped into him. Others bellowed the usual slogans, 'Down with Hu Yixi! If Hu doesn't surrender, he will face prompt and utter destruction!' Hu, a tough customer, insisted on his innocence. Having refused all criticism, he was arrested and thrown into jail. As Israel Epstein discovered, conditions in prison were harsh. He no longer had a name. He was a number. The light in his cell, protected by wire netting, was on day and night. From surrounding cells he could hear bashings and harsh commands: 'On your knees!' or a woman wailing, 'I want to go home.' His ears perked up whenever he heard the rattle of keys and the clang of bolts as doors were opened. He was always thinking, were they coming for him?

With prison a real possibility for one who had broken camp rules, Li Yao was not too upset at ending up in the May 7th Cadre School. His mother, now living in Jining, was harder to console. Her children were scattered, tortured by the Cultural Revolution, and every day she faced criticism. Li Yao tried to comfort her. The Cadre School, he said, would be much less severe than Yanggao. To his surprise, this turned out to be true.

Li Yao at the Cadre School, 1971

The school, on the grounds of an old labour camp, was in the Tumote Plain, a fertile area bounded on one side by a bend of the mighty Yellow River, on another by the Heihe River and on the third by the Daqing Mountains to the north. Summers were dry and hot, winters bitterly cold. In this well-watered area Chinese settlers grew spring wheat, millet, barley, potatoes, sugar beet, vegetables and flax. The camp housed a mixed population: candidates for re-education, farmers and released prisoners and their families. There was no escaping its military character. Internees were divided into companies and platoons although these were led not by PLA men but by capitalist roaders on the path to rehabilitation.

Li Yao shared his dormitory with eleven others, a better situation than in crowded Yanggao. Everyone in his dormitory had been pushed around, criticised and humiliated. They were tired of worthless slogans and tedious muckraking. Their new task was to raise pigs under the direction of their Muslim monitor, a journalist with a landlord background. He hardly seemed the best person to work with pigs, but he raised no objections. He was determined to improve his standing at the Cadre School. Singing 'Learn from the good example of Lei Feng', he worked tirelessly, doing good deeds, fetching hot water and studying Mao's works. He wrote a small pamphlet, *On the Relationship between a Human Head and a Pig's Head.* Li Yao looked it over and was bemused. It argued that studying Mao's works improved consciousness in ways that led to more effective pig raising and, of course, more and fatter pigs. The inmates of the dormitory thought the pamphlet was crazy stuff, nick-naming the monitor 'Marxist Theorist'. But he was on to something. One morning, bag packed and smiling broadly, he waved them all goodbye. He was returning to work on the *Wulanchabu Daily* while they were left behind to raise pigs.

Chinese poster promoting agriculture and pig-raising

Li Yao herded pigs with a woman named Yang whose husband had been released after a spell of reform through labour. They were a friendly couple from the north-east of China. Li Yao was surprised to see Yang was wearing white gloves. No-one else wore gloves, let alone white ones. He discovered that her left glove covered a prosthetic. Her hand had been cut off by a lawnmower. Li Yao wondered, 'Did she wear gloves to escape ridicule?' When it became clear he was not going to tease her, they became good friends. Learning that Li Yao was a compulsive reader, she would leave him reading under a big tree while she watched the pigs. She liked pigs. They responded to kindness and were never critical. Safe under his tree, Li Yao studied his English edition of *Jean Christophe*. Looking up, he smiled when he saw Yang's sunburned face as she ran up and down the slope with the pigs. She was like a bright star in the night sky, there was such goodness and beauty in her.

There was no more important day in China's calendar than the first day in October, National Day, when huge crowds gathered in Tiananmen Square, an unbroken tradition since 1949. Li Yao had seen the crowds there himself in 1966. In this year of 1971, everything was eerily different. At the Cadre School, internees were set to work digging trenches without a break. What had happened to National Day? All sorts of whispered rumours did the rounds. The Cultural Revolution had sharpened people's wits, but this time there were no answers. One of Li Yao's colleagues picked up a copy of *People's Illustrated* which had a large picture of Lin Biao, Vice Chairman of the CCP Central Committee, on the cover. The photograph had been taken by Mao's wife, Jiang Qing, while Lin Biao sat reading Mao's *Selected Works*. Across the image Jiang had written, 'Tireless Student'. In the photo, Lin Biao was hatless. That was unusual. Someone standing behind Li Yao exclaimed, 'Look—Lin Biao is bald!' And Li Yao thought, 'What a daring thing to say!'

Lin Biao was a man with an impressive military record. After the Japanese surrender, his forces had soundly defeated the Nationalist armies in the north-east of China and had gone on to occupy Beijing. As one of Mao's closest supporters, he was soon appointed to the Politburo and groomed as Mao's successor. During the 1960s, Lin Biao had led the way in promoting Mao's cult of personality, introducing *The Little Red Book* of Mao's sayings into PLA training and directing the Learn from Lei Feng campaign. Soon Red Guards were brandishing their copies of the *Little Red Book* at rallies all over China. By 1971, Lin Biao was the second most powerful figure in the country.

In 2014, David had organised a Foundation for Australian Studies in China (FASIC) Conference at Renmin University, Beijing, *The Big Picture: Lives, Landscapes, Homelands in Australian and Chinese Art.* One of the speakers was Shen Jiawei, an artist from Zhejiang province who now lives in Sydney. As he spent time talking to Jiawei, David came to appreciate that he was a remarkable 'history painter' with a deep knowledge of twentieth-century political turmoil in China and the USSR. One of his most famous works is *1966 Beijing Jeep* (2001). In this painting, Lin Biao is sitting up in the front of a small jeep smiling and holding up his *Little Red Book.* A reluctant Zhou Enlai is behind the wheel. In the back stands Mao. He is waving, wearing a white dressing gown, with his wife Jiang Qing smiling jubilantly beside him. This is clearly a jeep full of autocratic power and rivalries.

Back at the Cadre School, Li Yao couldn't help but wonder if something had happened to Lin Biao? He went to see his good friend, Deputy Company Commander Chuoluobuku, a CCP member. Chuoluobuku was a Daur, a Mongolic-speaking people from north-east China. When no-one was in the office, Li Yao asked quietly, 'What happened to Lin Biao?' Chuoluobuku looked out the window, then whispered: 'It's a party secret. Lin Biao tried to kill Chairman Mao, but his plot was discovered.' Li Yao asked, 'How could this happen? Lin Biao was Chairman Mao's chosen successor.' Chuoluobuku replied, 'It's a battle of two lines within the Party. We ordinary people can't understand it.' He added: 'The matter will be communicated to the whole country in a few days. Don't talk to anyone about it until after the official announcement. I can't say more.'

Lin Biao had plotted to kill Mao and take power. In March 1971, he had travelled in secret to Shanghai to discuss the details of his coup. When he gave the order to proceed, it was too late, Mao had been tipped off. Lin Biao's only option was to escape. With his wife and son he boarded a plane which crashed in Mongolia on its way to Moscow.

As the doomed plane flew towards the USSR, Jiang Qing was hosting a small gathering at her villa at the Summer Palace. She served fresh watermelon, a gift she told her guests, from Lin Biao as a symbol of his 'solicitude'. Evidently, she knew far less than her husband about what was happening. She soon caught up, describing Lin Biao as 'the devious over-reacher' who had wanted to become emperor.

Lying on a big *kang* with eleven other people, Li Yao could not sleep. The Cultural Revolution had dragged on for five years, a catastrophe for his troubled country. Now Chairman Mao's successor was dead. Li Yao tried to think what this might mean. Perhaps the Cultural Revolution would end. He thought about the long persecution of intellectuals by Lin Biao and his Central Cultural Revolution Committee. Their faces rose before him: Chen Boda and Zhang Chunqiao, the political theorists; Kang Sheng, in control of security; Jiang Qing, with her tight constraints on literature and art; the propagandists Wang Li and Yao Wenyuan; and Xie Fuzhi, who had incited the Red Guards to such violence. Surely Lin Biao's death would diminish their influence and be good for ordinary people? Li Yao lay staring into the dark. Hours later, a small ray of light came through the window.

The Cadre School was summoned to a big meeting for 'Great Revolutionary Criticism'. Throughout the day and late into the night, everyone studied documents castigating Lin Biao and his Anti-Party group, and then Lin Biao and Confucius. How were these two linked? No-one had much idea. One had wanted to murder Mao, the other was an ancient philosopher. Consulting editorials in the *People's Daily*, it became somewhat clearer. Lin Biao had revered the teachings of Confucius extolling the five basic relationships: ruler–minister, father–son, husband–wife, elder brother–younger brother and friend–friend. Confucius insisted that rulers, fathers and elder brothers should set a moral example, always conforming to proper ritual and tradition in their daily life. Mao was not a Confucian. He saw merit in the philosophy of Legalism, as practised by the Qin dynasty. Their approach to power had been very pragmatic, resources had to be used efficiently to build a strong army and a strong state. Mao linked Lin Biao with the traditional views of Confucius and set about attacking them both.

Two weeks after the big meeting, 'students' from the Cadre School were sent into rural and pastoral areas to teach the new line to peasants and herders. Chuoluobuku chose Li Yao and An Mi to accompany him. Then in his early forties, An Mi was a famous poet from Shandong, a member of the Writers' Association of China and the first real writer Li Yao had ever met. An accusation of 'Right opportunism' had sent An Mi to the Cadre School for re-education. As they travelled to the Donghongshen People's Commune, Li Yao, An Mi and Chuoluobuku became close friends. The commune was in Wuchuan County, just north of Daqing Mountain at the edge of the grasslands, a sparsely settled area where farmers had a reasonable life. The new arrivals settled into the office of the Xihongsheng Production Brigade, where an old peasant prepared steamed bread, noodles, eggs and even a little meat for them.

In this distant place they saw no need to rush into instructing the peasants on the failings of Lin Biao and his errant friend, Confucius. The peasants knew nothing about Confucius, so it was no easy task for the three wise men from the Cadre School to convey the nuances of the new doctrine to them. One eager peasant attacked Lin Biao for 'dressing himself up in a Marxist cloak'. 'Yes,' another added, 'Lin Biao's actions were very bad. He stole Marx's cloak to wear himself.' Then they asked, 'Was Confucius a member of Lin Biao's Anti-Party group?' When Chuoluobuku patiently explained that Confucius had lived more than 2000 years ago, the peasants were very surprised, 'More than 2000 years? Then how did he collude with Lin Biao?' Their teachers were making no sense. The meeting wrapped up as the farmers sat dozing in the dim light of a kerosene lamp.

The night sky was vast and the little village was silent. The three friends talked together quietly as they lay on the *kang*. They trusted each other and could share their thoughts, a rare experience. While the death of Lin Biao gave them hope, they could not understand how a great man like Chairman Mao could choose the wrong successor. They wondered about Mao's wife, Jiang Qing. A Shanghai actor, by 1971 she had gained significant political influence and a seat on the Politburo. Only at the dead of night and on the remote edge of the grassland did they dare talk about her.

One day, the three friends walked out into the deep snow looking for pheasants that had flown into the telegraph poles. Chuoluobuku, who had grown up among hunters in a forest in the north-east, was good at this. Back in the office, the old peasant rubbed his hands at the sight of the birds and cooked up a feast. That night the men sat together under the kerosene lamp, drinking the local *baijiu*. This was the good life: eating pheasant, chatting, singing and drinking. An Mi recited one of his poems:

> Wolf and camel
> Contested
> Who is stronger?
> Unhappily, the camel succumbed first
> Down on his knees wailing
> He let the wolf bite him
>
> About this
> My lips are sealed
> I keep silent for years
> And don't want to mention it again.

One month later they returned to the Cadre School where they learned that the leader of the Wulanchabu Military Control Commission, Li Kuiwu, was coming to the camp to assess their progress. That meant a big meeting. To his surprise, Li Yao was asked to speak. He delivered an impassioned address to over a thousand people including some PLA troops. Directing his words to Li Kuiwu, he outlined the crimes of Lin Biao's Counter-Revolutionary group. He had never been so openly critical before. But he was driven by the suffering experienced by his parents and by Jin Xigu's brutal execution. He hated the Lin Biao group. They had brought nothing but distrust and disaster. The audience burst into applause. Li Yao's speech had struck a chord. As Li Yao looked around at the cheering crowd, he thought how much he wanted to share this moment with his father.

A few days later, Chuoluobuku told Li Yao: 'You're in luck! To commemorate the 30th anniversary of Chairman Mao's *Speech at the*

Yan'an Forum, the Wulanchabu Bureau of Culture is going to organise a literary group. Li Kuiwu is selecting people for it. Your criticism of the Lin Biao Group impressed him. So, he has arranged with the Wulanchabu Military Control Commission to assign you to this new group. I've been asked to write a letter of recommendation.' Laughing, he added, 'Naturally, every word and every sentence will praise you, Younger Brother.' Li Yao was incredulous! Chuoluobuku continued, 'I'm not joking. An Mi, Qimude Daoerji and Zhang Yongchang have also been chosen. Don't thank me, thank yourself. Thank the pen in your hand.'

Mao had hosted the *Yan'an Conference on Literature and Art* in May 1942. Over 100 artists and writers and many officials had attended, listening intently as Mao outlined theoretical and practical issues that art and literature would encounter in a new proletarian China. Mao's approach to these cultural questions was very explicit, from now on permissible content would be precisely defined. What was past was dark, what was new was bright. Art, he argued, had to be drawn from the life of the people. They would provide 'materials in their natural form, materials that are crude, but most vital, rich and fundamental'. Art for art's sake was a dead end. Literature and art must 'serve (proletarian) politics' and 'serve workers, peasants and soldiers'.

That night, Chuoluobuku invited Li Yao and An Mi to dinner in his little cabin. They were joined his Han wife, a graduate of Sichuan University who now helped Li Yao raising pigs. The couple had done their best to prepare a good meal although it was very simple, just fried eggs and vegetables. Soon they were talking happily while drinking *baijiu*, singing songs from the model opera *Taking Tiger Mountain by Strategy*:

> When I look into the distance and think of my
> Comrades-in-arms, the army and the people,
> Waiting for the signal to attack these wolves, my spirits soar.

It was a still calm night, the distant mountains silhouetted against the darkening sky.

They all drank too much. What started as a joyful farewell among firm friends was suddenly overtaken by grief when Chuoluobuku, that 'man of steel', burst into tears. The men could say nothing. The pain was too great. Chuoluobuku had joined the Revolution when he was only sixteen. As a cadre from an ethnic minority, he had been entrusted with important tasks and once served as secretary to Wang Yilun, CCP secretary for the Inner Mongolia Autonomous Region. But in 1957, because of his wife's landlord background, the family were sent to Wulanchabu where they were accused of being members of the IMPRP and imprisoned. Their four children, aged seven to twelve, had been regularly bullied and beaten.

The next day, Li Yao left the May 7th Cadre School. Looking back at the big blue mountain, fading into the distance behind him, he could not help feeling some regret. He was leaving brave colleagues, true friends and kind Sister Yang, an excellent herder of pigs.

CHAPTER 16

Soaring peaks

In 1972, after Spring Festival, Li Yao and his three colleagues from the May 7th Cadre School, began to work for the Wulanchabu Literary Group. Li Yao was thrilled to be among published authors who might teach him a thing or two about imaginative writing. They were led by the famous Mongolian writer Monan who used the pen name Ankeqinfu (Hunter's son). Monan had grown up in a poor peasant family. After joining the Revolution when he was only sixteen, he had been a CCP cadre, an officer in the Propaganda Department of the Inner Mongolia Trade Union and then a professional writer. The Cultural Revolution abruptly upended his brilliant career. When criticised as a reactionary literati and capitalist roader, he did not take it lying down, arguing that his stories and novels had praised New China. This fell on deaf ears. He was jailed, then sent to a Mao Zedong Thought class in Hebei province before being assigned to the Wulanchabu Literary Group.

Another new colleague was Xue Yan, a prize-winning dramatist and author whose short stories had appeared in *Renmin Wenxue*, one of the best literary journals in China. Li Yao knew and admired his work. During the Cultural Revolution, Xue was criticised for his erroneous views on literature and art and sent to Zhuozi County. A third wrong-headed fellow was Yang Ping, editor-in-chief of *Grassland*, the sole literary magazine published in Inner Mongolia during the 1950s. Although celebrated for his children's books and short stories, Yang was denounced as a Rightist in 1957, sent to Zhuozi County, before being jailed at the onset of the Cultural Revolution.

Oddly enough, to commemorate the 30th anniversary of Chairman Mao's Speech at Yan'an, these mistrusted writers had been brought together again. But the old comrades wrote very little, they had been through too much. What they liked best was drinking and telling stories. Li Yao, like David, came from a non-drinking family. His new companions quickly introduced him to the bottle. Their liquor was very rough. Really good *baijiu* was out of their reach, let alone the proper accompaniments like pig's head and peanuts. It made them miserable just thinking about what they were missing.

The dramatist Xue Yan was a very funny man and a wonderful storyteller. The best drinker was Qimude Daoerji, the Mongolian poet. He spoke lovingly to his *baijiu* bottle, his 'dear ogre that was always beckoning to him'. Without it, he believed, he would have died long ago. Accused of being an IMPRP member, he had been imprisoned for two years. He had stopped writing. Perhaps he should have turned to parody, an old Mongol tradition developed under the Manchu when extravagant tales from the *Dalan Hudalch* (Monstrous Fibber) were common:

> I was looking after my grandfather's camels before my father was born. A female had given birth and I wanted to take her and her calf home. So I jumped on the mother camel and lifted up the calf, but we were too heavy, she could not carry us both. So I jumped on the calf and we carried the mother and we got home without any trouble.

A drinking man could be drawn to such tall tales and the Mongolian tradition of talking cows, goats and sheep, tricky fellows full of rascally schemes and clever deceptions. Qimude Daoerji loved telling them the story 'Words of a Chamois Being Chased by a Wolf'.

For Yang Ping, the literary editor, *baijiu* was an angelic spirit inspiring forgetfulness. Knowing he would be arrested, he bought a litre of strong local brew. After cooking a chicken stew for his frail old mother and his four children, he sat down and drank every last drop. It worked a treat. When the authorities came for him, he went off with them quietly. Once placed in his cell, he lay down on the narrow bed and fell straight into a deep sleep, snoring until dawn. No pain, no fear, no hope, nothing.

There has long been a strong drinking culture in Inner Mongolia where freezing winters last for months on end and hospitality demands sociability. Whenever Li Yao turned up in Jining or Hohhot with his strange Australian friends, out came the *baijiu* bottle. On special occasions, David and Karen joined the old friends in a *ger* on the grassland to share a meal of Mongolian lamb. In front of each guest would be a little glass and a small jug of *baijiu*. The host opened proceedings with a fine toast, welcoming the visitors. Glasses clinked. With a cry of *ganbei* each glass is emptied and shown to be so. Further toasts follow. Talk becomes merrier. A beautiful woman in Mongolian costume comes in, beads dangling from her conical hat. Draping a long blue scarf across her outstretched arms, she sings a song of welcome. She pours out a rice bowl of *baijiu*. Dipping her third finger lightly in the alcohol she flicks upwards to the Sky Father. The finger dips again and flicks downward to the Earth Mother. Then once again the finger dips and touches the forehead, of the singer, then the guest, who must take the bowl with both hands and drain it dry. Strong stuff, 60 per cent proof. Singing follows and everyone is the best of friends.

While the Wulanchabu Literary Group were expert drinkers, that had not been the purpose of bringing them together. The Director of the Cultural Bureau, a PLA man, was very unhappy to find that these brilliant fellows had done precious little writing. He glowered at Monan, brought his fist down hard on the table and told them all to get to work writing about workers, peasants and soldiers. Then he turned away and abruptly left the room. They got the message. Monan sent Li Yao off for a month to Qingshuihe County, one of the poorest areas in Inner Mongolia to gain first-hand experience in something other than excessive drinking.

Li Yao stayed with a poor farmer in the small village of Banmaozi. The villagers lived in caves built into the mountainside, like the peasants of northern Shanxi, sleeping on a *kang* of hard clay, without even the comfort of a straw cushion. Families often shared a single quilt. In the cave where Li Yao found himself, there was no stove and it was brutally cold at night. The farmer gave Li Yao his only quilt, so black and dirty it was impossible to make out the original colour. Li Yao didn't want to take it, but such kindness could not be refused. Each night he wrapped himself up in the filthy quilt. The villagers wore old clothes, wholly inadequate for the harsh conditions. One gaunt old farmer wore trousers made from blue plastic. He stared at Li Yao with glazed eyes. The village food was poor and monotonous, potatoes, millet and preserved cabbage. The children's 'schoolbags' were woven from sorghum stalks. Their classroom was a run-down cave house with 'tables' and 'stools' made from stacks of clay of different heights. It reminded Li Yao of the primary school in Bolitu where his mother had taught.

Banmaozi village was perched on a very high cliff above the Yellow River. Crops grew poorly due to the low rainfall. Inspired by Mao's campaign, 'Learn from Dazhai in Agriculture', the villagers decided they would show what they could do, directing the Yellow River up to the top of their cliff to supply drinking water and to use for irrigation. With no funding or materials, they had toiled away for over a year setting up a big pumping station. Watching them labouring away every day, Li Yao was impressed by their remarkable spirit and tenacity, even as he wondered if their dedication would prove successful.

Twelve girls aged sixteen to eighteen formed an Iron Girls' Combat Team living in a makeshift tent by the Yellow River. Subsisting mainly on potatoes, they climbed up and down the cliff every day carrying heavy steel pipes on their delicate-looking shoulders. Inspired, Li Yao wrote, 'The Iron Girls on the Cliff', a story which appeared in *Inner Mongolia Literature and Art* in 1973. The Director of the Cultural Affairs Bureau could now be told that something had at last been written. The other writers had also been busy. An Mi and Qimude Daoerji had finished some poems, while Xue Yan and Yang Ping had written a play for the Red Propaganda Team—Wulanmuqi. All these works praised workers, peasants and soldiers, celebrated Mao Zedong Thought and applauded the Cultural Revolution.

Jiang Qing's Australian biographer, Ross Terrill, has noted that without his wife's fiery opinions, Mao would probably not have used the term 'Cultural' Revolution. Jiang Qing constantly attacked traditional Chinese literature and art and anything tainted by Western influence. Artists and writers, she said, should always follow the CCP line, not draw on their own experience. The purpose of cultural works was to celebrate revolutionary heroism. Every work had to centre on one heroic figure, the clear leader. 'In-between characters' who were neither good nor bad must be avoided. They had no propaganda value.

As with literature, so with art. In 1974, Jiang Qing had organised a Second National Art Exhibition in Beijing to emphasise the contributions made to the Motherland by workers, peasants and soldiers. Hearing about the exhibition, Shen Jiawei submitted a painting which he called *Standing Guard for Our Great Motherland.* He had taken great care to ensure it conformed to Jiang's cultural principles: one heroic soldier is outlined against the sky as he stands on the platform of a high watchtower, while the dawn creates 'a ruddy warmth' on the faces of two subsidiary figures. The man is carefully watching out for any sign of hostile movement in the direction of the 'Soviet side' of the border which appears as required 'under dark clouds'. On travelling to Beijing to see his work exhibited at the National Art Gallery, Shen Jiawei was shocked to find that two of the faces had been reworked to give them ruddier complexions and fiercer expressions. Jiang had instructed her 'rectification team' to rework any exhibits that were not sufficiently Red and Revolutionary. In this state, Jiawei's painting was very well received. More than 200 000 copies were made and circulated throughout China.

Jiang Qing's own literary efforts were far from remarkable. In 1974 she sent a photograph of a mountain peak to *China Photo,* accompanied by her poem:

Overlooking the river is a soaring peak
Its face obscured in mists,
Mostly it is not beheld
Just occasionally its majesty is revealed.

The word she used for 'river' was her own name, *Jiang.*

In 1975, Li Yao was asked to collaborate on a novel based on Mao's directive: 'Learn from Daqing in Industry'. Daqing had been a nondescript little town in Heilongjiang province until oil was discovered there in 1959 and the town boomed. To write his novel, Li Yao needed to learn more about industry. He was sent to the Welding Rod Factory in Jining where he was handed a pair of overalls and told to get to work.

When Li Yao had difficulties understanding what was being done on the assembly line, he found the best people to ask were a young couple who were both skilled engineers. Although educated at the prestigious Tsinghua University in Beijing, they worked in the factory just like everyone else. One evening, Li Yao sat down to interview the woman, who was in her thirties. While responding to his questions, she suddenly removed her glasses and burst into tears. Li Yao was at a loss. What does a young man say to a woman crying in front of him? Seeing his discomfort, she apologised, adding: 'You're a writer, you should know what we've been through.' Li Yao nodded, 'Even if you don't tell me, I know what you've been through.' She continued: 'I just want you to know that our welding rod is very high quality and is used by the Shanghai Jiangnan Shipyard and by other important manufacturers. My husband and I developed the formula while undertaking labour under mass supervision. Conditions were difficult and it took some time, but we got there.'

Li Yao was intrigued. He began to think out a story featuring a Shanghai shipyard and an electric welding rod. Following the principles laid down by Jiang Qing, he needed a strong hero. It could not be someone like the woman's husband, an engineer and an intellectual. No, an intellectual could only be a villain, someone opposed to 'Learning from Daqing in Industry'. The couple from Tsinghua University became minor characters who obstructed the development of the advanced electrode. Now for the hero. Not a problem. He had to be an active member of the CCP, a technician from a worker's family. Li Yao called him Gao Dashan, 'Soaring Peak'. After dedicated self-study, Gao Dashan mastered all the knowledge and applied techniques needed to produce a wonderful welding electrode, one that could be used making massive ships in a Shanghai shipyard. To add just a touch of the grasslands to his story, Li Yao located his electrode factory in a remote northern town.

Within three months Li Yao had mapped out his storyline. He was then moved into a guesthouse at the Inner Mongolia People's Publishing House in Hohhot to finish the task. He worked day and night on his masterpiece, helped by an experienced editor, Li Yaoxian. One morning, Li Yaoxian, rubbing his stubbly chin thoughtfully, told Li Yao that his novel lacked real villains. Where were the hated class enemies in this story? It was a good point. Li Yao dreamed up a man called Qian Huairen, a nasty money-grabbing landlord who had escaped from Shanxi to the grasslands and was opposed to socialist ideas. Li Yao had been thinking of his Third Uncle who had escaped from Li village during land reform. Would he have tried to undermine socialism? Li Yao was quite sure he would not have dared, but his fictional villain was made of much sterner stuff.

While he was writing, Li Yao got to know two young women in the adjacent room, editors at the publishing house. Xijier was twenty-one, a graduate from the Mongolian Language College. Her Daur mother and Mongolian father, who had joined the CCP in 1946, had been sent out to the remote Xilingole League. During the Cultural Revolution they were accused of belonging to the IMPRP and were thrown into jail. The tortures used were dreadful. Left to fend for herself, Xijier, who was only fourteen, took her two younger brothers out into the grasslands. They wandered from place to place, doing their best to survive, but were often bullied and abused. As they trudged through the snow during the cruel winters, they were lucky not to freeze to death. Xijier developed severe rheumatoid arthritis and when Li Yao knew her, she was always in pain. To get herself up each morning, she would bite her lips and pull hard on a rope tied to the head of the bed. Then she would stumble out to do exercises, hoping one day to become strong. Li Yao joined her. Exercising together they became good friends. The name Xijier means 'as shiny as gold' in Mongolian. For Li Yao, her memory continues to shine.

Li Yao needed a second protagonist for his story. He made her a Mongolian girl called Gegentana, based on Wu Guiying, the girl who had suffered frostbite while herding sheep. Gegentana, a poorly educated shepherd girl, loved Chairman Mao and studied his writings closely. She was overjoyed to be selected to work at the new welding rod factory built in the grasslands and very honoured to help Gao Dashan to develop welding electrodes. Despite numerous difficulties, with guidance from Mao Zedong Thought the pair achieved brilliant success.

For six months, Li Yao worked hard in his little room, struggling to bring to life these improbable characters, invented scenes and fabricated stories. He had never been to Shanghai, and never seen a shipyard or any kind of ship, let alone one of 10 000 tons. But he pushed on. Gao Dashan and Gegentana went to Shanghai to test their electrode where they were warmly welcomed by the shipyard workers. Gegentana climbed up high on the ship's hull to weld steel plates. As Li Yao wrote of the great shower of sparks coming from the welding rod, he thought of the brave 'Iron Girls' on the cliff by the Yellow River. After eight months his novel was complete. It was February 1976.

Xijier shared her dormitory with a tall girl called Weng Rulan. One day, Weng stood sniffing at Li Yao's door: 'Oh my god! You are drinking coffee!' Li Yao, who had succumbed to the bourgeois coffee habit, quickly poured his visitor a cup. 'This is rare,' she said with a chuckle. 'I thought that in Inner Mongolia I would only be able to get milk tea.' Over coffee, Li Yao heard her story. Weng Rulan's father was Wen Dujian, a famous historian and educator. In 1939, after he had finished his Harvard doctorate on the Yuan dynasty and completed a post-doctoral year in Paris, he took up important positions in research and education in Beijing. Mongolian people were well aware of him but few knew about his daughter. She had enjoyed a carefree childhood in a beautiful courtyard house near Tiananmen Square, where it soon became clear she was a talented artist. By 1966 Weng Rulan was ready to graduate from the Central Academy of Fine Arts in Beijing. Instead, as Li Yao was shocked to hear, she ended up in jail.

As an artist in training, Weng liked to draw from life models. A classmate told her about a young African man who had escaped to China after a revolution in the Cameroons. Weng was excited. It was unusual to see a black person in Beijing. The young man agreed to sit while she did some drawings and afterwards, they kept in touch and sometimes corresponded. But suddenly, her friend was accused

Drawing of a Mongolian woman
by Weng Rulan

of working for the KGB and was expelled from China. Weng was then arrested and jailed for writing letters to a Soviet agent.

Her father wrote to Premier Zhou Enlai, who after a year, secured her release. After 'critical struggle' at her university and a year spent working on a farm, Weng was sent to the Inner Mongolia Publishing House, but suspicions remained that she might be a Soviet spy. Li Yao heard that she was about to be sent deeper into the countryside. She came up to him on the day she left wearing a white sheepskin cap still smelling of mutton and laughingly asked, 'How does this look? Am I pretty? Like a shepherd girl?' Li Yao nodded helplessly. She was so young, so very talented and had endured so much, yet somehow she remained cheerful. Li Yao did not see her again for some time. Once she wrote to him, 'Sometimes I feel like I'm living, not for myself, but for my enemies. So I have to be strong.' He remembers these words. After Zhou Enlai's death, Weng produced a famous work, *Premier Zhou, the Grassland People Love You*. At the end of the Cultural Revolution she migrated to the United States where she lived for many years, a well-known artist, until her death in 2012.

Just before Spring Festival 1976, Li Yao presented his editor with his final 300 000-word manuscript. He never heard anything more about it. His hero 'Soaring Peak' and his wonderful welding rod simply disappeared, completely lost to literature.

Every Thursday morning the History Department at the Research School of Social Sciences, ANU, held a seminar at which senior scholars, distinguished visitors and PhD students presented their work. Every trembling child had heard the frightening biblical tale of poor Daniel entering the Lion's den. The ANU seminar room seemed no less intimidating. Among the regulars was the head of the History Department, Professor J.A. La Nauze, known as 'Jack the Knife' for his demolition of those whose presentations failed to make the grade. Another 'soaring peak' was Professor C.M.H. (Manning) Clark, then steadily working through his multi-volume history of Australia. A third eminence was the snowy-haired Sir Keith Hancock, celebrated as the youngest professor in the British Empire after he had accepted a chair at the University of Adelaide in the late 1920s. Forty years on and many publications later, Sir Keith was doing a lot of fly fishing in the Snowy Mountains near Canberra while claiming to be writing a history of the Monaro high country. Some gossiped, was this a sign he was past his prime? Yet when Hancock's book *Discovering Monaro* came out, it was one of Australia's first environmental histories and remains one of the finest.

There was no escape for David. He had to present a paper. The usual practice was for the speaker to circulate a two- or three-page summary ahead of time and then to speak for forty minutes with added time for questions. The thought of speaking for so long alarmed him so much that he circulated a seventeen-page paper and, to everyone's surprise, spoke for less than fifteen minutes before taking questions. There were two problems with this innovative approach: busy ANU scholars did not read seventeen-page seminar outlines, and an emerging scholar pinched bits of David's seminar outline and used them for his own book. For his PhD, David wanted to explore the interface between Australian literature and history. This unusual approach in itself created controversy. There were historians who doubted it was 'real history'. Conversely, some literary scholars believed history was irrelevant to the study of literature, the text itself was all that mattered. So David's first ANU seminar did not go very well. Jack the Knife looked irritated. Sir Keith had his eyes closed. Professor Clark, who rarely attended these seminars, sat as silent as the Sphinx. Appearances can be deceiving. A few days later, Manning Clark wanted to discuss David's thesis with him. He thought it was an interesting topic. That was most encouraging. A little later, Sir Keith dropped by with some questions he wanted answered and suggestions about additional themes that would be worth following up.

The PhD thesis loomed before David like a mountain peak, 100 000 words or so which had to make an original contribution to knowledge. He chose to study four Melbourne-based literary figures who had started writing soon after Federation in 1901: the novelist Vance Palmer, the dramatist Louis Esson, the poet Frank Wilmot and the essayist Frederick Sinclaire. Australia's cultural history would be examined through the lens of this circle, four figures who often wrote or spoke together about pressing literary matters. Australians, as members of the British Empire, had inherited all the treasures of the English language. Were they then just a part of the great British reading public? Was there any real demand for a distinctively Australian national literature? How would a society preoccupied with the practicalities of settlement find a place for writers? Could a population of just over 4 million sustain literary journals and publishers? To Empire enthusiasts, the thought of an Australian literature seemed unnecessary and undesirable. Yet Vance Palmer was most unhappy with the idea that Australia should continue silently exporting its wool and soldiers to the Mother Country, but never its literature, art or ideas.

In a history thesis lots of scholarly footnotes are required, marking the journey the researcher has travelled. Vance and his accomplished literary wife, Nettie, had built up a very large collection of manuscripts—letters, diaries, drafts, newspaper cuttings—extending from the early 1900s to the 1960s. As was fitting for proponents of a 'national culture' and with an eye on their legacy, the Palmers left these voluminous papers to the National Library. David soon found a second home in the library's exclusive manuscripts room, working his way through the Palmer Papers. By 1976 he had been awarded his PhD and his thesis had been turned into a book, *Dream and Disillusion: A Search for Australian Cultural Identity*.

In 1901 there had been a lot of talk about Australia, the first new nation of the twentieth century. The new nation needed a new capital with an appealing name. Suggestions flooded in, among them 'Shakespeare', 'Myola' (new beginning) and 'Democratica'. Palmer, a keen democrat, liked to imagine the nation now emerging in what he called a 'new' continent, as an egalitarian community, free from the snobbery and class divisions of the old world. It seemed the right time for bold ideas and new beginnings. A 'new continent' needed a literature of its own.

For Palmer and his circle, cities, whatever they were called, (mercifully, Canberra was not called 'Democratica') did not express, and could not nurture, a distinctively Australian democratic spirit. It was only in the bush that 'real' Australian characters could be found. For Palmer, 'real' Australian characters were invariably male, rugged chaps valiantly fighting off bad feminising influences emanating from Australia's cities and their suburbs. Palmer's first book of short stories, pointedly titled *The World of Men*, focused on the lives of shearers, drovers and other bushmen.

One part of David's thesis explored how the 'bush formula' affected the work of the dramatist Louis Esson. Louis was a small and rather delicate boy, brought up and certainly pampered by two maiden aunts and two unmarried uncles, all of whom were devoted to 'Art'. Supported by this unusual family, as a young man Louis travelled to Paris where he fell deeply in love with the cafes, cabarets and artistic life of Montmartre. This was the life for him. Distant Australia seemed a terribly dull place, hostile to everything an artist needed: crowds, conversation, sparkling wit, wine, women and song. He then met the Irish dramatist J.M. Synge, whose plays, *Riders to the Sea* and *Shadow of the Glen*, had just been performed in Dublin as part of the Irish literary revival. Based on Synge's experience in the remote Aran Islands and written in a thick Irish brogue, they were acclaimed across the British theatre-going world.

Synge told the young Louis Esson that he must turn his back on the brittle and artificial world of the city. Truth would only be found in the lives of the toiling peasants, people close to the soil, bound by ancient customs and tested by adversity. At the time of his meeting with Synge, Esson had just completed a four-act play, *The Time Is Not Yet Ripe*. This was a play of manners, set in the city and wittily spelling out the deceptions, trickery and intrigue of contemporary Australian politics. It followed the fortunes of a political campaign for the seat of Wombat where the conservative prime minister, Sir Joseph Quiverton, stood against a handsome young socialist who had just become engaged to Sir Joseph's daughter. First performed in 1912, *The Time Is Not Yet Ripe* was full of shrewd observation and extravagant silliness in the tradition of George Bernard Shaw and Oscar Wilde. Melbourne audiences were enthusiastic, hailing Esson as Australia's most promising young dramatist. David and Karen saw a performance in Sydney in 1977. As a play it has held up well.

Yet when *The Time Is Not Yet Ripe* was first performed in Melbourne, Esson began to dislike his play, believing it was false, superficial and much too cosmopolitan. Having listened to Synge, he wanted to be at the forefront of an Australian literary revival. Now a fierce critic of the city and the suburb, he turned to the bush, looking for inspiration in Australia's drovers, shearers and itinerant rural workers even though he knew very little about them and had never lived among them. This new literary direction did not serve him well. Nothing that Esson wrote about bush workers through the 1920s and 1930s ever matched the wit and bravado of *The Time Is Not Yet Ripe*.

During his time in Canberra in the 1970s, as David sat thinking about Louis Esson and his struggles to establish a distinctively national drama, he became increasingly aware that at long last, Australian plays were making a comeback and filling theatres. One of the hits was *Don's Party* by David Williamson. Like the young Esson, Williamson had seen the comedic potential in Australia's contemporary politics. Also set in Melbourne, *Don's Party* is a witty satire on the defeat of left-wing hopes by conservatives in the federal election of 1969. Esson abandoned urban settings and modern themes but Williamson would fruitfully exploit them. In 2020, as David sits in locked-down Melbourne, avoiding the Grim Reaper, he learns that after more than fifty years as a celebrated Australian dramatist, Williamson has just announced his retirement.

CHAPTER 17

Endings

At the beginning of the 1970s, David was a PhD student in search of an argument for his thesis, weighed down on bad days by the looming prospect of having to serve as a conscript in Vietnam. By the end of the decade, things were very different. He had been liberated from conscription on the grounds of his very poor eyesight, he was a young married man with a small, spirited daughter, and he had a secure job as a lecturer in history at the University of NSW. While his future had changed, so had that of the nation. The decade had started with a royal tour and ended with Australia growing more distant from Britain and looking for a future in the Asia Pacific.

During the 1950s and 1960s, Australia had seemed secure in its membership of the English-speaking world. Australians saw themselves as British—just British living overseas, wonderfully improved by informality, sunshine and humour. Across the country, in a ceremony that David remembers well, primary school children would gather at morning assembly to salute the Australian flag bearing the Union Jack in its top left-hand corner. They would pledge:

> I love God and my country. I honour the flag. I will serve the Queen and cheerfully obey my parents, teachers and the laws.

'Cheerful obedience' was a nice British touch suggesting that no coercion was required.

Strategically, Australia had turned to the United States, strengthening its ties through the 1951 ANZUS Treaty. Even so, when they travelled, Australians still made a beeline for Britain. This was certainly the case for Gil and Glasson who made their first overseas trip in 1963, enjoying an exciting stopover in exotic Hong Kong before heading to London.

Through the 1960s, Britain had made several attempts to join the European Economic Community only to be knocked back by France. But the writing was on the wall, Britain was disengaging from Australia. An alarmed Menzies Cabinet feared that the Mother Country would break long-standing trading ties. One morning in 1969, when David went down to the foyer of University House, he was surprised to see a large figure in a crumpled grey suit. It was Sir Robert Menzies, the leader in whom his parents had placed so much faith. Now in retirement, much of what Menzies had stood for was fading away as a new giant, Labor's Edward Gough Whitlam, then still leader of the Opposition, prepared to take centre stage.

During the royal tour of 1954, the young Queen Elizabeth had been greeted with adoration. Prime Minister Menzies, who described himself as 'British to the bootstraps', had declared that the nation held 'the most profound and passionate feelings of loyalty and devotion' to their monarch. Three in every four Australians turned out to see their Queen, all of them waving flags. Her portrait was hung in schools, law courts and public buildings across the land. Just over fifteen years later, at the end of March 1970, and less than three years before Britain entered the European Economic Community, the response to a later visit by Queen Elizabeth was much more subdued. Although the *Canberra Times* tried hard to whip up enthusiasm for this 'living symbol of 900 years of unity of the British people', David, working away in University House, remained indifferent to the fuss. Perhaps as an historian he should have appreciated the efforts made to commemorate all possible anniversaries.

To mark the first fifty years of the nation's capital, Elizabeth II, in her role as Queen of Australia, accepted Britain's gift of a carillon. She inaugurated the Captain Cook Fountain in Lake Burley Griffin and laid a wreath of red velvet poppies at the War Memorial for the

55th anniversary of the ANZAC landing at Gallipoli. The biggest commemoration of them all took place in Sydney with the bicentennial celebrations for Captain James Cook. Leaving Plymouth Harbour on 25 August 1768 to observe the Transit of Venus in Tahiti, Cook had navigated the west coast of New Zealand before stepping ashore near Botany Bay on 29 April 1770, later claiming this 'new' continent for Great Britain. In 1970 more than 50 000 people gathered to see a re-enactment of Cook's landing.

The Queen entered Botany Bay on the royal yacht *Britannia*, escorted by three Navy ships and a flotilla of little boats. A golden carpet led her to a dais where she watched 'Captain Cook' as he was rowed ashore from a sailing barque rebadged as *Endeavour II*. Meanwhile Aboriginal actors caught a stingray from fake bark canoes and an alternate 'Captain Cook' was hustled away by police as he tried to claim the land 'in the name of George the Third and Sydney University'. Robert Askin, the conservative premier of NSW, explained to the crowd that Captain Cook had 'tilled the ground for the seeds of settlement under Governor Phillip' and that from these seeds had grown a great, free and predominantly British nation. For Indigenous Australians, these events were no cause for celebration. To mark the act of 'invasion', protestors threw funeral wreaths into the sea at La Perouse, led by the poet and activist Oodgeroo Noonuccal (Kath Walker). In Canberra, there was a torch-light procession to Parliament House in memory of 'vanished Australian tribes'.

For the 250th anniversary of Cook's landing in 2020, there were no such re-enactments. The global pandemic put paid to that. Instead, virtual exhibitions examined how the crew of the *Endeavour* first encountered Indigenous Australians. Historically, depictions of this meeting were based on the accounts of Sydney Parkinson, a young artist travelling with Cook, who described how Indigenous men had confronted Cook's party as they came ashore. Making threatening gestures with their spears, they had shouted '*warra wai*', to which the Europeans responded with musket fire. Descendants of the *Dharawal* people tell a more intriguing story. They explain that since '*warra*' meant 'white' or 'dead', the Aboriginal people on the beach were telling the Europeans 'you're all dead'. *Dharawal* people thought the white sails of the *Endeavour* were a low-lying cloud bringing dead spirits to their country. They shook their spears less in anger than to protect themselves from this ghostly crew.

As David grew into young manhood, the idea that Britain held the key to what was best in literature, art and culture was fading. He was a fifth-generation Australian whose family no longer had significant ties with Britain. Through reading the Palmer papers he came to understand that his country could do better than sticking with its narrowly British focus, it could open up to the larger world of Europe. The Palmers had often reviewed books by leading European writers. Nettie Palmer spoke both French and German and had studied phonetics in those countries. The Palmers had lived in Barcelona and, like many writers in the 1930s, had supported Republican Spain. They also knew and encouraged refugee artists who brought new trends including expressionism and psychoanalysis to Australia. The presence of these migrants helped local artists like Sidney Nolan, Albert Tucker and Arthur Boyd reimagine the Australian landscape.

On one wall of his room at University House, David had pinned a large print, Sidney Nolan's *Ned Kelly, 1946*. Kelly is seen from behind, riding towards the horizon on horseback in his black iron mask. Although David did not know it at the time, Nolan had been one of the first people to receive a Creative Arts Fellowship at the ANU, living for a brief time in 1968 with his wife Cynthia at University House. Nolan had recently completed one of his greatest paintings, the nine panels of the *Riverbend* series. They drew on childhood memories of fishing with his tram-driver father for Murray cod on the Goulburn River in northern Victoria. Ned Kelly is there among the trees, a tiny figure with the police in hot pursuit. But the power of the painting is the slow brown river as it moves past its banks with the mottled light filtering through the trees. Nolan said he wanted to paint the bush 'as the river sees it'. The first inklings of the painting had come to him many years before after reading a poem by Dylan Thomas about childhood memory:

And I saw in the turning so clearly a child's
Forgotten mornings when he walked with his mother
Through the parables
Of sunlight
And the legends of the green chapels.

David often studied the *Riverbend* painting while it hung in the ANU. Childhood memories returned him to the banks of the River Murray at Cadell and the peeling bark of the mighty river red gums.

The Nolans had barely settled into University House when Sid was keen to be off again. He wanted to take a look at China as 'from there perhaps we'll see what sort of a country Australia really is'. In her account of their trip, *A Sight of China* (1969), Cynthia explains that Nolan believed that 'in Australia we've grown up in half-Asia'. So for him, going to China seemed necessary to complete the experience of becoming fully Australian. When Nolan discussed his travel plans with Sir John Crawford, recently appointed as the university's next vice-chancellor, he found him very receptive. Like Vice-Chancellor Copland before him, for many years Crawford had promoted Australia's closer engagement with Asia. As an economist and public servant, he was among the first to appreciate that as Britain moved ever closer to Europe, Australia would need to find new friends and new markets in Asia.

In searching for new ways of painting Australia, Nolan argued that the Australian inheritance from Europe was mainly that of the 'whipper and the whipped'. He wanted Australians to understand that they were more than this convict heritage, they were people 'born in the East whether they like it or not'. Yet when the Nolans finally wandered through the streets of Beijing, they found themselves facing a culture for which they were totally unprepared.

In 1968, as the Nolans headed for China, Australia's prime minister was John Gorton, a conservative politician but a much more down-to-earth and Australian figure than the anglophile Sir Robert Menzies. Gorton is remembered for the support he gave to the emerging Australian film industry which, like Australian drama, had long been dormant. With Gorton's help, Australians could now see themselves on screen and continued to do so through the 1970s in films such as *Walkabout, Wake in Fright, Picnic at Hanging Rock, Don's Party* and *My Brilliant Career*.

Elected in 1972, the Whitlam Labor government continued the work Gorton had begun, making the nation more confidently Australian. Going further, they would withdraw Australian troops from Vietnam, recognise the People's Republic of China, promote Aboriginal land rights and appoint the first advisor to the Prime Minister on Women's Affairs. Whitlam also replaced the 'knights' and 'dames' of the old imperial honours system with an Australian Honours list.

In 1975, David left Canberra for a lecturing position in the History Department of the University of Auckland in his wife's old homeland. His undergraduate survey course in Australian history was the first to be taught in New Zealand. As an added bonus, he taught Australian cultural history to a group of bright MA students. One evening in November 1975 he was surprised to receive a call from the New Zealand Broadcasting Corporation. Would he come in immediately for a television interview? Australia's Prime Minister Gough Whitlam had just been dismissed by the Governor-General. Australian politics was in turmoil and they needed someone to explain what was going on across the Tasman. Clearly, a reformist but undisciplined Labor government had come to a very sudden end. The conservatives under the austere figure of grazier Malcom Fraser stood ready to take over. After his interview, David drove home in silence fearing no good would come of this day. The Whitlam government had introduced so many bold ideas to Australian society. Would there now be a return to another long period of political timidity?

In 1976, Li Yao was in Wulanchabu listening to peasants trying to sing opera. Li Yao loved Chinese opera, particularly the traditional opera of Shanxi. But during the Cultural Revolution, the fabulous tales and historical romances of Chinese opera were banned, replaced by Jiang Qing's *Eight Model Operas* telling the stories of farmers, workers and peasants. She brought in many innovations but let some traditional elements survive—high-pitched singing to the music of fiddles, lutes, drums and clappers, acrobatics, ritualised fighting and folk dance. A movement began to have the *Model Operas* performed by

A scene from the model opera *On the Docks*

amateur troupes. Two works seemed particularly suitable: *The Song of Dragon River* and *On the Docks*. Their songs were easy to sing. In *Dragon River*, a heroic CCP secretary dams a river to conquer a drought. The grand finale, 'Triumphant Song of a Bumper Harvest', celebrates his great success. In *On the Docks*, a resourceful woman belts out 'The Tempest Uplifts the Fighting Spirit' as she foils a plot to adulterate a cargo of rice. Once amateurs had mastered songs like 'I have carefully read the Communiqué from the Plenum', they were encouraged to compose their own works.

When the villagers of Xiao Jinzhuang became particularly good at performing amateur opera, Jiang Qing started another campaign: 'Emulate the Movement of Learning in Xiao Jinzhuang!' All over the country people started singing. Shangdu County in Wulanchabu did this so well that in 1976 people came from Beijing to see what they were up to. Led by Lv Lang, from the State Administration of Cultural Heritage, the visitors included several librarians from Beijing's Capital Library and a dozen worker-peasant-soldier students from Peking University. These students were young people sent to university as a reward for their patriotic work in the countryside. To keep them occupied as they were poorly equipped for further study, the universities sent them off for 'Open Door Schooling', undertaking social investigations in factories and farms.

When the Beijing group arrived, Li Yao and several other colleagues accompanied them to Shangdu County. The uneducated peasants at the People's Commune were not great poets but their rhymes written in strong local dialect were often funny and they performed them enthusiastically. One song compared Lin Biao and Confucius to groundhogs, demanding their overthrow because they did nothing but bask in the sun all day. Li Yao and his colleagues laughed loudly but the university students from southern China could not understand the local dialect and had no idea what was happening on stage.

Earlier in that year of 1976, there had been widespread mourning across China following the death of Premier Zhou Enlai. Australian papers reported 'black-bordered newspapers' and flags flown at half-mast. The *Canberra Times* praised Zhou as 'an architect of modern China' and 'one of the great survivors'. At the memorial service in Beijing, millions noted how Jiang Qing failed to remove her cap as she approached Zhou's bier. Watching on television in Guangzhou, a crowd began shouting, 'Beat her up! Beat her up!' Protests against the Cultural Revolution, Jiang Qing and her Gang of Four had begun. A poem in big black characters appeared at Tianenmen in Beijing: 'As in times past, the emperor is wrongly bewitched by beauty'. Following this, Tiananmen Square saw protests at which many were beaten and arrested. Rumour had it that the 'general standing behind the protest movement' was Deng Xiaoping, one of the five vice-chairmen of the CCP. A struggle for power began. With Mao backing him, Hua Guofeng rather than Deng Xiaoping succeeded Zhou Enlai as China's next premier.

Li Yao and his colleagues in Wulanchabu followed the news on morning radio. No-one dared express their feelings about the protests in Tiananmen Square although Li Yao sympathised with those beaten and arrested, hoping the Cultural Revolution would end. The worker-peasant-soldier students responded quite differently. To them, the Cultural Revolution was wonderful, it was giving them an education! Their monitor insisted on taking them back to Beijing immediately. They must aid the revolutionary struggle!

Alone with the librarians, Li Yao was free to talk about books. Although the Cultural Revolution was not yet over, libraries were starting to operate again as educated people began quietly looking for something to read. But there were very few books in Wulanchabu.

Lv Lang told them about a cache of books down in Shanghai, confiscated during the early years of the Cultural Revolution and now lying unread in the basement of the Huqiu library. Letters went back and forth and soon Shanghai agreed that if they would collect them, Wulanchabu could have them.. Early in September, Li Yao set off with colleagues from the Inner Mongolia Library to pick them up. Heading south, they planned an overnight stay in the guesthouse of the Ministry of Culture in Beijing. To their surprise, the guesthouse attendant told them to come to the meeting room at 4 o'clock to hear an important broadcast. This was unusual, hotels generally did not ask guests to listen to the radio. What was happening? Li Yao sat wondering. He hadn't seen Chairman Mao on television for quite some time. Could he . . . ? At 4 o'clock, a mournful voice announced to the packed room: 'Chairman Mao Zedong, the Great Leader and Mentor of the Chinese people, died in Beijing at 0:10 a.m., 9 September 1976.' All that could be heard in the silent room was the voice of the announcer describing Mao's great achievements. Suddenly, someone began to sob. Looking around, Li Yao saw people wiping away tears. Soon everyone in the room had begun crying.

After the broadcast, Li Yao and his colleagues walked out into the street where weeping people were cutting pine and cypress branches to make wreaths. Normally a bustling city, Beijing had become extremely quiet, the roaring giant was mute. They walked on to Tiananmen Square. It felt incredibly strange and powerful walking slowly, head down through its vast expanse. At Qianmen, Li Yao saw long lines of people outside the old silk store. They were buying black cloth, ripping it into strips for armbands. As evening approached, the Wulanchabu group entered an empty restaurant where they ordered beer. The waiter looked at them strangely as he put the bottles down on the table. Behind the waiter's back, one of their group, a CCP member, muttered, 'Is this a mistake? Chairman Mao is dead. Perhaps we shouldn't drink?' What could one say? They were all worried about getting into trouble. Then someone said, 'The beer is here, it's all the same whether you drink it or not' and he took a big gulp. Another said, 'Don't tell anyone. Let's just eat up and get out of here.'

That night Beijing was very dark. People spoke in low voices. Nobody dared laugh. From childhood, Li Yao's generation had shouted 'Long live Chairman Mao!' In every image, Mao had seemed so healthy, his face glowing red and his spirits high. How could he be dead? Government television sets were placed on the side of the road where crowds gathered to see Mao's body lying under a red flag. It was clear that an era had ended.

Australians joined the world in sending condolences. Prime Minister Malcolm Fraser said that Australians would 'understand and share the sorrow felt in China' at Mao's death. An 'outstanding figure in world history had passed from the scene'. Now in Opposition, Gough Whitlam, who unlike Fraser had met the Chairman, said Mao's death 'removed one of the giants of history'. One of the few discordant notes came from Queensland Premier Joh Bjelke-Petersen, 'Reds are Reds and I don't trust them.'

Several days later Li Yao and his colleagues flew on to Shanghai, the first time Li Yao had ever flown. Pressing his face close to the window, he looked down at the endless mountains, the winding Yellow River and then the Yangtze River. China's mountains and rivers were so magnificent, China's people were so hardworking and brave, but over the past ten years, they had experienced much hardship and suffering. Now Mao was dead. What would happen to their country? If the Cultural Revolution would only end, people could live a peaceful life. But Li Yao suspected the days ahead would not be peaceful.

This was Li Yao's first visit to Shanghai. He was fascinated by the beautiful vista of the Bund, the quay running along the western bank of the Huangpu River, just north of the old walled city. It was in the International Settlement and was lined with banks, consulates and beautiful European-style commercial buildings. Li Yao and his little group stayed in the Guest House of the Shanghai Revolutionary Committee, once a noted hotel. Founded in 1929, it was one of the first skyscrapers built in the East. In art deco style, this ten-storey building faced with granite and topped with a pyramidal copper roof still stands out. Originally it was called Sassoon House after its first owner, the Jewish businessman Sir Victor Sassoon, a noted figure of pre-war Shanghai society. At ground level there were banks and shops while upper floors housed 'the best hotel of the Far East'. Here, in 1930, Noel Coward shut himself into Room 314 to finish his classic play, *Private Lives*. Vicki Baum used the hotel as the setting for her best-seller, *Shanghai '37*. The novel follows the fate of nine disparate protagonists including a notorious character based on the feared head of Shanghai's 'Green Dragon Society'. All are killed on 14 August 1937 when the hotel is accidently bombed at the start of the Sino-Japanese War.

As the Guest House of the Shanghai Revolutionary Committee, the hotel was much less glamorous. Li Yao's group was given a simple room containing six beds where only the beautiful parquet floor indicated past luxury. Li Yao saw tributes to Chairman Mao everywhere in the streets of Shanghai. Yet among the crowds the Inner Mongolians felt uncomfortable. The Shanghainese seemed haughty, reserved and fastidious, superior even in grief. Their women were so smartly dressed, often with a small white flower in their hair. At night, people gathered in front of the hotel, to mourn and celebrate the life of the Great Leader. But across the road, on the banks of the Huangpu River, young couples were hugging and talking of love, not grieving for Mao. The Inner Mongolians felt strange and ridiculous as they walked along the Bund. Shanghai was another world.

They watched the memorial service in Tiananmen Square on television as over a million people heard Hua Guofeng deliver the eulogy for Chairman Mao. As funeral music played, people began to cry, many fainted. From Tibet to Inner Mongolia, from Heilongjiang to Hainan, China expressed its grief. In Shanghai, the government offices were closed, postponing the transfer of books. The group from Inner Mongolia wandered about, killing time looking at shops. They took short trips to Suzhou, Hangzhou and Wuxi, but there too, everything was closed. All they could do was enjoy the beautiful scenery of the Yangtze River delta and the great river running freely with its little boats and long bridges.

One day, by the edge of Taihu Lake, they saw two young women approaching. They looked so beautiful with their long straight hair, Hawaiian shirts, bell-bottom trousers and platform shoes. Had the beautiful Weaver Girl from the famous Chinese folk tale come down to earth from the stars? The Inner Mongolians wondered if they were looking at women from Hong Kong or perhaps overseas Chinese from the United States. All the women they knew had little pigtails sticking out like pot brushes or very short hair. It was a shock to see that women could dress up and look so beautiful. The girls smiled as they passed by.

That night as he stood at the hotel window looking out at the teaming crowds of pedestrians on Nanjing Road, Li Yao felt apprehensive remembering that Shanghai had been a major centre during the Cultural Revolution. It had seen the January Revolution and the February Countercurrent. While ignorant of struggles at the top, Li Yao and his colleagues knew a huge storm was brewing. Every night the workers' militia would seal off the mouth of the Huangpu River and the main arterial roads. Shanghai was in turmoil. Then on 7 October, in a shocking bolt from the blue, 'Down with the Gang of Four!' appeared on a large banner. The Inner Mongolians asked, could this really be happening? More big posters appeared. A seismic shift was underway. Despite desperate calls from the Shanghai Revolutionary Committee for workers to stop these protests, Shanghai people took to the streets in their thousands, calling for the overthrow of the Gang of Four.

The Inner Mongolians grew very excited. For ten years, the Gang of Four had inflicted untold suffering on the Chinese people. Retribution was now at hand. Li Yao wrote immediately to Chuoluobuku. They phoned colleagues in Inner Mongolia and, putting the receiver on the window, let them listen to the chants of the crowd below. In high spirits, they went to a restaurant and ordered 'Gang of Four' crabs, three male and one female, crunching through them with hatred while drinking the best yellow wine they could find. Li Yao drank too much, thinking of the suffering of his parents. He burst into tears.

At long last, arrangements were completed for the transfer of books. At the end of October the group returned to Beijing. Great changes were taking place. No sooner had they got off the train than they saw a large parade of people passing along the Avenue of Eternal Peace banging gongs and drums, beaming with joy and shouting 'Down with the Gang of Four!' Jiang Qing was in prison pending trial.

Back in Jining, Li Yao began to shelve books. Among them were many old 'friends': *Anna Karenina, Jane Eyre, Oliver Twist, David Copperfield* . . . After ten years in a Shanghai basement they came out into the light. Li Yao spotted *Jean Christophe,* one of his favourites. Written on the title page was 'Translator's own copy, 1952'. He imagined Red Guards rushing into Fu Lei's house, mercilessly criticising him, removing his property and books. As he looked at the many Chinese phrases drawn in red across the pages, he felt close to this great scholar whose accomplished translations had sustained so many Chinese readers. Fu Lei was clearly a perfectionist. Once again, Li Yao felt the desire to become a scholar. He would treasure this book and return it to Fu Lei as soon as possible.

In December 1978, the Eleventh Central Committee of the CCP made some momentous decisions. Class struggle would be abandoned, the oppressive labels of 'landlord' and 'historical counter-revolutionary' would be abolished. Hearing this, Li Yao took out his father's photo. Cutting out the image from the dark background he placed it on a new light blue card. In this way he would tell his dear father that the darkness had at last been banished. His son was no longer a dog's whelp!

One after another, members of the Literary Group left Wulanchabu. Monan became the director of the Inner Mongolia People's Publishing House in Hohhot. An Mi and Xue Yan rejoined the Inner Mongolia Literary Federation. Yang Ping took up his old position as editor-in-chief of *Grassland*. Li Yao knew it was time to send off *Jean Christophe.* He wrote to the Shanghai Translation Publishing House for an address, only to hear that Fu Lei and his wife, unable to withstand the insults of the Red Guards, had committed suicide in September 1966. Li Yao carefully wrapped up *Jean Christophe* to send to Fu Lei's second son, Fu Min. From then on, whenever Li Yao completes a translation, he writes on the title page of the original book, 'Translator's Own Copy'.

CHAPTER 18

Beginnings

In 1968, the University of New South Wales (UNSW) held a symposium called 'Australia: A Part of Asia?' One person who was asked to speak was Professor Frank Crowley, head of the Department of History. He forcefully declined, declaring that Australia never had been and never would be part of Asia. The son of an Anglican minister, Crowley was educated at one of Adelaide's top private schools and then at the University of Melbourne and Balliol College, Oxford. This experience, rather than turning him into a cultivated Oxbridge don, produced a provocative larrikin known for his loud behaviour and outrageous views. When at last prevailed upon to speak at the symposium, he somewhat surprisingly argued that although Australia clearly remained an 'outpost of Europe', it was essential for Australian universities to offer courses in Asian Studies. Frank was a 'know thy enemy' man.

On David's first day as a member of staff at UNSW in mid-1977, he was summoned to Professor Crowley's office mid-morning for a briefing on his new responsibilities. Crowley, now dean of the Faculty of Arts, welcomed David in, asking if he would prefer whisky or an ice-cold beer. Somewhat surprised, David accepted a whisky. He learned that he would be taking over a very large undergraduate survey course, 'Australia in the Twentieth Century'. He was also invited to teach an upper level course. David drew on his interests in popular fiction and the development of a distinctive national culture to create a new course, 'Literature and Society in Twentieth Century Australia'.

Until the 1970s, immigrants to Australia usually arrived by boat, approaching the continent from the west with stops at Freemantle, Adelaide and Melbourne, cities where many disembarked before the ship finally reached Sydney. With the abandonment of the White Australia policy in 1972, many more immigrants began coming in from Asia, most flying straight into Sydney and settling there. While there were few Asian students in David's classes, he noticed many around the campus.

UNSW had the largest intake of international students of any Australian university at the time. By the late 1970s, the UNSW History Department had expanded its teaching beyond East Asia, becoming well known for its Indian and South-East Asian history and its specialist courses on Vietnam, Indonesia and the Philippines.

By 1984, David had moved into a Federation-style house in Coogee with his wife and two young daughters. At UNSW he introduced another course for upper level students which he taught jointly with his friend John Ingelson. The idea for this course started on the squash court where David had regular contests with John, an authority on modern Indonesian history. In between games, the two men exchanged the odd grumble. John was finding that his students who were studying South-East Asian history had no interest in the history of Australia. Conversely, David grumbled that his students were intimidated by incomprehensible Asia. He was having some difficulty persuading them that Asia had influenced Australia's development. To bridge the divide, the sweaty scholars decided to draw students together in a single course, 'Australian Perceptions of Asia'.

Vietnamese people had begun arriving in Australia after the Vietnam War. By 1984, around 90 000 Indo-Chinese had entered the country, in world terms a significant number but less than 2 per cent of the total Australian population. In March of that year, on a wet afternoon in the Victorian town of Warrnambool, Professor Geoffrey Blainey spoke to members of the local Rotary Club. This distinguished historian, first chair of the Australia China Council, raised concerns that the influx of Asian arrivals was running ahead of public opinion. Was this a threat to 'social cohesion'? Once reported nationally, these remarks triggered the protracted 'Blainey debate' on immigration, soon to be seen on the front page of every newspaper in the country. Students became interested. Walker and Ingelson found that their boutique course 'Australian Perceptions of Asia' suddenly morphed into a very much larger affair.

The following year, the witty and engaging David Reeve appeared at the History Department at UNSW. Reeve was an ex-diplomat, returned from Indonesia after his satiric profiles of embassy staff were unfortunately revealed to a wider world. After a short stay in Sydney, Reeve intended to return to Jakarta to teach Australian history and society at Universitas Indonesia. Before he left, Walker and Reeve had many lively discussions about what the new course should examine. Not long after, the elder Rooster was appointed as a consultant to the Australian Studies Program in Jakarta, a role which allowed him to visit Indonesia on many occasions between 1986 and 1997, his first protracted encounter with an Asian society.

In 1989 David became editor of the journal *Australian Cultural History*. Given his current interests, he decided that the next annual conference for the journal would have the theme *Australian Perceptions of Asia*. Conference presentations published in the 1990 issue ranged widely across Asian Studies, histories of Asian engagement, teaching of Asian languages and stories of Australian writers and artists inspired by Asia.

Over the next thirty years or so, David's growing interest in Australian responses to Asia developed in parallel with a commitment to the development of Australian Studies programs at universities in the Asian region. He taught at Shiga University in Japan and Yangzhou Normal University near Shanghai and attended Australian Studies Association conferences in India. He published *Anxious Nation* and *Stranded Nation* and finished the last three years of his career with the support of FASIC as the inaugural BHP chair of Australian Studies at Peking University from 2013 to 2016.

Where was Li Yao? While David was moving towards Asia, Li Yao was moving towards Australia. But first he began to write about his immediate past. 'Scar Literature' was beginning to appear. This term is used to describe novels and poems that recall and examine the devastating effects of the Cultural Revolution. Li Yao too tried to express his trauma, writing short stories about Jin Xigu and Han Tong and a novella, *The Fire in September*, about his dear father and his own lost youth. After appearing in many newspapers these works were brought together in 1988 as *The Smile in Autumn*. Li Yao was then able to join the Writers' Association of China, a dream come true.

As China opened to the world, the country experienced a boom in literature. Long queues formed outside bookstores. There was a pent-up appetite for news of the wider world. Li Yao's thoughts turned to translation. His rendition of Dickens' story 'A Child's Dream of a Star' appeared in *Qinghai Lake* and was read on Beijing People's Radio. Encouraged, he finished translating *The Path of Thunder*, the South African novel that had helped sustain him in the Yanggao camp. He went on to translate Hemingway's *For Whom the Bell Tolls*, two short stories by John Steinbeck, and another by the Canadian writer Alice Munro. With Munro's work, he met with indifference from Chinese publishers who knew little about the flourishing literature of the British Commonwealth. They believed that the finest English writing came from Britain or America. Discouraged, Li Yao put his work away in a drawer. It seemed that China was not ready for translations of post-colonial literature.

At the end of 1980, Li Yao met Alison Hewitt, a school teacher from Perth who had arrived to teach English at Inner Mongolia University for four months, one of six teachers sent to China by the Australian Teachers' Federation. The Chinese government sent them all to Inner Mongolia, thinking they would cope with conditions there, as Australians were known to be 'tough'. Toughness was needed. Many university buildings were still damaged after the Cultural Revolution. A mask was sensible for any trip outdoors as the air was thick with soot. In Hohhot, Alison taught science students seeking sufficient fluency in English to enable them to study abroad.

Hearing of his interest in translation, Alison gave Li Yao a copy of Henry Lawson's short stories, to help him 'understand the Australian people'. All Li Yao knew about the country was its strange animals—kangaroos and koalas, parrots and black swans. He knew nothing of Australian writing. He was impressed by the 'heroic spirit of survival' in 'The Drover's Wife' and saw affinities between the vast spaces of

Alison Hewitt (seated centre)
with some of her students at Inner Mongolia
University. Photo: Alison Frere

Australia and Inner Mongolia. It was not long before his translation of Lawson's story appeared in *Grassland*. In 1944, the Australian painter Russell Drysdale put 'The Drover's Wife' on canvas as a large, drably dressed, stoic woman standing in a paddock devastated by drought. The famous image still speaks to settler Australia's troubled relationship with the land.

The next book Alison gave Li Yao was Patrick White's *The Tree of Man*. Vance Palmer had been no great fan of White, describing him as 'difficult to read' although reluctantly conceding he was 'one of the best novelists in the English-speaking world today'. In 1973, this verdict was confirmed when White became the first Australian writer to win the Nobel Prize for Literature. In China, the authority conferred by a literary prize can determine who matters and who does not. Li Yao now had an Australian book to translate that would command attention.

White, the son of a wealthy grazing family from NSW, served as an Intelligence Officer in Alexandria during the war. Here he met Manoly Lascaris, who became his 'central mandala' and partner for life. White was a product of the British Imperial world, while Lascaris' older, more aristocratic family were outcasts from the collapsed Ottoman Empire. At the end of the war, when the world of empires no longer needed them, these outsiders settled down on a farm near Sydney where White began writing *The Tree of Man*, an account of the lives of an Australian farming couple, Stan and Amy Parker.

Li Yao warmed to *The Tree of Man*, both to its earthy characters and rural setting. As he later told *China Daily*, 'White's elegant style and insightful thoughts were thrilling to my soul'. In it he found elements of social realist themes remembered from his early immersion in Soviet literature. But White offered something more: an imaginative response to language and landscape that Li Yao found very different to 'the dominant English literature in the West'. Li Yao admits that although he was initially drawn to translate Australian writing because there were few competitors in the field, over time, 'he came to love Australia and its literary works'.

Knowing he would need help translating White, Li Yao wrote to Professor Hu Wenzhong of BFSU who agreed to collaborate, giving Li Yao *The Concise Macquarie Dictionary* to help him decode strange Australian idioms. Hu Wenzhong was one of the 'Gang of Nine', nine literary scholars from across China who had studied linguistics and Australian literature at the University of Sydney in 1979. By 1986, Li Yao and Professor Hu were celebrating on the grassland in proper Inner Mongolian style, drinking and singing on completing their translation of *The Tree of Man*.

The *First International Conference on Australian Studies in China* was held at BFSU in 1988. Li Yao presented a paper on Patrick White. He met Australian writers Nicholas Jose, Rodney Hall and fellow Rooster Fay Zwicky and the academics John McClaren and Shirley Walker. Jose had been in Beijing for two years, teaching Australian literature at BFSU before becoming cultural ambassador at the Australian Embassy. He noted that the two best known Australian novels in China at that time were White's *The Eye of the Storm* and Colleen McCullough's best-seller *The Thorn Birds*, which was first translated into Chinese in 1983. Massive sales indicated that it struck a chord with Chinese readers. There was the exotic setting in Drogheda, a vast sheep station in outback Australia, overtones of 'Scar Literature' in the tragic story of forbidden love between 'Meggie' Cleary and a handsome priest, and the reliable appeal of a family epic dominated by an immensely rich and scheming old matriarch. Many Chinese women of that time chose 'Meggie' or 'Maggie' for their English name. At the height of the novel's fame, true devotees could even fly by 'Thorn Birds Air'.

While *The Thorn Birds* was widely read in Australia, it was dismissed by critics and never taken seriously as a contribution to Australian literature. The prominent critic Dorothy Green titled her utterly dismissive review of the book 'Porn Birds'. Others noted how its plot was implausible, the landscape and settings were botanically and geographically inaccurate and this story of European settlement left out the Aboriginal people. No Australian postgraduate student would think of writing about *The Thorn Birds* unless they were studying popular culture, but in China the book has sustained an extraordinary academic industry which has generated a run of theses, scholarly articles and conference papers. *The Thorn Birds* offers the Chinese a fantasy world in a place called 'Australia' which finds its parallel in that fantasy world called 'China' that has for so long fascinated the West.

Li Yao visited Australia for the first time in 1988 for the Tenth Conference of the Association for the Study of Australian Literature (ASAL) at the University of Sydney. Li Yao was surprised to see so many tall buildings of steel and glass, buildings unlike any he had seen even in Beijing or Shanghai. Walking around the city, he thought how wonderful that Australians had built all this in only 200 years. He was impressed by the variety of food in the supermarkets, the number of cars on the road, the hot water gushing out of the tap in the bathroom. In China, he could only dream of having a car and a big house with plenty of hot water. But now, forty years later, he has his comfortable apartment, hot water to spare and Beijing is full of tall buildings of glass and steel.

One sunny afternoon during his visit to Sydney, Li Yao rang the doorbell at 20 Martin Road, Centennial Park. The man who opened the door seemed much older than he had in his photograph. Patrick White was stooped but his eyes were still blue and shining. Leading

Li Yao with Patrick White, 1988

Li Yao into his living room, he called out 'Manoly, tea', and out came Manoly with a teapot. Both men were kind to their Chinese visitor as they sat talking about translation and writing. Li Yao gave White a copy of his own book *Smile in Autumn*, explaining how it had been influenced by *The Tree of Man*. White replied that literature has no boundaries, writers from all over the world should learn from each other. He himself liked China very much although now he was too old and sick to see it, but he was grateful his work had been published in translation. In this way, he had been to China after all. Giving Li Yao a copy of his autobiography, *Flaws in the Glass*, he wrote on the title page: 'To my brave translator Li Yao. May he and his readers be rewarded.' After photos in the garden, White suggested that Li Yao might like to come with him to the post office where he was going to collect his mail. Li Yao was impressed when the great writer spoke to the people serving behind the counter at the post office in relaxed and friendly terms. He watched as White walked away, such an old man now.

Li Yao later spent two nights in Sydney with Shirley Walker's son Don, in the seedy nightclub district of Kings Cross. Don was a musician and songwriter who wrote for the Australian rock band Cold Chisel. Li Yao would never have heard such music before. David pictures him drifting to sleep to strains of 'Khe Sanh'.

This music and Kings Cross itself would have been an entirely different world.

Li Yao caught the bus to Cobargo, a tiny town on the NSW south coast. When David hears this name all he can think of is a wall of flames. In the dreadfully hot summer of 2019–2020, beautiful old Cobargo was devastated by a catastrophic bushfire. Climate change had arrived. But in 1988, Li Yao sat on the bus enjoying a beautiful view of thick forest and ocean. Then he noticed no-one had come to sit beside him. Were his clothes dirty? Did he smell bad? No, it must be because he was Chinese. He tried to comfort himself by thinking, when chickens meet another strange chicken, they always chased it away. He was a strange chicken from China, of course Australian chickens might look askance.

The writer Rodney Hall met the traveller off the bus. At dinner, Li Yao presented his gifts: a Chinese painting and his translations of Hall's poetry for a Chinese magazine. Rising early the next morning, Li Yao looked around the unusual house, built of round timber slabs and stringy bark, its floor covered with cowhides and sheepskins. A large stone fireplace dominated the living room. A single dim lightbulb hung from the ceiling. There was no television or sign of any electrical appliances. Pointing to the wonderful views of ocean and bush, Hall explained that he enjoyed living close to nature. He had everything here he wanted except a bigger water tank and a larger electric generator.

Li Yao was surprised that a famous writer would live like this. Hall would stand in front of his Canon typewriter drafting his novels and poems, then abruptly stop to take his dog for a walk in the bush. Cobargo is close to the Wabilliga region of rugged mountain ranges, tall gum trees and pockets of rainforest. Over the next ten days, Li Yao went with Hall into this 'primeval forest' learning about its flowers and birds: the red bottlebrush that looked like a brush, the birds that sang like the crack of a whip or like a bell. He began to recognise different kinds of eucalyptus and wattle. He now understood why the anthills rose so high. He gained bush knowledge invaluable for a translator of Australian literature.

Cobargo was the ancient home of the Djiringanj south coast Yuin people. As a doctor, Hall's wife Bet often visited their communities. She introduced Li Yao to an eighty-five-year-old Aboriginal elder named Gabo. He was wearing a white T-shirt on which Li Yao read the characters *Wan Sui*, 'long life'. When he looked surprised, Gabo explained that his mother had come from Guangdong. Li Yao wondered why she had come to Australia and joined an Aboriginal community? He thought of White's novel *A Fringe of Leaves*. Gabo had little to say about his mother but was keen to tell stories about 'his mob'. He sang some songs:

> Our beautiful mountains and forests were taken over by White men,
> Our beautiful lake and river were taken over by White men,
> Nothing left for us,
> We have to wander around
> We have to wander around!

As a social activist and poet, Gabo was well known. He had been photographed with the Dalai Lama. After presenting Li Yao with a collar woven from yellow, black and red thread, he explained that these were the colours of the sun, the earth and the people, colours now seen on the Aboriginal flag. Li Yao dates his interest in Australian Aboriginal peoples from this visit.

Li Yao travelled to Melbourne to stay with the literary critic John McClaren. To his bulging suitcase, another book was added, Brian Castro's *Birds of Passage*. As he read it, Li Yao was fascinated by the lives of Seamus O'Young, an Australian-born Chinese man and his ancestor Lo Yun Shan who had come to Australia to search for gold in the 1850s.

Li Yao's visit to Australia strengthened his resolve to become a translator. His own writing inevitably drew him back to the painful experiences of the Cultural Revolution, to the fate of his father, his mother's pain and the deaths of Jin Xigou and Han Tong. During this 'Time of Chaos', Li Yao had sought various means of escape, lying on his bunk writing his novel, reading English in a field with the pigs, drinking too much *baijiu* with trusted friends, escaping to the grasslands, but events always caught up with him. Had he continued as a writer, these sad experiences would always return. Australia was a world remote from China, offering new landscapes and a new literature. This was a world he could enter and bring home unburdened by bitter memories of the past.

In 1988, Li Yao began to translate *Flaws in the Glass*, a book in which White explores the 'contradictory characters' within his personality, ending with some spiteful portraits. Queen Elizabeth has a 'cold China voice' and Prince Philip a 'Glucksberg scowl'. White is scathing about Sidney Nolan's intellectual pretensions, complaining that at dinner 'Sid' could never resist running up 'a flag with "Kierkegaard" on it during the soup'. Similarly, White had no time for the Australian opera diva Dame Joan Sutherland who had been incautious enough to tell him 'she had not read a word' of what he had written, but 'could not put *The Thorn Birds* down'. Of the literary critic Leonie Kramer, who had been host to the 'Gang of Nine' scholars, White wrote: 'ambivalence has given me insights into human nature, denied, I believe, to those who are unequivocally male or female—and Professor Leonie Kramer'.

After a wonderful launch of his translation in August 1990 at the Australian Embassy in Beijing, Li Yao hurried home to wrap up a volume to send to White. Too late. *The Sydney Morning Herald* arrived to tell him: 'Patrick White, author and stirrer, dies at 78.' David wonders whether, in his fascination with this literary giant, did Li Yao notice White's nasty streak and understand just how much of a 'stirrer' he had been?

It was not always easy to get Australian writing published in China. Without the profile of British or American literature, it did not deliver reliable profits to publishers. One difficult project was Castro's *Birds of Passage*. Fearing a small readership, the publishing house cancelled their promised print run. All they could offer was the manual typeset manuscript. Li Yao set off to collect it, travelling by train 'hard seat' to the capital of Jilin province, over 1500 kilometres away. Once there, he faced a further two-hour bus trip in bitterly cold weather to Nongan County, where a very heavy bundle of typeset pages were waiting to be lugged back to Hohhot. Li Yao found a printing house prepared to produce 1000 copies for an amount equivalent to his salary for the next five months. Gritting his teeth, he decided to go ahead, he might be able to recoup his outlay. A friend designed an elegant cover with birds flying over the ocean. By 1991, 1000 birds perched in Li Yao's apartment. Some were sent off to friends across China, but at least 900 still sat there regarding him in silence. Li Yao has to admit that he might be a good translator but he is not a good businessman.

Over the next decade, Li Yao continued to translate Australian literature. When his work on Alex Miller's *The Ancestor Game* won a translation prize, Li Yao was delighted to learn that the author would attend the award ceremony in Beijing. Author and translator celebrated together at dinner in the famous Quanjude Roast Duck restaurant in Qianmen. Not long after, Nicholas Jose, the great literary enabler, sent Li Yao a copy of *Carpentaria* by Alexis Wright, an Indigenous writer whose great-grandfather was Chinese. Li Yao was excited. Since meeting Gabo, he had been very interested in Aboriginal culture. He had translated *Benang: From the Heart* by Kim Scot and *Who Am I? The Diary of Mary Talence* by Anita Heiss, books about Aboriginal children 'stolen' from their families and forced to assimilate into 'white' society. Now he decided he must translate *Carpentaria*. He found it full of splendid and unusual scenes illustrating the contradictions between the totems, legends and myths of the ancient ways of thinking, and the problems and difficulties of modern life. He admired the book's innovative style and artistic appeal. But he soon found it was not easy to translate.

Initially, Alexis Wright had no thoughts of her book appearing in Chinese. Corresponding with Li Yao, she quickly came to appreciate his difficulties with 'Aboriginal dialects, the customs of my hometown, Carpentaria, and the world view of Indigenous peoples'. Li Yao explains that it was not just a simple matter of finding the Chinese equivalent for an Aboriginal word. Establishing meaning was troublesome but not difficult. The real problem lay in the wider context. To make a good translation he needed to gain more understanding of Indigenous culture, their ancient legends and myths, and the protracted conflicts within the tribe. He read widely and had long talks with the artist Zhou Xiaoping, who had lived with Aboriginal people in northern Australia for many years.

Gradually, Li Yao began to understand how the Aboriginal relationship to the land reverberates in their stories. Each rock and creek could be an 'actor', even sand dunes and trees had witnessed legends. The Great Serpent, the sea monsters, the fish, parrots, heavy seas and violent tornados began to metamorphose into vivid symbols. The characters became more lifelike, figures with whom Li Yao could converse as he sought to understand their loves and hates. Finally, he felt ready to undertake the translation. In March 2010, at the Fourth Australian Writers' Week held at the Australian Embassy in Beijing, Li Yao met Alexis Wright in person for the first time. She read extracts from *Carpentaria*, then Li Yao read his version of the story in Chinese. Two years later, the complete translation was launched. At this glittering embassy event, Tie Ning, chairman of the Writers' Association of China and the Chinese Nobel Prize winner Mo Yan both spoke. Soon after, Li Yao began to translate Alexis Wright's *The Swan Book*.

In 2005, despite having become 'legally blind' from macular degeneration the previous year, David started teaching short courses as a visiting professor at Renmin University of China in Beijing. A very active Australian Studies Centre had been developed there under the determined leadership of Professor Zhang Yongxian. He was an authority on Australian English and like Li Yao, a graduate of IMNU. After a hearty banquet and some *baijiu* he would often stand and recite Dorothea Mackellar's:

> I love a sunburnt country
> A land of sweeping plains,
> Of ragged mountain ranges,
> Of droughts and flooding rains

On one later occasion, he gave a complete rendition of this famous poem to Australia's governor-general, Quentin Bryce. There was rousing applause.

In his annual visits to Renmin, David greatly enjoyed the teaching. The students were thoughtful, hard-working and keen to know more about Australia. They were always happy to ferry him around ensuring that he navigated Beijing streets without mishap. Before long, Professor Zhang and his students took on the sizable task of translating *Anxious Nation*. Facing objections about some negative stereotypes of Chinese in late nineteenth-century Australia which appeared in the book, Professor Zhang pressed on, emphasising that it was important for Chinese readers to understand these racial opinions in their historical context. Professor Zhang explained that they clearly did not represent modern Australian thinking or the views of the author.

As he came and went from Beijing, David became aware that the leading translator of Australian writing into Chinese was a man called Li Yao. He caught occasional glimpses of this elusive scholarly-looking fellow at Renmin University and at functions at the Australian Embassy. Eventually, in 2012, Nicholas Jose suggested that Li Yao would be the perfect choice to translate David's personal history, *Not Dark Yet*. The two Roosters met and discussed the project. Karen remembers how excited David had been on learning that this great translator was interested in his book. The timing was perfect, they would be able to meet and talk as the translation progressed since David would soon be working at Peking University. Professor Zhang was not so happy, insisting that David belonged at Renmin and should not fly off anywhere else.

As David takes out his face-mask and prepares to go on his daily walk in locked-down Melbourne, he finds an email has arrived from Li Yao working away in Beijing on his translation of Mary Gaunt's *A Woman in China*. This is his thirty-eighth Australian translation. Li Yao says that Mary's book, first published 106 years ago, contains 'many precious accounts' of a China that is now long gone. Each morning the old chap gets up at dawn to eat a solid breakfast, downing a strong cup of black coffee before settling down to convert more pages of the text into two thousand or so carefully chosen characters. He has been doing this regularly for over forty years. Although there were more characters per day when he was younger, now he has become very selective with his choice of words. A lifetime of deep reading allows him to write 'beautiful Chinese', which he observes is an 'increasingly rare skill' in modern China. He says on this point he likes to 'blow trumpet'.

CHAPTER 19

Reading deep in willows

The years 2013 to 2016 were a very good time to be living in Beijing. Australia and China were getting on well. In November 2014, China's President Xi Jinping addressed a special joint sitting of the Australian Houses of Parliament in Canberra and celebrated the signing of a China–Australia Free Trade Agreement. President Xi spoke of the bilateral relationship as one that would be as enduring as China's Great Wall and Australia's Uluru. Back in China, interest in the Australian Studies program was growing, with new centres opening in Hohhot, Shenyang, Shantou and Harbin. Australian Studies was well supported by FASIC and by the Australian Embassy in Beijing, led by its ambassador, Frances Adamson.

David and Karen lived in a fourth-floor apartment in the main Shaoyuan Guesthouse, Peking University. Their enclosed balcony looked out to the Western Hills, home to many revered temples: the Daoist Miaofengshan, the Temple of the Sleeping Buddha and the Monastery of Clear Pools and Wild Mulberry. Early one morning in mid-April 2013, heavy snow fell overnight. David and Karen rushed to take in the scene. As dawn broke, the trees, regarding their reflection in the glassy waters of Weiming Lake, began to turn a golden pink. The staggered eves of the pagoda-like Boya water tower were edged with snow. Mysterious stone pathways led into wooded groves. A small pavilion offered a moment of oriental serenity before a bevy of dedicated photographers appeared, leaving tracks in the snow where none had been before.

Snow at Peking University, 2013

As soon as it had come, the snow was gone, and the campus reverted to a mass of bare black branches and dry yellow grass. The greyness was soon challenged by yellow patches of *ying chun hua*, one of the very earliest spring flowers. Grass slowly turned green. Pink followed yellow as peach, cherry and plum trees burst into flower. An old almond tree was covered in blossom. Waiting in turn were the white and purple magnolias, early lilac and the cheerful red of flowering quince. Willows, gingko and plane trees came into leaf. A venerable wisteria growing over the arched gateway to the courtyard of the Australian Studies Centre was a mass of soft purple flowers. Near a lake, David and Karen came unexpectedly upon a statue of Cervantes standing before a backdrop of white flowers. As summer approached, the peonies, freed from their winter wrappings at last, displayed magnificent blooms of white, pale pink, dark pink and deep magenta. By summer, convolvulus and snake gourd vines had crept everywhere. Each walk revealed new pathways, pavilions and rockeries as awareness grew that this was a university built over a series of antique gardens.

Chinese friends said little about the history of Peking University, only that it had once been the garden of a Manchu prince and that before Liberation it had been the site of Yenching University. Nationally it was clearly an important place. Every weekend, long queues formed at the gates as parents sought permission from the guards to show their children this famous campus. The children were told that if they studied really hard they might come here one day. How proud their parents would be!

In 1919, John Leighton Stuart was appointed as the first president of Yenching University. A man with a deep appreciation of Chinese history and culture, Leighton Stuart was born in Hangzhou, the son of American protestant missionaries. Seeking to create a fine liberal arts university, Leighton Stuart employed an American architect to design a suitably imposing campus set in its own garden, the *Yan Yuan*. While making full use of modern building materials, its halls, dormitory buildings and library spoke to their Chinese heritage and were placed with proper regard to *feng shui*. By 2013, these buildings, covered in grape ivy, had aged gracefully, looking wonderfully Chinese, in sharp contrast to the modern buildings of glass and steel pushing upwards around the university's East Gate.

David and Karen frequently walked over to the extensive gardens of the nearby Yuanmingyuan (Old Summer Palace). They had first been taken there one harsh winter in 2004, when the site seemed to consist of barren lake beds, broken masonry and bulldozed mud. By the spring of 2013, the place had been transformed. The willow branches were long and green, sparkling lakes were edged with the intense yellow of weeping forsythia and artfully rounded mounds were thick with cherry blossom. How had so many trees grown so fast? The Chinese are expert at transplanting mature trees, trucked in from the countryside, their roots carefully protected with hessian and rope. Seeing rows of newly planted bare trunks, the Australians can't believe this will work, but this is China. In spring, the trunks break obediently into leaf. Among the old stones and broken bridges of the *Yuanmingyuan*, a narrow path leads to a shady spot called 'Reading Deep in Willows'. In summer, little canopied boats move through the lotus flowers and waterlilies on the lakes. In late autumn, defiant orange persimmons stand out on bare branches.

The *Yuanmingyuan* was founded in the seventeenth century by the Kangxi emperor, and greatly expanded during the long rule of his grandson, Emperor Qianlong. It contains stone ruins of what had once been the Western Mansions, a series of European-style palaces, fountains and gardens designed for the Chinese emperor by Italian Jesuits. David and Karen are well aware that in 1860, the *Yuanmingyuan* was burned to the ground by Western imperialists. The two Australians enter a crowded exhibition hall with some caution, but the Chinese treat them with courtesy as they examine traditional paintings and intricate models revealing the layout and past beauty of the gardens and indicating the extent of the wanton destruction. On display are replicas of the twelve bronze animal heads of the Chinese zodiac that had adorned the great clock fountain in front of the Western Mansions. The message coming out of the new *Yuanmingyuan* was that in the later years of the Qing dynasty China had been too weak to defend its borders and incapable of protecting and feeding its people. This would never be allowed to happen again.

In *Place and Memory in the Singing Crane Garden*, Vera Schwarcz tells a deeper history of the Haidian district. As its name ('shallow sea') implies this was an area well supplied with water, ideal for gardens, places where an overburdened courtier could withdraw from the travails of imperial governance. The exiled Ming courtier Mi Wanzhong was one of the first to settle here. His garden, which he loved to paint, was the Shao Yuan (Spoon Garden). As 'Mi the friend of rocks', he avidly collected large stones of appealing shape and texture for his garden. Peking University commemorates this garden through the Shaoyuan guesthouses, but any traces of a garden in the immediate vicinity are long gone. Sounds from the busy tennis and basketball courts are more prominent.

Even so, fragments from the elusive past recur across campus. On a little island in Weiming Lake, a graceful octagonal pavilion stands among old trees. It is named after Henry W. Luce, a past vice-president of Yenching University. In front of this pavilion, standing at the edge of the lake, is the base of an old marble boat, a great place for students to pose for graduation photographs. It is also a reminder that here in the eighteenth century there was once a sumptuous Manchu garden, the Shu Chun Yuan, the property of a corrupt favourite of the Qianlong emperor.

One of the most celebrated of the many princely Manchu gardens established in Haidian, belonged to Prince Mianyu. He built it on land given to him after his successful defence of Beijing during the

Taiping Rebellion and it included part of the old Shu Chun Yuan. Prince Mianyu's garden lay between Weiming Lake and what is now the West Gate of Peking University. It was given the name, Ming He Yuan or 'Singing Crane' garden. Cranes were traditional symbols of eternity, fidelity and high-mindedness. Perhaps Prince Mianyu wished his garden to become a refuge for 'crying crane scholars', quiet men of learning who preferred the shadows of lake and garden to the glare and self-promotion of public life.

The Ming He Yuan was reached by a marble bridge. Turning left, 'an enclosed passageway' opened onto a rear garden 'filled with lilac'. To the right were the public spaces, a library, a large hall and a courtyard with a stage for opera. In the centre lay the peaceful 'studio for rethinking one's career' and pens housing several pairs of cranes. Two marble lions guarded a side entrance while behind the crane enclosure were rounded hills, further pavilions and a gourd-shaped lake. Unaware of its history, David is often drawn to the little Yi Ran Ting pavilion, set on a high mound with a fine view of green foliage and little lakes.

At the beginning of the year 1860, Prince Mianyu retired to his garden. Like a crane perhaps he hoped to 'thrive in the shade, while tigers roar on the mountains'. Defence of the capital was left in the hands of the Mongol General Sengkelinqin. Yet by September, danger grew near as British and French armies approached Beijing, intent on forcing the Qing to open up China to trade. The French were led by a cultured diplomat, Baron Gros, and the British by James, the eighth Lord Elgin, whose father had taken the marble statues from the Parthenon. The Qing court expected elaborate negotiations with these foreigners according to the stylised rituals of their tribute system. Lord Elgin was having none of it. He sent a delegation off to the capital to set the Chinese 'straight' before winter set in. Faced with the intractability and great rudeness of these foreigners, General Sengkelinqin promptly arrested Elgin's delegation, an action interpreted as a provocative insult. As misunderstandings accumulated on both sides, conflict became inevitable. A smuggled message, embroidered on a shirt in Hindustani, warned the European prisoners that Elgin and Gros planned to attack.

On 5 October, Western troops were at the gates of the Yuanmingyuan. For three days, furniture, jewellery and art, the accumulated wealth of three centuries, were ransacked from fourteen large palaces and many pavilions spread across the gardens. One French soldier reported that the troops seemed overcome by 'temporary insanity', all they could do was 'plunder, plunder, plunder'. Matters deteriorated further on 16 October, when twenty coffins bearing bodies from Elgin's delegation were returned to the European armies. Looking down at the tortured remains, including those of Thomas Bowlby, correspondent to the London *Times*, a man he knew well, Lord Elgin made the fateful decision that the Chinese emperor had to be taught a lesson. He ordered the looted Yuanmingyuan to be put to the flames. Burning continued for days, darkening the skies over Beijing. Fires soon spread to the nearby princely gardens including the Ming He Yuan. The 'yellow crane flew off, never to return' and the once enchanting gardens were left to decay into a mass of 'broken marble arches, weed-infested lakes, bramble-thickened paths and peeling pavilions'. In 1875, instead of rebuilding the Yuanmingyuan, the Dowager Empress, Cixi, made herself a new garden retreat, the Yi He Yuan or New Summer Palace near Kunming Lake.

In 1899, the Sydney-born Chinese cartoonist James See (also known as Xie Juantai) published a famous map showing China being torn apart by a number of predatory beasts representing the Western powers. To the north looms a fierce Russian bear, out to conquer Manchuria, Mongolia and Korea. In the south, a British bulldog paws at the coast, keen to control the Chinese market. An American eagle hovers over the South China Sea, ready to stand beside Britain. France, Japan and Germany are there too, represented by the witty cartoonist as a frog, a sun and a sausage. This widely circulated cartoon signalled China's humiliating vulnerability to the world. Following the collapse of the Qing dynasty in 1911, Chinese intellectuals wearing scholarly robes gathered among the ruins of Haidian to maintain their smouldering rage against the foreign aggressors. How had mighty China become so weak? Had it been too soft and feminine, too corrupt?

No writer caught the mood of critical self-reflection better than Lu Xun, whose short story 'The Diary of a Madman', published in 1918, marked the beginning of Chinese modernist writing. Trapped in a world of antiquity and menace, the madman declares, 'I can't bear to think of it. I have only just realised that I have been living in a place where for four thousand years they have been eating human flesh.'

In their early walks around Peking University campus, David and Karen often passed a mysterious broken-down house, locked away behind bolted gates and flourishing bamboo. They were told it had been the home of Leighton Stuart. By 2015, after serious and sensitive renovation, this house, which had a contemplative aspect looking through trees towards a little lake, never failed to impress visiting delegations. Over the decades, the reputation of Yenching University has undergone similar demotion and repair. Founded as a progressive Christian enterprise, its backers had great hopes that it would become an institution able to transcend political and cultural differences, a place where Chinese might benefit from exposure to Western civilisation and where Americans might develop a deeper appreciation of China. For a time, this might even have seemed possible until international events intervened. In 1937, as Japan invaded China, Yenching University shrank to a small American enclave within the occupied capital, where Leighton Stuart continued to teach and speak out against Japanese aggression while refusing to fly the flag of their puppet regime. After Pearl Harbor, he was incarcerated until the end of the war. Appointed as the new US ambassador to China, he was then given the impossible task of fostering American interests while mediating between the Guomindang and the Communists as the Civil War commenced.

Mao's response to Leighton Stuart's diplomacy was scathing. Accusing America of trying to 'turn China into a US colony', Mao insisted that Stuart had practised deception in pretending to love 'both the United States and China'. For Mao, foreign attempts to sponsor education in China just concealed political and cultural imperialism. He gleefully applauded the fact that Stuart had been forced to 'take to the road, his briefcase under his arm'. An event worth celebrating. Soon Yancheng University ceased to exist. Stuart died in 1964 without ever seeing China again. Meanwhile, under Mao, China's century of 'national humiliation' at the hands of Western powers was constantly emphasised. Mao claimed that only the CCP had been strong enough to stand up to the outside world to make China great again.

While Yengching University remained in the capital during the Japanese occupation, Peking University moved from its original site near the centre of Beijing to the relative safety of southern China. In 1952, this university returned to Beijing to replace Yenching University. Now called Beijing Daxue or Beida in Mandarin, in English it remains 'Peking University' perhaps to emphasise its long scholarly pedigree. It was the first modern university in China, founded in 1898. Mao was not fond of the institution. He was snubbed as a young man by university lecturers on the old city campus for his provincial accent and lowly status as assistant to the Peking University librarian.

By the 1960s, it became the turn of Peking University educators and leading scholars to undergo mass criticism. Learned intellectuals became 'ox ghosts' and 'snake spirits' confined near the area around Democracy Hall and the old Foreign Languages Building. Schwarcz records that more than 200 intellectuals were confined here in sheds called ox pens. They were treated by Red Guards with a 'clumsy brutality' that inflicted 'deep spiritual wounds'. Over 1000 academics were accused of being traitors and spies. More than fifty took their own life. Among the academics who committed suicide were Professor Jian Bozan, former chairman of the History Department, and his wife. An unobtrusive lake near the Yi Ran Ting pavilion became a favoured place for suicide by drowning.

While David and Karen looked intently at their surroundings at Peking University, noting so many architectural details and seasonal changes in the gardens they walked through, they missed much of the historical and cultural significance of what they saw. Schwarcz reminds us that 'gardens are not merely earthly stuff they occupy grounds in the mind as well'. Since becoming legally blind in 2004, David has given quite a bit of thought to the many ways in which we do not see. Not knowing the history of a place is a common form of 'sightlessness'.

Working with colleagues at Peking University, David struggled at first to overcome his inherent Western programming which without due care might lead him to conclude that a different way of seeing the world reflected error or mischief or bad faith. All societies are prone to think their own ways are the right ways. Listening is both an act of courtesy and a way of learning. Too often we fail to do this.

Full agreement may not come about but common ground will never be reached without gaining some understanding of the Chinese view of things.

Just as we see what we want to see, we often only hear what we want to hear. Neither David nor Karen speak Mandarin. China had to be translated for them by Chinese who spoke English. The years of travelling about by train with Li Yao provided time for deeper listening. Fengzhen, Yanggao, Hohhot and Jining were no more than obscure place names until Li Yao recounted family stories of what had happened there. Then imagination lent life to the narrow streets, and to the little houses and courtyards. Small details also spoke volumes. As Li Yao's brother-in-law leaned forward, pushing back his hair to reveal the scar on his forehead, the anti-Japanese war ceased to be a distant event. The hands of the brothers Li Yao and Li Xin spoke of how the Cultural Revolution had delivered different paths through life.

On their long train journeys together, David and Li Yao discuss how certain phrases in *Not Dark Yet* were best translated. Different understandings often emerged. In Australia, the bush was a nurturing place, an escape from the artificiality and pressure of city living. While the Chinese still see the countryside as a place of exile and punishment, Australians retreat to the bush in search of relaxation and spiritual renewal. Chinese are more likely to find solace among gardens, many of which are now open to all, not just the elite. Chinese people also like the warm feeling of being among others in their big cities. Australians often prefer to wander alone along a beach or in the bush. Li Yao had translated several Aboriginal writers, raising the question of how best to translate the word 'country' as used by Indigenous peoples? The indigenous idea of 'Country' is very different from the Chinese idea of 'the countryside'. The ethnographer Deborah Bird Rose has described Country as 'a living entity with a yesterday, today and tomorrow, with a consciousness and a will towards life'.

There are profound differences in how Chinese and Westerners see the world. Rui Yang, a Hong Kong professor with a deep understanding of cross-cultural education, has argued that just as Orientalism has 'shackled and misled the West in coming to know China', the Chinese must grapple with how they see the West. In the traditional *Tianxia* way of thinking, China stood at the centre while Western 'barbarians' roamed the periphery. Later, this view of the West coexisted uneasily with the attractions of Western modernity in culture and science. Still later views of the West were complicated by Sinocentric interpretations of socialism and Marxism.

Whatever they may think of individual Chinese, Australians harbour a deeply embedded and largely unacknowledged distrust of geopolitical China, often seeing it as a bad actor on the world stage. The two countries have different understandings of threat and vulnerability. Thinly populated Australia expects the world to understand that it has a vulnerable northern border, open to Asian invasion. While believing this, not one Australian in ten thousand could identify the fourteen countries with which China has a land border. They do not know how, over China's long history, those borders have been repeatedly violated and challenged, not least by Western powers. The differing vulnerabilities of Australia and China, their different cultures, mythologies and patterns of thought make it critically important for the two countries to develop educational programs that allow students to study the other and understand how and why they see the world as they do.

Now in the dreadful years of the plague 2020/21, the sharp deterioration in the China–Australia relationship is troubling. Today there is suspicion on both sides. How will things look in 2022, fifty years after Australia first recognised the People's Republic of China? The two Roosters are old fellows now. Will they be able to meet once again in Beijing?

Perhaps the last word can go not to the vexatious present but to a voice from Australia's past. In 1966, at a time when China seemed to be at war with both itself and the wider world, the senior Liberal politician and accomplished historian Paul Hasluck, then minister for external affairs, told an audience in Adelaide that 'no-one but a fool would think that China can be ignored, or destroyed or reduced, or forced to be something else other than China'. Australia would have to learn to deal with this perplexing nation.

Acknowledgements

Many people have helped this book become a reality. Generous BHP funding for the Chair of Australian Studies at Peking University (PKU), allowed David and Karen to spend three rewarding years in China. The Australian Embassy in Beijing and Kevin Hobgood-Brown, Shirley Gao and Stephanie Lowe at FASIC have championed educational links between Australia and China and the translation of Australian writing into Chinese. Liu Shusen and Liu Hongzhong from the Australian Studies Centre (ASC) at PKU, Li Jianjun at the ASC, BFSU and Zhang Yongxian (ASC, Renmin University) continue to be good friends and academic colleagues. Nicholas Jose first introduced David to Li Yao. Ding Dou and Changwei Chen of PKU, Bruce Connelly (formerly of Beijing Radio) and Wu Haiyan and Wuyungaowa of IMNU showed their visitors places that few foreigners are lucky enough to see. Chen Bing of PKU translated valuable historical information. Li Ruilian described traditional child rearing practices in Inner Mongolia. Our thanks go to Greg Lockhart, Geoff Raby, Jing Han, Lyu Lipan, Chengxin Pan and Greg McCarthy for sharing reflections on Australia–China relations. Owner of the Red Gate Gallery, Brian Wallace, introduced David and Karen to contemporary Chinese art. The artists Zhou Xiaoping, Shen Jiawei and Michael Downs joined discussions on cross-cultural relations. Bruce Clunies Ross remembered bookshops in Adelaide and Alison Frere (Hewitt) shared memories of meeting Li Yao in 1980. We also thank Chen Qinglin and Qian Fengqi for warm hospitality and interesting discussions over many years. Special thanks must go to Graeme Davison and Renata Osborne for their comments on the completed manuscript while Ipsita Sengupta provided insightful feedback on an early draft. David and Karen would like to thank their daughters, Zara Parker and Veronica Walker, and their wonderful grandchildren, Zamina, Iris, Meredith, Remi and Sebastian for continued distraction and good humour during the COVID pandemic. Li Yao would like to thank his daughter Li Yiqun for reading proofs and useful advice, his son Li Yilun for writing the dedication in Chinese and his lovely grandchildren, Hako, Jun and Kiko who are the future of the Li family. Finally, the authors thank all members of the extended Li family, particularly Li Xin for sharing memories and for many family banquets and expeditions to sites of great relevance to this book.

Select Bibliography

Balina, M and Rudova, L, eds, *Russian Children's Literature and Culture* Routledge, New York, 2008.

Billé, F and Urbansky, S, eds, *Yellow Perils: China Narratives in the Contemporary World*, University of Hawai'i Press, Honolulu, 2018.

Bridges, D, (ed), *Helen Palmer's Outlook*, Helen Palmer Memorial Committee, Sydney, 1976.

Brown, K, *The Purge of the Inner Mongolian People's Party in the Chinese Cultural Revolution, 1967–69*, Brill, Leiden, 2004.

Brown, N, *A History of Canberra*, Cambridge University Press, Canberra, 2014.

Crookshank, FG, *The Mongol in Our Midst: A Study of Man and His Three Faces*, WP Dutton & Company, New York, 1924.

Davis, M, *Late Victorian Holocausts: El Niño Famines and the Making of the Third World*, Verso, London, 2001.

DeFrancis, J, *In the Footsteps of Ghengis Khan*, University of Hawai'i Press, Hawai'i, 1993.

Edgerton-Tarpley, K, *Tears of Iron: Cultural Responses to Famine in Nineteenth Century China*, University of California Press, Berkeley, 2008.

Epstein, J, *My China Eye: Memoirs of a Jew and a Journalist*, Long River Press, San Francisco, 2005.

Farquhar, MA, *Children's Literature in China: From Lu Xun to Mao Zedong*, Routledge, New York, 2015.

Gaunt, M, *A Woman in China*, T Werner Laurie, London, 1914.

Gaunt, M, *A Broken Journey: Wanderings from the Huang-Ho to the Island of Saghalen and the Upper Reaches of the Amur River*, T Werner Laurie, London, 1919.

Harrison, H, *The Man Awakened from Dreams: One Man's Life in a North China Village 1857–1942*, Stanford University Press, Stanford, 2005.

Hartcher, P, 'Red Flag: Waking Up to China's Challenge', *Quarterly Essay*, vol. 76, 2019, pp. 1–89.

Hyer, P and Jachid, S, *A Mongolian Living Buddha: Biography of the Kanjura Khutughtu*, Sri Satguru Publications, Delhi, 1983.

Johnson, D, *Night Skies of Aboriginal Australia: A Noctuary*, Sydney University Press, Sydney, 1998.

Johnson, I, *The Soul of China: The Return of Religion after Mao*, Pantheon Books, New York 2017.

Judd, E, 'China's Amateur Drama: The Movement to Popularise the Revolutionary Model Operas', *Bulletin of Concerned Asian Scholars*, vol. 15(91), 1983, pp. 26–35.

King, R, *Milestones on a Golden Road: Writing for Chinese Socialism, 1945–80*, UBC Press, Vancouver, 2013.

Leung, L, *Morning Sun: Interviews with Chinese Writers of the Lost Generation*, ME Sharpe, Armonk, 1994.

Li, K-S, *A Glossary of Political Terms of the People's Republic of China*, The Chinese University Press, Hong Kong, 1995.

Li, N and Cribb, R, *Historical Atlas of Northeast Asia 1590–2010: Korea, Manchuria, Mongolia, Eastern Siberia*, Colombia University Press, New York, 2014.

McDougall, BS (ed), *Popular Chinese Literature and Performing Arts in the People's Republic of China, 1949–1979*, University of California, Berkeley, 1984.

Mair, VH and Bender, M, *The Columbia Anthology of Chinese Folk and Popular Literature*, Colombia University Press, New York, 2011.

Marinelli, M, 'Names and Reality in Mao Zedong's Political Discourse on Intellectuals', *Journal of Global Cultural Studies*, article 5, www.journals.openedition.org (viewed January 2010).

Meaney, N (ed) *Under New Heavens*, Heinemann Educational Australia, Port Melbourne, 1989.

Meinig, DW, *On the Margins of the Good Earth: The South Australian Wheat Frontier, 1869–1884*, Rigby Ltd, Adelaide, 1962.

Nolan, C, *A Sight of China*, Macmillan, London, 1969.

Ochirbat, N, 'Political Parody: The New Image of Mongolian Contemporary Art', PhD thesis, Curtin University, Perth.

Proudfoot, PR, *The Secret Plan of Canberra,* University of NSW Press, Sydney, 1994.

Rinpoche Z, *The Rituals of Kalachra Empowerment,* Gerlin Monastery, Tong Liao City, 2010.

Roberts, R, and Li, L, *The Making and Remaking of China's 'Red Classics': Politics, Aesthetics and Mass Culture,* Hong Kong University, Hong Kong, 2017.

Schwarcz, V, *Place and Memory in the Singing Crane Garden,* University of Pennsylvania Press, Philadelphia, 2008.

Scott, R (ed), *Strange Flowers: Australia–China Encounters in Writing and Art,* Wakefield Press, Kent Town, 2011.

Shen, J, *Painting History: China's Revolution in a Global Context,* Cambria Press, New York, 2018.

Sneath, D, *Changing Inner Mongolia, Pastoral Mongolian Society and the Chinese State,* Oxford University Press, Oxford, 2000.

Strahan, L, *Australia's China: Changing Perceptions from the 1930s to the 1990s,* Cambridge University Press, Cambridge, 1996.

Sullivan, LR, *Historical Dictionary of the Chinese Communist Party,* The Scarecrow Press Inc., Lanham, 2011.

Tanner, HM, *China: A History. Volume 1. From Neolithic Cultures through the Great Qing Empire 10,000 BCE–1799 CE,* Hackett Publishing, Indianapolis, 2010.

Tanner, HM, *China: A History. Volume 2, From the Great Qing Empire through the People's Republic of China (1644–2009),* Hackett Publishing, Indianapolis, 2010.

Terrill, R, *Madame Mao and the White-Boned Demon: A Biography of Madame Mao Zedong,* Hale & Iremonger, Sydney, 1995.

Van Fleit, HK, *Literature the People Love: Reading Chinese Texts from the Early Maoist Period (1949–1960),* Palgrave Macmillan, New York, 2013.

Volland, N, *Socialist Cosmopolitanism: the Chinese Literary Universe, 1945–1965,* Columbia University Press, New York, 2017.

Walker, D, *Dream and Disillusion: A Search for an Australian Cultural Identity,* Australian National University Press, Canberra, 1976.

Walker, D (ed), 'Australian Perceptions of Asia', *Australian Cultural History*, vol. 9, 1990, pp. 1–134.

Warrior, F, Knight F, Anderson S, and Pring A, *Ngadjuri: Aboriginal People of the Mid-North Region of South Australia*, SASOSE Council Inc., Prospect Hill, 2005.

Weatherford, J, *Genghis Khan and the Making of the Modern World*, Crown Publishers, New York, 2004.

Yang, H, *Genocide on the Mongolian Steppe: First Hand Accounts of Genocide in Southern Mongolia during the Chinese Cultural Revolution. Volume 1*, Xlibris, Milton Keynes, 2017.

Ying, L-H, *The A to Z of Modern Chinese Literature*, The Scarecrow Press, Lanham, 2010.

Yu, O, 'A Century of Oz Lit in China: A Critical Overview (1906–2011)', *Antipodes*, June 2011, pp. 65–71.

APPDENDIX

LI YAO: TRANSLATIONS OF AUSTRALIAN WRITING INTO CHINESE

No	Chinese title	Date	Publisher	Australian title	Author
1	当代澳大利亚中短篇小说选 [1]	1993	Beijing Publishing House	*Selection of Contemporary Australian Short Stories*	
2	漂泊的鸟	1991	Jilin Publishing House	*Birds of Passage*	Brian Castro
3	人树 [2]	1991	Shanghai Translation Publishing House	*The Tree of Man*	Patrick White
4	长安大街	1991	The Times Literature Publishing House	*Avenue of Eternal Peace*	Nicholas Jose
5	树叶裙	1993	China Literature Publishing House	*A Fringe of Leaves*	Patrick White
6	浪子 [3]	1995	Chongqing Publishing House	*The Ancestor Game*	Alex Miller
7	苦旅	1996	Chongqing Publishing House	*The Shiralee*	D'Arcy Niland
8	内海的女人	1996	China Literature Publishing House	*Woman of the Inner Sea*	Thomas Keneally
9	澳大利亚文明 [4]	1997	China Literature Publishing House	*Australian Civilisation*	
10	黑玫瑰 [5]	1997	China Literature Publishing House	*The Rose Crossing*	Nicholas Jose

11	镜中瑕疵	1998	SDX Joint Publishing Company	*Flaws in the Glass*	Patrick White
12	纳瑞斯金公园最后的散步[6]	1999	Chongqing Publishing House	*Last Walk in Naryshkin Park*	Rose Zwi
13	守望者	2000	Chongqing Publishing House	*The Custodians*	Nicholas Jose
14	心中的明天[7]	2003	Chongqing Publishing House	*Benang From the Heart*	Kim Scott
15	凯利帮真史	2003	People's Literature Publishing House	*True History of the Kelly Gang*	Peter Carey
16	为什么去中国[7]	2004	Shandong Pictorial Publishing House	*Why China?*	Charles Patrick Fitzgerald
17	摩根的旅程[8]	2005	People's Literature Publishing House	*Morgan's Run*	Colleen McCullough
18	古尔德的鱼书	2005	World Literature	*Gould's Book of Fish*	Richard Flannagan
19	呼唤	2006	Writers' Publishing House	*The Touch*	Colleen McCullough
20	红线[9]	2007	People's Literature Publishing House	*The Red Thread*	Nicholas Jose
21	别了，那道风景	2008	People's Literature Publishing House	*Landscape of Farewell*	Alex Miller

22	多特和袋鼠	2009	People's Literature Publishing House	*Dot and the Kangaroo*	Ethel Pedley
23	亡命天涯	2010	Writers' Publishing House	*His Illegal Self*	Peter Carey
24	卡彭塔利亚湾 [10]	2012	People's Literature Publishing House	*Carpentaria*	Alexis Wright
25	我是谁?	2012	Zhonghua Publishing House	*Who Am I ?*	Anita Heiss
26	光明行	2014	People's Literature Publishing House	*Not Dark Yet : A Personal History*	David Walker
27	煤河	2016	Foreign Language Teaching and Research Press	*Coal Creek*	Alex Miller
28	李尧译文集	2017	Qingdao Publishing House	*Li Yao's selected translations*	10 volumes 10 authors
29	哈尔滨档案 [7]	2018	San Lian Publishing House	*Secrets and Spies, the Harbin Files*	Maria Moustafine
30	神秘的布丁	2019	Beijing Union Press	*The Magic Pudding*	Norman Lindsay
31	诺亚·格拉斯之死	2020	The Writers' Publishing House	*The Death of Noah Glass*	Gail Jones
32	金色国度	2020	Qingdao Publishing House	*The Golden Country*	Tim Watts
33	吉米的颂歌 [11]	2021	Foreign Language Teaching and Research Press	*The Chant of Jimmie Blacksmith*	Thomas Keneally

34	耻辱与俘虏 [11]	2021	Foreign Language Teaching and Research Press	*Shame and Captivity*	Thomas Keneally
35	天鹅书	2021	Shanghai Translation Publishing House	*The Swan Book*	Alexis Wright
36	地平线上的奥德赛	2021	Beijing Union Press	*Odyssey of the Horizon*	Alexis Wright
37	石天金山	2021	Beijing Culture Development Publishing House	*Stone Sky Golden Mountain*	Mirandi Riwoe
38	中国游记	2021	Chinese Workers' Publishing House	*A Woman in China*	Mary Gaunt
39	月亮骨的故事	2021	The World Literature	*The Story of the Moon-bone*	Nicholas Jose
40	特莱庞的爱情	2021	The People's Literature Publishing House	*The Twyborn Affair*	Patrick White

[1] co-translator, Hu Wenzhong
[2] co-translator, Hu Wenzhong, republished 1995 and 2001
[3] ACC Inaugural Australian Translation Prize 1996
[4] co-translator, Liu Ximin
[5] Commendation prize, ACC 2008
[6] Silver Prize for Translation, Asia Pacific Book Awards, 2000
[7] co-translator, Huan Zhong
[8] co-translator, Li Yiqun
[9] co-translator, Huan Zhong, ACC Translation Prize 2008
[10] ACC Translation Prize 2012
[11] co-translator, Liu Yang

David and Li Yao in Shanxi 2016

David Walker is an Australian historian who holds honorary professorships at the University of Melbourne, Western Sydney University and Deakin University. From 2013–2016 he was the inaugural BHP Chair of Australian Studies at Peking University, Beijing. For many years he has studied Australia's responses to Asia. His books include *Anxious Nation: Australia and the Rise of Asia, 1850–1939*; *Stranded Nation: White Australia in an Asian Region* and (with Louise Johnson and Tanja Luckins) *The Story of Australia: A New History of People and Place.*

Li Yao is a member of the Chinese Writers' Association who teaches translation at Peking University. He has translated more than thirty Australian books into Chinese ranging from novels and memoirs to children's literature, work that has been acknowledged by the award of honorary doctorates from the University of Sydney and by Western Sydney University where he is an adjunct professor. He has received many prizes including a life-long achievement award from the Foundation for Australian Studies in China (FASIC).

Karen Walker is a research scientist and academic. After obtaining her PhD at the ANU she worked at the ANU, the University of Auckland, the University of Sydney, Deakin University and Monash University. Since her retirement she has been able to indulge her long-term interest in history and writing.

Index

Page numbers in **bold** indicate illustrations.